Suffering

Contents

CONTENTS

CONTENTS

CONTENTS

Translator's Preface

There is little need to justify the publication of a book on the subject of suffering. One can hardly refrain, however, from noting the specific considerations that render the present work significant: the universality of the experience of suffering; the continuing effort to find its meaning; the rich array of biblical materials and insights pertaining to the subject; and the resources of mind and spirit that are contributed by the authors, one of them a specialist in the Old Testament and the other in the New Testament. It is my hope that the appearance of the book now in English translation will help in the search for understanding and will serve, at least indirectly, to diminish the pain of humanity.

I should like to express my thanks to Sara and Stewart Newman, friends who have demonstrated a profound sensitivity to those who suffer and have lightened the burdens of distress for a great many. My warmest thanks must go to my wife Donnie, whose help in this work, as always, goes beyond her own awareness and beyond my powers of expression.

JOHN E. STEELY

Wake Forest, North Carolina
January 1979

A.
SUFFERING
IN THE
OLD TESTAMENT

I. Suffering—then and now

1. Individual and social dimensions of suffering

"Everyone has a cross to bear. I must deal with my sufferings by myself." This is a frequently heard utterance that reflects life experience. Anyone who deals with suffering people also knows how much timeless truth is contained in these words, even when they are used lightly. Any suffering, even if it is imaginary, is in a mysterious way my personal affair. Even under the most favorable circumstances I cannot simply put aside pains, fears, or uncertainties the way one puts hat and coat in the closet. Whatever troubles, hampers, embitters me, whatever threatens to cripple me in body or spirit, belongs, in spite of all counter-measures, to me myself. The pain, and in a certain sense this holds true also for all its causes, and for evil itself, is something alien, fearsome, from which I would like to escape. But it has a grasp on me and does not let me go.

That suffering is most profoundly sensed as personal fate is the one basic experience of man (Prov. 14:10). But if the sufferer thinks only of himself and his pain, he ends up in despair or in dull resignation. The latter is by far the more common; the statistics on suicide do not refute this. Suffering can stunt a person, or even kill, long long before physical death occurs. The sufferer accepts his fate, perhaps even as divinely willed, and can finally die without a struggle—the only comfort of silent endurance. But such an attitude appears to be rather a carryover from man's prehistory at the animal level than the fruit of typically human knowledge. Man is concerned with comprehending himself and his world actively. Hence he must also reflect on the source and the aim of suffering. Indeed, the experience of the calamitous and painful, of privation and want, has perhaps been an important impetus toward the development of the ability to think.

Hence we must consider suffering rationally, that is, critically. Then it immediately becomes evident that neither in its origin nor in its consequences—nor as long as man is actively engaged in dealing with it—is it an exclusively personal, private experience. The fact that now and then one must suffer entirely dependent upon oneself is only a basic experience of man that must be analyzed from case to case. As for others, my suffering unites me with others. It is not simply that I arouse sympathy and find comfort in others. The connections between the suffering of the individual and his environment are stronger and more complex than that. Suffering never develops only in the individual man, as though from his own personal fault. Others are involved also, as the ones who cause it, as onlookers, or as friends. The pain that torments an individual never affects him alone; he then would have to be and remain utterly lost and forgotten. Anyone who dies abandoned and forgotten, under a bridge somewhere or in an asylum, will at least in his death affect those who bury him; oftentimes there will be someone else who joins in the funeral procession. The causes and consequences of suffering have, in the broad sense, a fellow-human dimension, and any struggle against the necessity of suffering all the more involves the environment as well.

Now if suffering occurs in interplay with the environment, then when and where a person suffers cannot be a matter of indifference. The subjective experience of violence that oppresses, dishonors, and defaces may be the same or at least comparable in various situations. Otherwise it would hardly be possible for us to concern ourselves with the sufferings of another person. But in any case the outward circumstances also have a part in determining the quality of the suffering. It makes a difference whether one is going hungry and losing weight in a prison camp, in the slums of a large city, in a hospital, or in an Olympic-training camp. Moreover, the position held by the person who suffers is far from unimportant; the means available for his relief are dispensed to him in accordance with his standing in society. Further, what is regarded at one time as a terrible calamity can, under other circumstances, be dismissed or heroically glorified. Thus, again and again parents have sacrificed their children in patriotic or religious intoxication. In short, social relationships, cultural value-systems, and conceptions of faith in the context of which suffering occurs are of major importance for the critical observer in any case. The person who is "pursued by misfortune" may temporarily lose sight of these connections. But he too must be freed from the misery that isolates, if he is not to be vanquished by it.

2. Suffering in the context of the Old Testament world

From what has been said it follows that the suffering which we encounter in the Old Testament also had its times and circumstances. We would like to know in what frame of reference suffering was experienced in that time, so that we can compare the experiences of the biblical witnesses with our own. For this purpose it is necessary to sketch, at least in broad outline, the world in which the Israelite found himself. We shall note significant differences between our reality and that of the Old Testament, but shall not over-emphasize these differences. The person who is subjected to suffering and is tested by suffering remains the same in the various cultural systems and historical epochs. Pain comes and makes its impact in varied ways; it forms the personal experience of suffering. For a critical evaluation of suffering that is remote from us it is essential to recognize these differences. An understanding mind, however, will see the similarity of all suffering. What happens in a different garb or in a different stage setting is clearly recognizable as human suffering by the way in which it points beyond itself and calls man into question.

a) Forms of society in ancient Israel

The people of Old Testament times (approximately 1200 to 200 B.C.) lived predominantly in the Semitic language-world of the Near East, which is characterized, even down to the present day, by the contrast between desert and arable land; that is, by the tension between the respective social systems. The settled peoples of Mesopotamia, Asia Minor, Syria, and Egypt set the tone politically, culturally, and religiously. However, their city cultures were constantly being both threatened and enriched by nomad groups who saw in the agriculture a secure basis for living and in the cities half-repulsive, half-enticing wicked luxuries (Gen. 19:1-9). The Israelite tribes were originally such bands of poor herdsmen. They drifted into the land of Canaan, became farmers, and in the end even adopted the city way of life. The Old Testament writings still allow us to perceive the various social orders and values of Israel. For example, the practice of exacting blood-revenge (Gen. 4:23-24; 2 Sam. 3:27) dates from the nomadic period; the court held by the elders in the gate, together with the laws aimed at compensation for injuries (Ruth 4:1-12; Exod. 21:2–22:16), reflects village and bourgeois circumstances. The royal court of judgment (2 Sam. 15:2) is an innovation of the central power of the state, and the priest's authority even in civil matters (Ezek. 44:23-24) belongs to the time after the collapse in 587 B.C. (the beginning of the Babylonian exile). We can assume that the various forms of organization did not simply follow in succession, but that in the course of history they were interwoven with each other, blended into each other, and often enough came into conflict with each other (cf. Jer. 35; 1 Kings 21; Judg. 9; Ezek. 45). We may further assume as certain that every form of human life together has its own peculiar points of irritation and therefore produces characteristic fears and possibilities of suffering. The ancient Israelite was concerned first of all with the continuation of his family, the security of the inheritance, and personal and national freedom—always against the background of the political and cultural conditions of that time.

b) Understanding of the world in personal terms.

The world of ancient man was shaped and dominated by personal powers (cf. Ps. 114:3-8; 148). Behind all that existed stood an intentional intellectual activity, basically comprehensible to man because it corresponded to his capacities. Mountains, streams, trees, rocks—all nature had the character of handiwork and at the same time possessed a soul. The human relationships and conditions—in short, history itself—formed the realm of activity of lesser and greater spirits, ranging from legendary animals to man, angels, demons, and even to the gods. In antiquity there certainly was no lack of what we call "a way of looking at the world in terms of natural science." Man was always an inquiring being who liked to observe and catalog. The ancient investigator, however, reckoned with a personal basic structure of reality. Today the relationship appears exactly the reverse: the mechanical, causal, functional, technical, or in any case the impersonal view of reality is so prominent that it is also applied to human relationships. The will is no longer an instrument for the interpretation of the world; its place has been taken by "natural laws." It is often asserted that this depersonalizing of the world was already introduced in the Old Testament, by its concentration of all power in God, to the exclusion of all opposition to God, and the vigorous assumption by man of the governance of the earth that has been released from the forces of magic (cf. Deut. 6:4; Isa. 44:6; Ps. 8). In actuality the personal interpretation of reality was never abandoned in the Old Testament. Yahweh contends with other deities for the preeminence and rules through them (cf. Ps. 82; Jer. 2). And where suffering is involved, the Israelite does not see bacteria, processes of change in matter, or psychological aberrations as possible causes, but rather personal powers (cf. 1 Sam. 18:10; Ps. 3:1; 11:2; 91:5-6). Thus suffering was not accidental, but intentional.

c) The world as comprehensible

The universe that was known at that time was certainly imposing, mysterious, and unexplainable, for personal being is not subject to calculation. But at the same time the totality of the world was to an enviable degree closed, comprehensible, and in balance. Every phenomenon had its name, its function.

The world was not fragmented into isolated phenomena and was not swallowed up in boundless space and time that can be expressed only by unreal mathematical symbols. The universe rather resembled a communal entity or a household; it was far from one of those major industrial concerns that can hardly be surveyed from the executive level of the central administration. At that time the danger was seen to be that the existing harmony might be threatened from without or within; the floods of chaos could again break into the well-ordered world (Gen. 6–9), and the peoples might endanger peace in foolish arrogance (Ps. 2; Isa. 14). Basically, however, the world is secure under God's care. The earth rests upon firm pillars (Ps. 75:3), and the vaults of heaven form a solid roof, a shelter against the primordial floods (Gen. 1:6-8); above there, God dwells in his palace (Ps. 33:13; 104:3). What does such world-order mean for the experience of suffering? Man always draws meaning for his life from the structure of the world. In doing this, he strives also to fit in what is contradictory and painful. One wonders whether this is better achieved in a cosmos that is comprehensible and cozy than in a universe that is expanding at the speed of light, that possibly contains a large number of worlds likewise inhabited by intelligent beings.

d) Anthropological constants: tribal relationships

In the personal and ordered world, human society was set in structures as nature is. The individual's course of life was mapped out from birth onward. For example, there was hardly any possibility of personal choice in the selection of a career or a life-partner. In the settled population even one's place of residence was fixed once and for all. The person belonged through good times and bad to his tribe and his family. The roles one had to play in the community were clearly defined; rights and obligations of every member were permanently fixed. Opportunities for advancement (one may think of Joseph and David) were remarkable exceptions. The wanderings of the patriarchs were already regarded, in the time when they were written down, as examples of a turbulent and dangerous way of life. Sojourns abroad were at most the task of princes, diplomats, and merchants who imported and exported goods, if one disregards military undertakings. Deportations by foreign conquerors then appear to have forced Israel to be more mobile. In any case the books of Ezra and Nehemiah attest a certain amount of travel between Palestine and Mesopotamia. Nevertheless the predominant impression conveyed by the Old Testament is one of a stable, patriarchally ordered society. Breaking away from the fathers' customs means calamity (Jer. 6:16; Prov. 15:10), and loss of the protection of the family is the worst of fates (Mic. 7:6; Job 19:13). Anyone who doubts the authority of the elders makes himself a criminal outsider (Lev. 19:32; Prov. 30:17). It will be evident that in our times we are compelled in a quite different way to try the new and to test and to change the customs and norms that have been handed down.

e) Intellectual equipment; the state of knowledge

The intellectual equipment that was available to a man of Old Testament times can hardly be stated in a formula; there is too much variety in the currents which we encounter in the Old Testament. The general state of knowledge corresponds to what we have said above about social history, structure of the world, nature, and society. It is significant that antiquity often posed different connections between familiar phenomena from those that we establish, or gave them different interpretations. A sufficiently strong will could, for example, stay the sun (Josh. 10:12-13), because it moved across the sky, whether on its own impetus or being drawn, by the power of will (Ps. 19:5-6). The breath was an element of life bound up with the person, so that to breathe upon something meant the same as to vivify it (Gen. 2:7; 2 Kings 4:34). If at the time of conception the cattle saw a striped or spotted pattern, then they produced their young with a corresponding pattern (Gen. 30:37-39). The strength of the Nazirite, who was consecrated to God, lay in his hair (Judg. 16:17). As is shown by contemporary fashions, splendidly illustrated for example in the musical "Hair," such prescientific associations and interpretations of reality are by no means extinct. The best example of this perhaps is the Babylonian belief in the stars, which survives in contemporary astrology. Technology and industrial production, however, today prohibit any unprogrammed utilization of our knowledge, or they restrict it to the private sphere. Still more important for our subject would be the fitting of suffering into the intellectual climate of its time and of the stratum of society in which it occurs. The vagaries of Israelite history and the diverse interests and conditions of the social groups within Israel (clans, tribes, classes, ranks, regions) render this task difficult. In the Old Testament we encounter proud songs of the victorious people (Exod. 15; Judg. 5; Ps. 68) and a despairing, guilt-conscious explanation of history (2 Kings 17; Ezek. 16; Neh. 9; Ps. 106). Forthright belief in reason and progress, frequently characterized as "Solomonic enlightenment" (1 Sam. 16–2 Sam. 5; 1 Kings 5) stands alongside profound pessimism (Eccles.). Rustic cunning contends with priestly or worldly cleverness (Gen. 27; Lev. 13; Prov. 4), and prophetic pronouncement of calamity contradicts national self-assurance (Hos. 1:9; Jer. 7; Ps. 46).

f) The significance of belief in Yahweh

In this ebb and flow of the sense of life in Israel the belief in Yahweh certainly was the decisive factor. This is true particularly for the conquest of suffering in the national as well as in the personal sphere. We observe in the Old Testament, when we apply generally scientific methods, a growing concentration of belief in the one God of Israel. In the early period there were obviously various family and tribal deities, which from Exodus 3 onward are absorbed into Yahweh. In the cultivated area then many local shrines existed for centuries side-by-side. It can hardly be assumed that they all observed one unified religion. People worshiped Yahweh acording to local tradition and custom, and it was not uncommon for a person to become a worshiper of a Canaanite Baal-deity without any conflict of conscience (Judg. 6:25-32; Hos. 4:13). Prophetic criticism, royal interests, and later the priestly reorganization of the exilic community gradually led to a unifying of belief which we encounter in the final version of the Old Testament. The unprecedented intensity with which Yahweh contends for his people and subjects all other peoples to Israel (Exod. 34:10-16; Isa. 45:14-17; Ezra 9-10) is an idea born out of the situation of distress in the Exile. Hand in hand with this theological claim of Yahweh's sole sovereignty goes the setting-apart of Israel as a "holy nation" and the establishment of priestly rule in the community that was subject to alien rulers. A direct consequence of this development, however, was also the revival of local cults (Jer. 44; Ezek. 13). The world-ruler Yahweh was so far removed from everyday life that he appeared hardly any longer to be able to help the person in distress. Hence people sought helpers in their distress on a lower plane of the world's hierarchy. We shall do well to keep in view both of these dimensions of belief in God in Israel: the universal, which was bound up with organizational forms of state and nation, and which served their purposes; and the private, whose sphere was the life of the individual and his immediate environment. The Old Testament offers abundant testimony that the family's worship of God was extremely important for the Israelite; to what extent he equated the "familial deity" with Yahweh is an open question. In any case, important contracts were sealed in the presence of the house-deity (Exod. 21:6); some clans owned their own statues of the gods (Gen. 31:34; 1 Sam. 19:13), and many even had a regular private chapel with a priest installed (Judges 17). The laments of the individual in the Old Testament psalter (e.g., Pss. 17; 22; 31; 35; 38; 55; 59; 69) moreover prove, in my opinion, that outside the official state-cultus, and very likely often in the home of the patient, services of prayer and healing were held for individuals who were ill. The story of Hezekiah's illness (Isa. 38) offers some clues to this.

3. Can we learn from the suffering of that time?

We live more than two thousand years after the latest Old Testament witnesses; moreover, we are not direct descendants of the Israelites. The question is obvious: How can we at all gain access to these ancient writings? What do they mean to us? One bridge back to the Old Testament undoubtedly is the history of faith. Present-day Christianity is inconceivable without primitive Christianity, as is the latter without the Old Testament. Ancient Israel begins to speak of a loving God who assuages suffering in his own fellow-suffering. There begins the struggle for an understanding of the self and the world that corresponds to the message of the love and solidarity of God. A second bridge, which should not be underestimated, is created simply by the fact that in the Old Testament, believing and suffering men still speak audibly today. Our being human binds us to all other men. And in any case it is rewarding to hear testimonies of faith, love, and suffering.

However we may evaluate our relationship to the Old Testament, one thing should be clear: we have only scattered literary witnesses to that time. They cannot provide us with a complete picture of that millennium of Israelite history. Still less are the ancient documents suited to draw for us a direct, well-rounded portrait of life as it was lived. That is difficult even today, when we have the help of tape and film recordings. The accounts preserved in the Old Testament are in any case representations of reality of that time which have undergone repeated thinking-through and structuring. With reference to our subject, this means that anyone who wants to become acquainted with present-day suffering will not want to draw his information solely from books and reports. He will seek out the suffering persons: those suffering from cancer, the homeless, orphans, prisoners, illiterates, oppressed minorities. Through personal contact and perhaps in sharing the suffering he will gain a conception of the lot of these fellowmen. This direct access to the individual man of the Old Testament times is not available to us. In the Old Testament texts we have before us portrayals of suffering that have been reflected upon many times and set in schematic patterns, portrayals that have been drawn with various intentions. We are dealing with narratives, court documents, wisdom, priestly and liturgical materials, and other types as well. This requires consideration when one is engaged with the Old Testament. But it cannot in any case prevent us from seeking, along with and during the investigation of the Old Testament, the physical proximity of those who suffer, when we can find them today. And if there is one thing sure, it is this: there is suffering very close at hand, wherever we may be. A proper study of the Bible must actually be accompanied by such an orientation of our perspective.

II. Experiences of suffering

1. Loss

a) The loss of property

Job's way of suffering begins with his being deprived of his possessions. "Satan" (originally: "Accuser," Ps. 109:6; Zech. 3:1-2), correctly estimating human nature, challenged God: "But if you destroy what belongs to him, he will curse you" (Job 1:11). And the irreproachable man, whose wealth and fear of God—the two complement each other (Prov. 22:4)—cause amazement (Job 1:1-5), in a series of four catastrophes loses his flocks and herds, his slaves, and his children (Job 1:13-19). Job's reaction shows how deeply he is affected: the rending of garments and the shaving of the head are signs of lamentation for the dead (Job 1:20).

The loss of property not only means the immediate pain, but torment and mortal danger. The person who is without property stands on the edge of the abyss (Prov. 10:15; 1 Sam. 22:2); he lacks the very foundation of existence. It is understandable that the Old Testament throughout joyfully affirms personal (or, better, family) possessions, regards them as a gift of God's beneficence (Gen. 33:11; Job 42:10), and quite obviously assumes that everyone will fight (2 Kings 4:1; 8:3) or work for his possessions, frequently even with impure means, as the stories about Jacob show (Gen. 27; 30:25-43). Further: the norms that were in force in Israelite society were from the very first strongly oriented to the security of possessions and the regulation of any injuries or damages that might be suffered (e.g., Exod. 21:2–22:16). The ideal even of prophetic preaching, as well as of many messianic predictions, is that every clan can live on its own territory independently and with human dignity (Mic. 2:2; Isa. 5:8; 61:7). One can say that in ancient Israel, property was a "highest good," with which perhaps only "honor" could compare in the scale of social values. The free Israelite of the male sex and head of a family stood or fell according to what he possessed. His possessions did not merely keep him alive, but they moreover secured his position in society and assured him of the continuing faithfulness of his God. The New Testament attitude of "Sell all you have" (Matt. 19:21) is not found anywhere in the Old Testament. In rare exceptional situations, for example in order to protect a guest or to keep a vow (Judg. 11:3-39; 19:24-29), a person was obliged to stake his possessions—even his wife or his daughter. But possessions meant life, and loss of property meant suffering and mortal danger (cf. Lev. 25). In many situations poverty must have been a real nightmare (2 Kings 4:1). For because possessions belonged to a person as closely as his clothing, one without possessions was naked (Job 1:21; Ezek. 16:9-13). He was utterly helpless and could be "consumed" like a bit of wild game (Hab. 3:14; Prov. 30:14).

Here we can only indicate that in the context of this total perspective, in the course of the thousand years of Old Testament history, of course there also were changes in the attitude toward property, and consequently shifts in the experience of suffering are to be noted. In the beginning, in Israel it was chiefly the flocks and herds that counted as family possessions. Conflicts arose over rights to pasture and water and the ownership of livestock (Gen. 26:15 ff.; 30:28 ff.). After

the migration into the land of Canaan there were houses and
lands as well; now people feared and lamented lost harvests and
devastated settlements (Judg. 6:3-4; Deut. 28:30, 33, 38-40). In
the centuries after the introduction of the monarchy, then,
Israel's social order was exposed to great burdens. There
developed, hand in hand with the central royal administration,
an elite stratum of large landowners and a rural as well as an
urban proletariat. The new settlement of the northern part of
the country, after it had been annexed by the Assyrians (722
B.C.), and the expropriation and reallocation of the land in the
one-time nation of Judah by the Babylonians (after 587 B.C.; cf.
Jer. 39:10), further shook the structures of society. In
connection with these events and as a consequence of
far-reaching rearrangements in Israel's belief and thought,
then, there gradually developed a certain mistrust toward
earthly goods (Prov. 28:20, 22; 30:8-9; Eccles. 2:4-11), and even
poverty appeared in a different light (Prov. 15:16-17; 17:5; 19:1,
17; 28:6, 11). In the view of these later people it was connected
with virtues such as sincerity and cleverness, and it even
claimed God's special attention (Prov. 14:31; 19:17). Thus a
bridge extends from the impoverished farmers of the period of
the monarchy to the community of the Exile who called upon
Yahweh as the Lord of the poor, the deprived, and the
wretched (Ps. 113:7; Isa. 66:2).

It certainly will be helpful at this point to make it clear that
the Old Testament concept of property does not coincide with
ours and therefore must occasionally appear to us strange and
even offensive. We probably no longer enumerate our
possessions in terms of so many head of cattle, but we have
different items of value: money, stocks, pension rights, life
insurance, savings accounts. But this difference in kind—which
certainly also brings with it other forms of anxiety and
distress—is unimportant in comparison with the fact that
Israel, like all other ancient peoples, could also without
hesitation count persons among one's possessions. Classical
lists of items of property include, for example, "wife,
manservant, maidservant, ox, ass" (Exod. 20:17), or "sheep,
maidservants, menservants, camels, asses" (Gen. 30:43). It

makes no difference now to assemble from the Old Testament the fairly numerous indications of the emancipation of women (e.g., Judg. 4:4-5), of children not being subject to their parents (e.g., 1 Sam. 20:27-32), and of the relative independence of slaves (1 Sam. 9:7-10). Nor does it make any difference for us to cite the considerable and steadily growing concerns for legal guarantees and properly human existence for those in society who are weak; one may compare Job's great confession (Job 31:13-15)!

The fact remains that in a patriarchal-feudalistic society the master of the house is the real and sole owner of the servants and the members of the family still in their minority; this right of possession embraces the obligation to care for these persons and the power of disposing of them. Certainly the Israelites were not so dull as to place subordinate persons on the same level as the cattle or the household furniture. They knew very well, in their world that was personally animated, how to make a distinction among many kinds of "objects," each of which had its own justification for existing. The slave had thoroughly human claims; only they were subordinated to the will of the owner (cf. Exod. 21:4). All power issued from the head of the family. And in a serious case this could mean that he could beat his slave to death. If he struck the fatal blow intentionally, the owner was punished; in the case of mistreatment that later resulted in death, he went unpunished, for the slave was after all "his money" (Exod. 21:20-21). Similarly the master of the house could—and under certain circumstances, according to the laws of the society of that time, he was *obliged* to—have power over his wife and children (Exod. 21:7; Judg. 11:39; 19:25; 1 Sam. 14:44; Prov. 19:18; Deut. 21:18-21).

Two consequences appear to me inescapable. First, we must evaluate the Old Testament expressions within the then-prevailing social system and cannot too hastily apply our own standards of values. Second, we may, if we are to make the testimonies of the Old Testament our own, inquire after suffering man and the loving God in the reality of that time and now. We shall then discover in the Old Testament some concerns for humanity, for example, the concern that the owner be protected against loss. But we also encounter the victims of the system, the dishonored wife, the daughter who is sold, the "prodigal" son, the maltreated slave. For the submissiveness with which Jephthah's daughter accepts her death sentence from her father (Judg. 11:36) certainly corresponds more to the wishful thinking of the dominant father than to the anxiety of the victim. It should be added, as a reminder to us, that we resist the idea of treating a person as a piece of property. Rightly so. But in the social systems of today there are forms of dependence and of exploitation that are far more cruel than anything that was possible in Old Testament times. Will it suffice to call to mind the two hundred million or more undernourished children? For them there is not even a patronage relationship that would include the obligation of someone to provide for them.

Let us go back to the "loss of property according to the Old Testament." A little later we shall have to speak further about the causes that led to impoverishment. At this point it is sufficient to say that the Israelite was aware that his possessions were threatened by various machinations of the mighty (Amos 2:6; Neh. 5:1-5), by attacks from neighboring peoples (Judg. 6:3-6), by natural catastrophes (Jer. 14:1-6; Joel 1:15-20), and even by his own indolence (Prov. 24:30-34). Against this background we shall inquire further into what the loss of possessions meant for the man of Old Testament times and how he reacted to it.

With the multiplicity of Old Testament writings and the frequency with which the subject of property and threat to property is touched upon, it is amazing that nowhere is there a fuller description of the frame of mind of those who have been deprived of everything. We do not possess any "portraits of the soul" of the unfortunate, such as are offered in Homer, Shakespeare, Dostoyevsky, or many modern authors. The Old Testament texts which apparently offer something comparable have an aim entirely different from that of the literary scenes that are familiar to us. Seen as a whole, the Old Testament is quite sparing with words when it comes to the distress of those who are deprived and devoid of possessions. In the Job narrative it is indeed expressed how deeply injured is the man who is tormented by Satan (Job 1:20), and later the portrayal of his suffering is given its artistic climax by the representation of the horror of Job's friends (2:11-13). But what is put in words there are hardly the feelings of the individual, but predominantly the socially determined manifestations of pain, sympathy, and mourning. We may assume that actions such as throwing dust in the air (2:12), sitting in silence (2:13), tearing one's outer garments and shaving one's head (1:20), just like putting on black mourning clothes (Ps. 35:13), fasting (1 Sam. 12:16), and wounding oneself (Jer. 16:6), were meant to serve to ward off evil spirits and to do penance before God. If one adds that after the blows of fate that reduce him to nothing, Job utters a prayer (of praise!): "The Lord has given it, the Lord has taken it away . . ." (Job 1:21), we once again are confronted with an extremely important state of affairs. Because God is the Creator and Giver of all that is good, the loss of possessions, like every other distress, is therefore related to God. Yahweh has given or lent every possession, the land (Lev. 25:23), the harvest (Ps. 65:9 ff.), the herds (Isa. 30:23), as well as wife (Prov. 19:14) and children (Ps. 127:3), and indeed all wealth (1 Kings 3:13). Psalm 127, which we have just cited, shows that God's readiness to do good to man counts for more than diligence and skill in labor (cf. Lev. 26:3-13; Deut. 28:3-14). The same view is expressed in the old German inscription placed on houses: *An Gottes Segen ist alles gelegen* [i.e., "Everything depends on God's blessing"). Then, if misfortune strikes, possessions are destroyed, or property seized, God's beneficent will, his care and his presence, are called into question. The loss and the accompanying threat to life become a problem for faith. To this extent Satan is entirely correct in his challenge in Job 1:9-11. God creates the basic presuppositions for human life, from the beginning of the world to its renewal (Gen. 2:15-18; Isa. 65:21-25). This foundation for life is not simply at hand; it is prepared by design. If it disintegrates, the person who is affected must conclude from this that his God has turned his back on him. Thus poverty is a sign of Godforsakenness. Why then should it be surprising that the poor man is neglected in human society also, or even hated (Prov. 19:4, 7)?

From the perspective of such utterances of belief, it becomes fully understandable why the most detailed portrayals of suffering generally—this includes the pain of the person who has lost everything—are to be found in the context of worship in the Old Testament. Loss and pain, threat and uncertainty demand to be considered in prayer. Hence the loss of possessions also is reflected in the lament before God or before his representative. The distress after the capture of Jerusalem by the Babylonians, when the food supplies are used up, destroyed, or confiscated, is portrayed, for example, in Lam. 2:10-12:

> Jerusalem's old men sit on the ground in silence,
> With dust on their heads and sackcloth on their bodies.
> Young girls bow their heads to the ground.
>
> My eyes are worn out with weeping; my soul is in anguish.
> I am exhausted with grief at the destruction of my people.
> Children and babies are fainting in the streets of the city.
>
> Hungry and thirsty, they cry to their mothers;
> They fall in the streets as though they were wounded,
> And slowly die in their mothers' arms. (TEV)

What we read here is not a documentary report, but an appeal to Yahweh, made in the context of worship, to see the misery of his people and to have mercy on them. The prayer of lamentation describes, as example, the death struggle of little children; this is intended to move God (cf. Lam. 1:10-20; 4:4-10; 5:1-18). But with a slightly shifted accent in the same intention, in a liturgical text the effects of drought are described (Jer. 14:1-6), where in place of the suffering children there appear the animals that are doomed to death (v. 5-6). And a third example: in Neh. 5:1-5 those who are endangered do not turn directly to God, but to those whom he has commissioned:

1) Men and women loudly protested against their Jewish brethren: 2) Some said, "We must barter our children for grain in order to survive." 3) Others said, "We must mortgage our fields and vineyards in order to get bread." 4) Still others: "We have borrowed money in order to be able to pay the royal tax. 5) But we are Israelites, too. Our sons are as good as the children of our fellow believers. Yet we must make slaves of our sons and daughters. Some of our daughters have already been sold into slavery. We are helpless. Our land and our vineyards too belong to others."

The rich obviously are exploiting the distress of the small landowners and are acquiring their possessions through questionable transactions. This is a violation of God's commandment, which is intended especially to prevent the abuse of lending practices, of securities taken for loans, and the enslavement of Israelites for indebtedness that was often connected with these practices (Exod. 22:25-27; Deut. 15:1-18). And because the divine commandment is at the same time a law of society, the Israelites can hope that Nehemiah, their fellow Israelite and special commissioner of the Persians, will enforce it (Neh. 5:6 ff.).

All this shows that in the Old Testament, economic distress, the loss of the material basis for existence, is wholly embedded in faith and in a relationship with God—and this automatically means also, in worship. In some of the following chapters we shall have to deal with this state of affairs.

b) Loss of other persons

But now it would be mistaken to try to consider every experience of loss in Israel altogether under the rubric of property. A person can, for example, also lose other persons who "belong" to him, though not in the sense that he has the right of disposition over them. Then, as now, a person "had" or "has", for example, father and mother, friends, and neighbors, teachers, models, etc. Loss of these fellowmen is, from the perspective of suffering and its conquest, altogether to be equated with the loss of property (cf. Gen. 50:1-14; Ps. 35:14; 1 Sam. 25:1; 31:4-5; 2 Sam. 13:19; Ruth 1:6-21). Like the other peoples of the Near East, Israel felt the pain of bereavement with peculiar intensity. If a member of the family or an important personality of "public life" died, a lamentation for the dead was held, in the family or the circle of friends, or on the "national" level. For this occasion, professional mourners (Amos 5:16; Jer. 9:16-17) were called in, and these then were responsible for a part of the ceremonies. In the course of the ritual actions—these included putting on mourning clothes, wailing, weeping, throwing dust in the air, fasting, rending of garments, and so on—songs were also sung to the deceased. The most moving Old Testament example probably is David's lament over his friend Jonathan. The two young men had sworn absolute loyalty (1 Sam. 18:1-4). "Jonathan bound himself to David, for he loved him as himself" (v. 1). This personal commitment of the crown prince to the secret pretender to the throne is exposed to severe tests, but it survives all the strains (1 Sam. 18–20). When Jonathan then falls in battle against the Philistines, David arranges the lamentation (2 Sam. 1:12), and he himself sings the dirge (1:19-27), the climax of which is the lament over his lost friend:

> The brave soldiers have fallen,
>   they were killed in battle.
> Jonathan lies dead in the hills.
>
> I grieve for you, my brother Jonathan;
>   how dear you were to me!
> How wonderful was your love for me,
>   better even than the love of women.
>
> The brave soldiers have fallen,
>   their weapons abandoned and useless.
>   (vv. 25-27 TEV)

The difficult question is how the lamentation for the dead is fitted into the belief in Yahweh. For Yahweh was not originally the Lord of the realm of the dead; the dead could not praise him (Ps. 88:10-12; Isa. 14:4-21). Thus the deceased had emigrated, as it were, from the region of Yahweh's dominion. What then is the aim of the extensive lamentations that are mentioned in the Old Testament? Can they comfort or overcome the pain? It is likely that Israel considered even this last stage of human life in the light of its God, perhaps at first only with respect to those who were left behind, until, when much later, Yahweh became the Lord of the dead also (Job 26:6; Ps. 139:8).

c) Loss of honor

There are in the Old Testament a number of peripheral situations in which a man is brought to the brink of the abyss by the loss of an "ideal" good. Anyone who loses his home wanders "fugitive and restless" through the world, at every moment threatened by uncontrollable powers (Gen. 4:12; Ps. 120). Anyone who surrenders his critical reason and no longer orients himself to the prevailing norms of conduct, that is, anyone who lets himself be led away from them and thus led astray, is racing to his own destruction (Prov. 1:10-19; 5:6; 7:1-5). Anyone who loses his credibility becomes a liar who is dangerous to the public and whom no one any longer trusts at all (Lev. 19:16; Jer. 9:2-5; Ps. 1:1; 26:4-5). Such a man is already in himself a veritable bundle of contagious "misery," "calamity," and "delusion" (Job 15:35).

As an example, we will best choose the ancient Israelite sense of honor; here it can be most impressively demonstrated what the loss of a "nonmaterial" possession can mean. "Honor" in the Old Testament sense is the weightiness and dignity which would make a man, in keeping with his "position," a full member of society. It is that self-esteem and that regard without which life in the community becomes impossible. The honor of the man is closely intertwined with his masculine roles: it is asserted in his effectiveness as head of the family and worker in his vocation, as a soldier and a member of the council. Obvious prosperity (Gen. 45:13; Isa. 61:6; Ps. 49:16) confirms the reputation of the man just as much as do honesty, integrity, faithfulness, generosity, etc. (cf. Job 31:1-23). The honor of the woman is manifested--and here the fundamental values appear to have remained even more stable over the millennia—in a well-ordered household, children who turn out well, and marital fidelity, combined with a constant diligence (Prov. 31:10-31).

We actually have in the Old Testament very little conduct that would affect one's honor, that is, of people who themselves place their honor in jeopardy. There certainly is no lack of warnings. But the Old Testament narrators, if we bracket out the writers of the deuteronomic history, who pronounce their judgment in retrospect, are quite restrained in their presentation of real scoundrels. Abimelech is one such (Judg. 9), and possibly the sons of Eli (1 Sam. 2:12-17) and the Korahites (Num. 16). Otherwise, dishonorable conduct is to an amazing extent excused in the Old Testament narratives or even accepted with approval (cf. Gen.27; 30:25-43; 38; 2 Sam. 11). There may occasionally be good reasons for this; taking the narratives as they stand for our point of departure, we can nevertheless say that as a rule "honor" is threatened by external acts of violence (see below, 3). A very reliable historical account, which however no longer allows us clearly to discern all the motives of the participants, provides a specific case (2 Sam. 10). David sends an embassy to the new Ammonite king, Hanun. Officially, it is supposed to be bringing a message of condolence to the new king on the death of his father and to confirm the "covenant of friendship" between the neighbors. In the traveling diplomacy of our times such missions are not at all unfamiliar. However, mistrust toward the king of Jerusalem, who is becoming very powerful—Or is it exaggerated national pride?—prompts some tribal princes to suggest to Hanun: "Was it really David's intention to honor your father, when he sent you this message of condolence? Weren't his envoys rather sent to spy out the city, so that he then could capture it?" (2 Sam. 10:3). These words fall on fertile soil. "Then Hanun had David's messengers seized and had half of their beards cut off. Then he had their cloaks cut off at the waistline, and then let them go" (2 Sam. 10:4). These men are greatly humiliated; they must wait in Jericho until their beards grow back full (v. 5). The national humiliation that is felt is the occasion for the outbreak of war between Israel and Ammon (v. 6 ff.).

Equally vivid and realistic is the story of Tamar, the half-sister of Amnon. She refuses to have sexual relations with him (outside of marriage). For the man to have such relations is a minor fault, but according to the Israelites' code a maiden must remain untouched (2 Sam. 13:12; Deut. 2:13-21). Amnon follows the advice of his "experienced" friend, deceives Tamar, but then rejects her instead of marrying her (2 Sam 13:14 ff.; Deut. 22:28-29). Now the girl's shame is complete; she leaves home, with all the signs of horror and grief, and apparently lives thereafter in a kind of quarantine in the home of her full brother Absalom (2 Sam. 13:16-20).

We probably cannot readily share the feeling that destruction of one's self-esteem and regard—the loss of honor—must bring a person into a profound crisis. The different cultural conditions in Israel, however, bring it about that the dishonoring events occasionally appear to us unreal or even laughable. Imagine a negotiating delegation of one of the great powers of today, with each member exhibiting a disfigured beard and wearing cut-off trousers! Of course, against the background of ancient values and ideas the humiliation becomes obvious. The beard was the sign of masculine authority and dignity (2 Sam. 20:9; Ps. 133:2), and the exposure of the private parts was for both sexes the most disgraceful humiliation (Gen. 8:20-25; Ezek. 23:10). We can go further: to strike someone in the face or to spit in one's face, to take off his shoe, can be a fatal insult (Deut. 25:9-10; 1 Kings 20:37-38). A curse can utterly destroy another person (2 Sam. 16:5-12); the same holds true for malicious gossip (Jer. 20:10; Ps. 41:7; 64:3-6), and probably for the use of malicious enchantments through the manipulation of one's name (Exod. 20:7). Thus honor is endangered precisely because it is exposed to sinister forces. On the other hand, the esteem in which a person is held is closely bound up also with the outward appearance presented by his life. Loss of property (Num. 27:4)

or the dying out of the family (Ruth 4:10), defeat in games (Judg.
14:15) or in battle (1 Sam. 17:46) are just as injurious to honor as
a verbal affront. An Israelite whose honor was assailed felt that
his life was in danger. Honor was something like the psychic
skeleton of a man (cf. Ezek. 28:1-10). If it collapsed, death could
seize one, and to be refused burial was the ultimate dreadful
dishonor that one could undergo (Isa. 14:19; Jer. 19:7).

2. Illness

Even after that first affliction Job is not granted any rest.
Satan undertakes once again to pressure him to denounce God.
This time he gives the rationale for his plan thus: "A man will
give up everything in order to stay alive. But now suppose you
hurt his body—he will curse you to your face!" (Job 2:4-5 TEV)
Thus the Old Testament narrator regards physical
suffering as the most severe test. Man seems self-centered
enough to detach himself from his dearest possession, and even
from wife and child, if thereby he can save his own skin. But if
his life itself is directly affected, then his trust in the beneficent
God, the "dear God," must collapse. And a hideous illness
immediately befalls Job. "Ugly abcesses" break out all over his
body (Job 2:7). Obviously the narrator is thinking of leprosy (cf.
Deut. 28:35; Lev. 13).

a) Kinds of illness

The way Job's illness is presented and numerous other
passages in the Old Testament show how great the Israelites'
fear of serious illness must have been. Not that people in that
time were excessively sensitive; minor indispositions or not yet
completely diagnosed complaints certainly were hardly worth
mentioning in the Israelites' daily life. They were disregarded
or were treated with home remedies (2 Sam. 13:5-9). Wounds
and fractures were properly cleansed and rubbed with oil or
bandaged (Isa. 1:6; Ezek. 30:21). The Shunamite woman simply
held her sick child on her lap—Did he suffer a sunstroke? Or

meningitis? Or some other fever?—until after a short time he died; a picture of uncertainty and maternal helplessness (2 Kings 4:20). On the other hand, if danger was identified—and this ordinarily occurred through the diagnosis by the specialist, the priest or prophet—then began for the Israelite the life-and-death struggle. For every "genuine" illness is a harbinger of death (Job 33:19-22).

Of course, we can no longer today determine with exactness what illnesses were known in Israel and how they are related to the phenomena that are familiar to us. The identifications of illnesses in the Old Testament are too imprecise and the descriptions of symptoms are too ambiguous for such determination. Besides, our state of knowledge is different, our consciousness of illness has changed, and every age, every cultural milieu has its own major illnesses. But the medically exact and complete identification of the ailments of that time is not so important for us. We note that the Old Testament man especially feared a number of afflictions, among them leprosy (Num. 12:12-16; 2 Kings 7:3; 2 Chr. 26:19-21), bubonic plague (1 Sam. 5:6–6:9; 2 Sam. 24:11-15), consumption and various kinds of fever (Deut. 28:22; Ps. 9:5-6), smallpox (Exod. 9:8-12), and some mental illnesses (1 Sam. 19:8; Dan. 4:26-30). All of them appear to have been regarded as punishments (or as extraordinarily severe punishments) sent from God. Leprosy and certain forms of mental derangement even led to exclusion from all human society (Lev. 13:45-46; Dan. 4:29). It is not easy to say how the Israelites ranked other "natural" impairments to life, for example, blindness, mute- ness, the weakness of old age, infant mortality, and deformities; more than in the case of the diseases mentioned earlier, this probably depended on the respective circumstances.

b) Attitudes toward illness

How did the Israelite experience his affliction? How did he understand his fear? Let us begin with the healthy person. Of course, here one may not simply project backward our own conceptions, as though at that time a particular illness was regarded as fatal according to its own laws—as cancer in its advanced stages is for us—or as though according to the Old Testament sickness and health were purely physical conditions which one could affect with medication. Today the awareness that precisely in suffering, body and soul form a unity is still quite new and is far from being universally recognized; in those days it was a self-evident presupposition of thinking: Your will to live can sustain you when you are sick, but if you lose it, your last hope is gone. (Prov. 18:14 TEV)

The Israelite accordingly had a comprehensive understanding of human well-being, body, soul, spirit, human security, and success in all one's undertakings were always included when he spoke of the "healthy" (i.e., "happy," "sound," "strong," etc.) man. The essence of the all-round healthy condition, however, was the blessing of Yahweh. One should enjoy God's protective concern with gratitude (Deut. 12:7; Ps. 128:3-6). The amazing thing is this: in spite of a profound recognition of man's perversity (Gen. 8:21; Ps. 14:3) and in spite of frightful experiences in history (Ps. 124:1-5; 129:1-3), the Israelite accepted the unspoiled, intact world as the foundation of his existence.

c) Causes of illness

The harmony between God and man—the precondition for the equilibrium of the world that is peopled by spirits—is seriously threatened by illness. What is the cause of illness? The ancient Israelite would say: evil, which is inexplicably but just as obviously present in the world as was the serpent in Paradise (Gen. 3:1). In contrast to many theoreticians today, however, the Old Testament man would not try to localize evil unambiguously and once-for-all. It can be lodged in man himself. Perhaps he has, knowingly or unknowingly, out of fear or presumption in the great "household" of the world, offended one of the powers or broken a rule (Ps. 38:3, 18). In the course of Israel's history the written law of Yahweh more and more came to be the norm, the violation of which produced illness (2 Chr. 21:12-20). But it would be a distortion to try to read the Old Testament solely from the perspective of one's own guilt. Many illnesses were undoubtedly caused arbitrarily by evil powers. Indeed, the dreadful thing about the story of Job is that God himself acknowledges to Satan: "You persuaded me to let you attack him for no reason at all" (Job 3:2 TEV). How much more mischief, then, could one expect of demons (Ps. 59:6, 14; 91:5-6) or from hostile men (Pss. 3:1; 11:2). The worst thing in a case of illness, it seems, was the tormenting uncertainty about its implications. Some symptoms might be regarded as unmistakable. Thus leprosy or the plague were "punishments" from God. Nevertheless, even in these cases official confirmation was required, as is shown in Leviticus 13 and 1 Samuel 5 and 6. In the latter passage, the Philistines immediately recognize the connection between the pestilence and the war booty they had brought from Israel, the ark of Yahweh (5:7). Nevertheless they want to get to the root of the matter. If the oxen take the ark back to Israelite soil, "then he has sent this plague upon us." Otherwise, "we know that it is not he that has punished us, but someone else" (6:9; the expression in this verse that usually is translated as "perchance," or something of the sort, only indicates the continuing uncertainty about the source of the pestilence).

d) Diagnosis and cure

The necessity of gaining some certainty as to the cause, nature, and seriousness of the illness led then, as it does now, to the development of techniques of diagnosis appropriate to those times. Though quite different as to their contents and results, ancient and modern practices can be placed, functionally speaking, altogether on the same level. The patient needs the counsel of the specialist, and society is interested in identifying any threatening illnesses as soon as possible. Unfortunately the Old Testament provides us with only scanty information about the methods of diagnosis used in Israel. From the rest of the ancient Orient we are familiar with

an abundance of mantic practices, for example divination on
the basis of drops of oil that were sprinkled on water or on the
basis of the shape of the liver that was taken from a sacrificial
animal. Such efforts to ascertain the future were strictly
forbidden in the latter half of the Old Testament era (Deut.
18:10-11; Ezek. 21:26), just as was conjuring up the dead, which
was nevertheless practiced (1 Sam. 28). But we have sure
indications that down to the time of the late monarchy certain
kinds of divination were allowed even in Israel, for example,
through the interpretation of dreams, by casting lots, and by
prophetic utterances (1 Sam. 28:6). In earlier times the prophet
himself was even called the "seer" (1 Sam. 9:9). In the
underground, in the folk-religion, moreover, all sorts of
questionable cults and practices continued (Jer. 44:15-19;
Ezek. 13:17-18), even in the period of the strict observance of
the law.

Before we take up specifically the prophetic practice of
diagnosis, a further word on the role of the priest in the
evaluation of illnesses. We have seen that when leprosy was
suspected the priests had authority to judge (Lev. 13; Deut.
24:8; 2 Chr. 26: 20). The reason for this is easy to see. The
priests had to decide in general whether or not an Israelite
could participate in the services of worship, whether he was
"clean" or "unclean" (Lev. 11–15). Because those suffering
from leprosy were in no way eligible for participation in the
cult, it fell to the priests also to check the symptoms of the
illness. Thus their judgment was not primarily a diagnosis that
served in the treatment of the sickness, but a protective
measure for preserving the purity of the cultus. Possibly there
were in Israel also other illnesses or defects that were cultically
significant in this way and required priestly evaluation. We
have suggestions of such in Deut. 23:2 and Lev. 21:16-23, for
example, but explicit directions to the priests to take an interest
in such cases have not been handed down.

And diagnosis by the prophet? The patient or his family
had one concern: whether he would regain his health (2 Kings
1:2; 8:8; 1 Kings 14:1-3). In any case, the texts referred to report

a question on this point, and only this, addressed to the prophet. The answer from God that is given through the prophet's mouth, however, is often more comprehensive than the question suggests. It may even have included, as a rule, both diagnosis and suggested treatment, even though we can no longer document this. In any case, both elements are contained in counsels that are given to the sick, as in 1 Samuel 16:15-16; 2 Kings 5:10; Isaiah 38:1. In what manner the prophet ascertained God's answer in private consultations cannot be determined now with certainty. It is probable that, as in the case of inquiries on matters of national concern, he went into a state of ecstasy or sought an oracle by casting lots (2 Kings 3:15-16; Num. 27:21; 1 Sam. 30:7-8). The "seer," the "man of God," or the "prophet" appears as the competent authority to consult in time of illness.

The diagnosis had to be followed by a treatment of the illness; whether it followed immediately and was performed by the diagnostician himself is not clear. However, traces of prophetic healing practice are found in several texts (Num. 12; I Kings 13:4-6; 17:17-24; 2 Kings 4:18-37; 5:8-14; Isa. 38; Job 33:19-30). The later tradition presumably has partially suppressed narratives of healing because they offered occasion for misunderstandings. They could easily be interpreted as magical performances; but any form of magic was strictly prohibited (Exod. 22:17; Deut. 18:9-12; Isa. 47:9). In the exilic and postexilic era even the free prophetic proclamation of the word had to yield to the religion of the priests and the law (Zech. 13:2-3). For the authors of the late books of Chronicles, which in fact like 2 Samuel and 1 and 2 Kings portray the time of the monarchy, prophets are only spokesmen of the law (cf. 2 Chr. 15:1-7); any trace of their practice of healing is missing. The existing passages, however, suffice to allow us to discern in outline the surely widespread treatment of illness by the prophets. It appears that a central place was held by the supplication of the man of God (Num. 12:13; 1 Kings 13:6; 17:20-21; 2 Kings 4:33; Job 33:24-25; cf. Gen. 20:7; Num. 21:7; 2 Kings 5:11). In addition, the prophet performed symbolic-ritual actions (1 Kings 17:21; 2 Kings 4:34-35) and had medicinal-cultic remedies applied (Isa. 38:21-22; 2 Kings 5:10; cf. Num. 17:11-13; 21:8-9).

The story of King Hezekiah's illness, preserved in Isaiah (in shorter form also in 2 Kings 20:1-11), sets us on still another track. Along with the account of the prophet's activity, it contains a prayer of petition and thanksgiving of the sick man on his bed. The same situation is presupposed by Job 33:19 ff., while 1 Kings 8:37-40 *inter alia* speaks of the prayer of the sick man in the temple. From such indications we conclude that in ancient Israel, just as among other peoples of the Orient, there must have been regular religious services of prayer for the sick. In such services a "religious functionary" (prophet? priest? singer?) probably was the leading figure, for a sick person did not know how he should pray in his particular situation of distress. Now in the Old Testament Psalter we have preserved, among the many prayers of petition and lament for suffering people, some which could be used, even if not exclusively, in the case of serious illness (e.g., Pss. 6; 38; 41; 69; 102). Such prayers belonged, along with various rites of expiation and purification (cf. Pss. 26:6; 51:7), to the home and temple services by means of which the sick person hoped to gain healing. The drastic portrayal of his suffering was supposed to move Yahweh to banish the illness.

> Thy indignation has left no part of my body unscarred;
>   there is no health in my whole frame because of my sin,
> For my iniquities have poured over my head;
>   they are a load heavier than I can bear.
> My wounds fester and stink because of my folly.
>
> I am bowed down and utterly prostrate.
> All day long I go about as if in mourning,
>   for my loins burn with fever,
>   and there is no wholesome flesh in me.
> All battered and benumbed,
>   I groan aloud in my heart's longing.
> O Lord, all my lament lies open before thee
>   and my sighing is no secret to thee.
>   (Ps. 38:3-9 NEB)

Here a person speaks of his pain, of the deterioration of his body, and of his fear of death. But it is not the voice of an isolated individual that we hear, but the cry of the many who have recognized a connection between their sickness and the earlier conduct of their lives. They may confess their guilt and expect to be healed (Ps. 32). Others, convinced of their innocence, may attribute to God all the responsibility for their suffering (Pss. 7; 17; 26; Job 9:15-24, etc.). Such a breadth is exhibited by Israel's liturgy and life of faith in the time of the Old Testament.

3. Violence

It is possible to take the position that all human suffering consists essentially of experiences of loss and deprivation. In such a view of things, man is reduced to his various roles as possessor. The Old Testament, however, sees in man not only the manager and owner of the property entrusted to him, but to a large extent a partner, a person in relation, in a social context. The unhappy, and indeed often inhuman, state of interpersonal relations is a further source of suffering, regardless of whether and to what extent personal losses arise in that connection. When David chooses from among the three punishments offered as options to him—of all things the judgment of God, namely the plague, because men are more cruel than God (2 Sam. 24:14)—this expresses what is also the contemporary view of a very realistic estimate of human "nature." Man can in fact exhibit unsuspected strength and imagination when he wants to prevail over his rivals, and in an ultimate way when he has the opportunity to inflict pain upon others.

Let us pause for a moment and ask: Must it actually be so? It may be that mankind has not much more time to answer this question and to get human aggressiveness under control. There are many researchers and thinkers who are intensively concerned with acceptable solutions to this problem. Here we can say with respect to our subject that wherever men live together there are forms of hostile and injurious encounters.

But it is equally evident that here and there on our earth, whether among the Indians of South America, in the South Sea islands, or in Swabia, more peaceable communities have existed or still exist than seems possible, according to reports and observation, in the Near East and the Middle East. Another question: Is the particularly strong aggressiveness of the inhabitants of that region between the Arabian desert and the Mediterranean Sea perhaps a direct consequence of the extraordinarily harsh living conditions? And could Christianity's above-average power to prevail, which frequently has issued in the persecution of "others," perhaps be in part an Old Testament-Jewish legacy?

The Old Testament does not treat our problem theoretically and systematically. Yet the utterances of Old Testament narrators, poets, and writers, made with the most widely diverse intentions, allow us to recognize that man's use of violence against his fellowmen has something to do with the general intellectual equipment and the capacity for power. God's final creation shares in his dominion (Gen. 1:26, 28; Ps. 8:5-8); this participation is made possible through the effective recognition of reality (Gen. 3:8; Prov. 22:12). An unexplainable hunger for knowledge and power drives man beyond himself; he wants to be sole ruler (Gen. 3:6; 11:4; Ps. 10:3-11; Ezek. 28:12-19). And the boundlessness of his claim in relation to God is matched by the ruthlessness of his conduct toward his fellowman. This is shown in the last two passages cited as well as in many others (cf. Judg. 9:1-6; Amos 1:13; Prov. 14:31).

a) Violence in the family and the clan

Now we shall examine the misuse of power and the suffering that it caused at the various levels of social organization in ancient Israel. The smallest unit was the (larger) family and clan, bound together by ties of blood, elemental human needs, and obligations of support, as they prevailed among kinsmen from earliest times, and by common daily work. Normally the individual found a measure of security in the family unit, such as we in the age of social regroupings (nuclear family, urbanization) can only dream of. In spite of that, we may not simply regard the Israelites' family life as paradise on earth. Then, too, tensions could arise in the most intimate circle which could then be discharged against a member of the group—with devastating consequences for the one affected. In this connection we shall speak only in passing of the numerous court intrigues that even down to the present regularly decimate ruling Oriental families (cf. 1 Kings 2:13-25; 2 Kings 8:7-15; 11:1-3). They belong more to the upheavals that are set off by superimposed power structures. Instead, we restrict ourselves to the misunderstandings, estrangements, and outbreaks of hatred which can make life a hell for people who are closely bound to each other.

What must have appeared as improbable, in view of the parental absolute authority even over children of marriageable age and in view of the possible plurality of wives, nevertheless could occur. There were all sorts of tribulations of love. A collection of wedding songs, now combined under the title, "The Song of Solomon," tenderly and touchingly describes the yearning of lovers. The story of Jacob's earning his bride (Gen. 29), the marriage narratives in which Samson is the chief figure (Judg. 14–16), the accounts of the fateful love of Amnon (2 Sam. 13), and the marriage of Michal and David, which was overshadowed by political events (1 Sam. 18–19; 2 Sam. 6), or of Bathsheba with David (2 Sam. 11), contain scanty and yet psychologically fine indications of love and the pangs of love. Thus the social forms of ancient Israel, though foreign to us, did not prevent those age-old human feelings; though it is true that concrete experiences of suffering, for example, were actualized in a different system of coordinates. Jacob had to serve twice seven years (Gen. 29:20, 30; "It seemed to him like only a few days, because he loved her so much," v. 20). Samson was twice betrayed by his wife (Judg. 14:17; 16:15-20), his eyes were put out, he was sentenced to penal servitude (Judg. 16:21), and he finally died along with his enemies in a violent act of revenge (Judg. 16:30). Saul's daughter Michal, who loved her husband

more than her father (1 Sam. 18:28; 19:11 ff.), was abruptly
given to another man (2 Sam. 25:44). After a long time
David—who in the meantime had a considerable harem and six
sons (2 Sam. 3:1-5)—demanded Michal back (For political
reasons? 2 Sam. 3:13-16); this meant new suffering for the
woman, although it is reported only that her second husband
ran after her, weeping, when she was taken away (v. 16).
Finally, Michal had to suffer God's punishment because she
criticized the king, who in ecstatic dance before the Ark of the
Covenant (and in public) had thrown off his clothing (2 Sam.
6:20-23). The fate of a woman some three thousand years ago?
To be sure, it appears that the woman's subjection to the man's
will and often enough the silent suffering under his arbitrariness, in spite of all the efforts at emancipation, are still a long
way from being overcome. Conversely, this holds true when in
many marriages, the wife subjects the husband to her skillful
management.

In Israel the awareness of the problem on this point
certainly was different. In the Old Testament there are, it is
true, still traces of matriarchal conceptions, as for example in
the very ancient saying in Genesis 2:24, and perhaps in the
peculiar form of the commandment ("Honor your mother and
father") in Leviticus 19:3. But for the rest, the principle prevails
everywhere "that every husband should be the master of his
home" (Esther 1:22 TEV). And so the woman gives in (Ps.
45:11), and nothing is said about her daily burden in house and
garden. It is only in a roundabout way that we gain an
impression of the weight of her tasks. Proverbs 31:10-31 sings
the praises of the diligent housewife—of course one-sidedly,
from the man's perspective. According to this passage she
labors from early morning until late evening (v. 15, 18), and is
always cheerful (v. 25). She takes care of her husband (v. 11-12),
while he apparently has lots of time for important conversations
"in the gate" (v. 23; we would say "in the marketplace" or "in
business"). However, so far as we know, no one in Israel
complained about this apportionment of roles. Should we
therefore speak of an unconscious suffering? The complaints of

women have to do especially with the troubles of pregnancy
(Gen. 3:16); in the same context, it is the man who (still?) earns
the daily bread by the sweat of his brow (Gen. 3:17-19).

The real problem for a woman begins—and again this is
seen from the man's perspective—when she becomes unfaithful to her traditional obligations. Open rebellion against the
clear command of her husband (Esth. 1:12) was very likely an
unprecedented exception, more legend than actuality. But the
suspicion of marital infidelity could fall upon her (Num.
5:11-31), even if only because of jealousy on the part of her
husband (v. 14). And then what happened? The woman had to
undergo a religious ritual of judgment that is, to our way of
thinking, degrading. If she was found guilty, the death penalty
was certain (cf. Lev. 20:10; Deut. 22:21-22). Or the husband
could simply grow tired of his wife. He did not need to give any
reasons, but might simply "send her away" (Deut. 24:1-4; the
justification in v. 1 should be translated, "because he has found
something about her that doesn't please him"). According to
the Old Testament, divorce is nothing more than the unilateral
renunciation of the marriage contract by the man; the woman is
protected against this only in exceptional cases (Deut. 21:10-14;
22:28-29; cf. Exod. 21:7-11). But then what is the fate of the
woman who is divorced? If she cannot find a new husband (cf.
Isa. 4:1) and cannot return to her parent or kinsman, then she
belongs, along with many widows and orphans, foreigners and
manumitted slaves, cripples and mentally ill persons, among
those living on the periphery of society. It is true that the quite
considerable social legislation in Israel provided protective
measures for some categories of these unfortunate persons (cf.
Exod. 22:20-23; Lev. 19:13-15; Deut. 24:14-22), yet the
divorced woman who had no one to care for her is not included
among these. The only way left open for her was prostitution (cf.
Gen. 38:14 ff.).

The Old Testament attests with relative frequency still
another crisis in the life of a woman. She could remain childless,
and because the biological functions of the body were not
understood in detail, and the cause of infertility would never

have been sought in the man, the woman was held solely responsible. The torments of soul that resulted for a woman from her barrenness are vividly portrayed by the story of Hannah (1 Sam. 1:6-8, 10-16; in this case, the husband, Elkanah, is sad, too, and in spite of everything he still loves the childless woman; v. 5). The rivalry among an Israelite's wives, whether they were equal in rank or not, could lead to violent conflicts (Gen. 16:4-6; 29:31–30:24). This particular problem of the Israelite family apparently was always felt as an oppressive one. The figure of the barren woman whom God himself has "sealed" moves the Old Testament authors (cf. Gen. 11:30; 25:11; Judg. 13:2-3) and plays a role, in symbolic elevation, in the promises of the future (Isa. 54:1-4; 66:7-9). Apparently the curse of childlessness will finally be set aside only in a new order that will be achieved by God (Exod. 23:26; Deut. 7:14; Ps. 113:9).

All this is not intended to create the impression that the life of the woman in ancient Israel was one of unrelieved misery. Human courage for living can also transform adverse circumstances. And the Old Testament on the whole, precisely because it does not need to whitewash the dark side of life, allows free course to the joyous affirmation of life. This holds true even for the relatively few passages in which, according to the biblical testimony, we have before us the unfalsified opinion of women (cf. Exod. 15:20-21; Judg. 5:1 ff.; 1 Sam. 2:1 ff. = hymns of praise about events that are important to men; Ruth 2:13-14 = gratitude for acceptance by a man. But frequently the woman made the decisions for the family: Gen. 3:6; Judg. 4:17 ff.; 1 Sam. 25; 1 Kings 21:5 ff.; 2 Kings 22:14 ff.). Our examination should rather, by way of example, make two things clear: the Old Testament tells of painful individual experiences which take place in the context of the primary social groups, and we can readily feel a sense of solidarity with the suffering people. And in a critical reading of the Old Testament we encounter, even in the context of the family circle, structurally conditioned sufferings that probably were not consciously felt in this same way at all by the people of that time.

Studies similar to that which we have undertaken on the role of the woman obviously could be conducted on the other members of the Israelite family group. We have already spoken of the almost unlimited authority of the fathers of the household over children and servants (cf. Deut. 21:18-21; Prov. 19:18). We connect this report with our own situation: thousands of cases of child abuse every year, many of them with fatal outcomes, and this in a civilized and allegedly Christianized country that displays a powerful apparatus of law, justice, and social services for the protection of children. How did Israelite parents react when their children brought them grief (cf. Prov. 17:25)? We do not know, because such accounts of day-to-day matters are not preserved for us. And we can go on to ask at once: How was it with other weak members of the family, the sick, the mentally ill, the cripples, the aged? Were they subjected somewhat to rebuffs from the group? What was the relationship of the children to each other? Were there in Israel typical situations of conflict and suffering? And finally, because even the head of the family certainly did not simply stand above the tensions: In what way was the father involved in the sufferings of those under his protection by way of sharing in them?

We can take up these questions only quite briefly. Certainly the solidarity of the family protects the weak. But it occasionally develops that the weak person becomes a burden or even a danger for the others. The cultural history of humanity offers numerous examples of the exposure of deformed newborn infants or of aged persons no longer able to work. And in Israel? We have seen (above, 2) that those suffering from leprosy and the mentally disturbed were thrust out of human society. In other cases, morality and law demand humanitarian help and consideration (Lev. 19:14, 32; Prov. 16:31), while again certain bodily defects exclude one from religious practices (Deut. 23:2; Lev. 21:16 ff.), and therefore perhaps these are not unimportant in the family circle also. The conclusion is suggested that for some special cause a person could lose the protection of his family. And actually the prayer-literature of the Old Testament in particular has preserved the laments of those who are outcasts and isolated (cf. Pss. 41:5-9; 71; 88:18). Rivalries among siblings often become a major theme in the Old Testament; one need only think of the stories of Jacob and Esau (Gen. 25:19-34; 27) or of Joseph and his brothers (Gen. 37-50). Furthermore, Cain's murder of his brother (Gen. 4), Solomon's conduct of his office (1 Kings 2:13 ff.), the rejection of Jephthah (Judg. 11:1-7), and the bloody tyranny of Abimelech (Judg. 9:5) belong here. It appears that the Israelite family was especially susceptible to disruptions in matters involving the sons' claims to property and the inheritance. The head of the family ultimately could only look on in helpless sorrow when the sons departed from the right way (Prov. 10:1; 19:13). Impressive narrative portrayals of paternal suffering are found (e.g., in Gen. 37:32-35; 42:36; 43:14; 44:18-34; 2 Sam. 18:19-19:9; 1 Sam. 2:12-26).

Thus according to the Old Testament, self-destructive forces are at work even in the most intimate circles of human society. The announcement by the prophet of approaching disaster can simply represent the disintegration of the family as the essence of all evil (Isa. 3:5; Mic. 7:5-6). When a man cannot escape suffering even where of all places he might be secure, how then can he survive in other, that is, in larger and more impersonal contexts?

b) Violence in secondary forms of organization

Secondary forms of organization of society function according to different principles from primary groups. In the latter situation, direct human contact and comprehensible, limited aims (e.g., the acquisition of food) are the crucial factors, while the larger communities must be built upon more abstract foundations, upon morality, law, political or social means of constraint, and religious or ideological conceptions of values. This logically leads also to other, different experiences of suffering. Anyone who has ever been caught in the thicket of the bureaucracy, for whom the consequences of demagogic campaigns or of economic and political decisions of principle have become manifest, will be able to make a clear assessment of the autonomy and the anonymous power of secondary organizations.

As we have already indicated in the Introduction (I. 2. a), in the Old Testament quite different forms of society and groupings according to interests can be discerned. Again, we propose only to touch upon a few in passing, from among the abundance of possible points of view, in order then to allow the texts to speak more in detail in a few exemplary cases.

The tribal structure of the early period—quite apart from the fact that it did not afford adequate protection against enemies from without—held sufficient inflammable material for inner-Israelite conflicts. Because there was no overarching association or union, the private interests of the tribal groups were much stronger than similar phenomena in the regions of a contemporary federal state or in the wings of our parties. The Old Testament mentions, for example, culpable indifference toward common aims (Judg. 5:13-18, 23), disputes and wars over claims to territory (Deut. 33:20-21; 1 Kings 15:16-22), problems of leadership in the religious association of the tribes (Gen. 49:10-12; Judg. 8:1-3; 12:1-6), disunity in cultic polity (Josh. 22:9-29), and a punitive expedition against a tribe (Judg. 19–20). Such reports suggest a slight suspicion that smouldering and occasionally erupting tribal disputes claimed many a victim.

The monarchical structure of the state in Israel (from the tenth to the beginning of the sixth century B.C.) brought the tribal conflicts under control to some extent. In their place, the new central power brought new dangers for the people. Freedom-conscious Israelites had always feared tyrannical assaults of a king (Judg. 8:22-23; 9). The conduct of office on the part of at least some rulers confirmed these evil suspicions (cf. 1 Kings 12:4, 14; Jer. 22; Ezek. 34). A later writer of history has Samuel set forth in a comprehensive way how much the populace would have to suffer under their own king (1 Sam. 8:11-18). Other sources are less fundamentally judgmental on this point. For them, a good king is a genuine blessing (Prov.

20:26, 28; cf. Ps. 72), yet the wrong man in such a position of power is a misfortune (Prov. 30:22).

Ancient Israel's economic order was, as already indicated (above, 1), not without its problems. During the period of the monarchy many farmers lost their land; they were out-maneuvered by large landowners and made tenants or bondservants (Isa. 5:8; Mic. 2:1-2; Jer. 34:8-11). The misery of those affected is easily imagined (1 Sam. 22:2; 2 Kings 4:1 ff.). We can only infer from hints to what extent royal business enterprises (1 Kings 9:26-28; 10:22, 26-29), administration (2 Sam. 20:23-26), or military organizations (1 Sam. 11:6-7; 2 Sam. 10:7, 17; 15:17-22; 2 Chr. 25:5-6; 26:11-15) exhibited specific—or even typical, all-too-human—weaknesses and hence imposed burdens upon people. It is certain that in the army, contests over leadership were often settled with the dagger (2 Sam. 3:22-30; 20:8-10). From generals such as Joab, Jehu (2 Kings 9-10), or even David himself (1 Sam. 22:2; 25:39; 2 Sam. 8:2) one may not expect any compassion that is out of keeping with their position. In the world as it was governed at that time, "advocacy" certainly was a favorite means of achieving one's aim (2 Kings 4:13; Jer. 38:7-9), for in the maintenance of power, people were not as a rule supersensitive, regardless of all the consciousness of right. At any rate, the Old Testament is full of complaints and accusations against open and hidden acts of violence, in which, as a rule, the circumstances of the period of the monarchy are presupposed (cf. Isa. 1:15-17; 10:1-2; Jer. 6:7; 7:9; Pss. 94:3-7; 109:2-3).

At one point, it becomes particularly clear how people in Israel thought about the evil in society. It is the point at which prophets and preachers, poets and sages must speak about the violation of law. Israel shared with its neighbors a liking, indeed a zeal, for the legal ordering of all things. Law is almost cosmic force (cf. 2 Sam. 23:3-4; Pss. 45:6-7; 89:14; 98:8-9); it is above all the norm for human behavior and a kind of basic substance of any interpersonal relationship. One could say that for the Israelite, "law" and "justice" are something like oxygen, in which alone life is possible. It is rewarding to use a concordance and look up the Old Testament passages on "law," "justice," "peace," "salvation," and "life," and to reflect upon them. To abide within this sphere of life appears to have been a high goal for the Israelite (cf. Gen. 38:26; Job 2:3; Ps. 119; Ezek. 18). The transgressor, on the other hand, is the person who disrupts the healthful state of things and thereby brings upon himself and others endless grief (cf. Deut. 27:15-26; Ps. 109; Isa. 5:8-23). That is to say, the man of the Old Testament had a very keen sense and feeling for justice and for injury done to justice; here we touch his very life-nerve.

In this section our consideration is not restricted to suffering in its personal aspects alone. Therefore we cannot avoid asking how, then, right was institutionally preserved in Israel. In the pre-exilic period this was done essentially on three levels. For cases involving punishment and for civil cases, the full assembly of the citizens in the gate was in principle responsible (the gate was the public meeting place). In certain cases of cultic offenses, or in unclear criminal cases that made a divine judgment necessary, the priests decided. Finally, the king as God's deputy had a certain right of supervision over matters of justice. When good order suffered injury, these institutions and the persons responsible for them therefore were directly involved. We recognize this most clearly in the sharp criticism by the prophets in the eighth and seventh centuries B.C. They call the injustice of their time by name. Thus, for example, the prophet Amos:

I know all your crimes.
I know how many wrongs you have done.
You persecute the innocent, you take bribes;
You refuse the poor his rights in the gate.

(Amos 5:12)

They turn justice into gall
And turn righteousness upside down.

(Amos 5:7)

They sell the righteous,
For the price of a pair of sandals they barter the poor.

(Amos 2:6)

The attack against those who pervert justice obviously is made under commission from God and in solidarity with those who are deprived of their rights. Quite similar outbursts against the perversion of judicial power and the destruction of rights are found in the prophet Hosea (5:11; 10:4), Micah (3:1-3; 6:9-12), Isaiah (1:21, 23; 5:22, 28:7), Zephaniah (3:1-5), Jeremiah (2:8, 34; 5:1-5; 8:8; 22:17), and Ezekiel (7:10-11; 9:9; 18:8). Indeed, the later prophet Zechariah, who appeared shortly before 500 B.C., is able to see in their stand for the right and in the battle against injustice the main task of his earlier colleagues (Zech. 7:7-10). With the same resoluteness Old Testament laws and wisdom-texts warn against the destruction of justice and right (cf. Exod. 23:1-3, 6-8; Lev. 19:15-18; Deut. 5:20; 16:18-20; Prov. 10:2; 11:19; 12:17; 16:10; Eccles. 3:16; 4:1). Finally, narrative texts give us a glimpse now and then of injustice that occurs. Naboth, an Israelite farmer, refuses to sell his vineyard to King Ahab. He falls victim then to the machinations of Queen Jezebel. Perjured witnesses testify against him, he is condemned and stoned to death, and his land is confiscated (1 Kings 21:1-16). In another place the prophet Nathan uses a story that was taken from life in order to speak to King David's conscience. A rich man took the last sheep of his poor neighbor. The just verdict—so David spontaneously declared—must be death for the guilty one and fourfold compensation for what was stolen. Then Nathan said, "You are the man!" David had unwittingly exposed his own bending of the law. He had tried to cover up adultery and murder (2 Sam. 12:1-9). Or again, a prophet named Uriah, unknown to us, was put to death by King Jehoiakim because he had prophesied against the nation of Judah. Jeremiah barely escaped the same fate in a highly charged judicial proceeding, because he found defenders who prevailed against the priests and prophets (Jer. 26:7-24).

The concern for a deliberate, reflective order of law can be traced throughout the entire Old Testament. The concern is also for the settlement of conflicts and for "wise" guidance of all human affairs. Any disruption of the sphere of right and justice is a catastrophe for those affected and at the same time is disastrous for the community. For injustice works like poison or

like an explosive. It is true that an entire nation may be blinded and
unwilling to see the evil consequences (cf. Jer. 5:21, 31; 8:7; Isa.
6:9-10; Ezek. 3:7-9). But those who have been denied or deprived
of their rights and the possibility of living certainly have become
aware of their situation. Their voice also can be heard in the Old
Testament, and indeed once again primarily in the formularies of
prayer, which are not meant to portray the individual's fate but
typical suffering.

> O Lord, my God, I seek refuge in you;
> > save me from my persecutors, snatch me from danger.
> Otherwise they will fall upon me like lions.
> They will tear me in pieces, and no one can help me.
> O Lord, my God, if I have done these things,
> > if my hands are stained with such wrong,
> > if I have injured those who wanted peace,
> > if I have despoiled anyone without cause,
> > then let my enemy pursue me,
> > then he will seize me and cut me down to the ground,
> > then I belong under the earth.
>
> (Ps. 7:1-5)

Such prayers of those who are persecuted without cause and of
the disenfranchised concentrate upon petitions for help, the
declaration of innocence, and denunciation of the persecutors;
and they allow us moreover to see that the suffering of the
innocent affects body and soul and brings one into a crisis of
faith (cf. Ps. 17; 26; 73; Jer. 11:18-20; 18:19-23). We shall return
to this in connection with Job's sufferings.

We should at least briefly call attention further to the
sufferings which, in theology and church, are preferably swept
under the rug. I refer to those that are internally created, that
is, hardships and distresses that are caused by the church's own
teaching and structure. Like every other human society, the
"fellowship of the saints" also sometimes produces specific
forms of organization which contain within themselves a
corresponding division of power and hence particular possibi-

lities of conflict. Everyone knows that not infrequently bitter struggles over leadership and direction arise within congregation and church. These are usually grounded in a claim made by individuals or groups that their theological views or forms of religious life are the only correct ones. Everyone knows also how absurd and tragic the misunderstandings, accusations, and mutual injuries among brethren in faith often can be. Were there similar occurrences in ancient Israel?

This question obviously must be answered in the affirmative. The challenge to be holy, which was already made in the Old Testament (cf. Exod. 19:6; Lev. 19:2), never resulted in a community free of conflict. On the contrary, the radical claims themselves of the Old Testament community of faith perhaps are partly responsible for many regrettable conflicts, and it is even possible that many of the problems and their solutions presented in the Old Testament continue to have their effect in the situations of conflict and suffering in contemporary Christianity.

We do not know how much historical truth is found in the stories from the time of Moses. In any case, however, the various accounts of rebellions during the wandering in the wilderness (e.g., Exod. 16:2 ff.; 17:2 ff.; 32:1 ff.; Num. 11:1 ff.; 14:1 ff.; 20:2 ff.) point to more or less early conflicts within the cultic community. Frequently the entire nation is dissatisfied, quarreling and grumbling over living conditions and the organization of the community. Especially vivid and painful is the story of "Korah's company" (Num. 16), who in the name of a "universal" priesthood rose up against Moses and Aaron (Num. 16:3). According to the account as we have it, Yahweh cast the ringleaders, together with their families, alive into the underworld (Num. 16:32-33), while 250 of their followers were burned up in a blaze of divine fire (Num. 16:35). In its present form the narrative is supposed to account for the preeminent position of the Aaronic priestly family (Num. 17:5). We value it as an evidence of long-lasting quarrels among the tribes that had the religious leadership in Israel (cf. the expulsion of Abiathar in 1 Kings 2:35 and the subsequent legitimizing of the Zadokites in 1 Chr. 6:1-8).

Another internal problem within the community arose out of the fact that the Israelite was not automatically admitted to the religious services. A kind of "church discipline" prevailed. In this connection we are not talking about persons of lesser rights, who certainly never possessed the full cultic rights, but of males who were full citizens. Even for them certain limitations and restrictions were in force. Various illnesses rendered them unclean and therefore excluded them from attendance at the religious services (Lev. 13:45-46; 15:31); many infirmities, and descent from the Ammonites or Moabites alike were irreconcilable with membership in the community (Deut. 23:2-7). In addition, there were ethical and cultic demands that had to be observed if an Israelite wished to participate in the life and blessing of the community's worship (Ps. 15; Isa. 33:14-16). From Jeremiah we even learn that one time he, for reasons unknown to us, was not permitted to go to the temple (Jer. 36:5). To be cut off from the very source of life must have been for a man of that time an immense burden. We can read Psalms 42 and 43 as the prayer of those who were still able to cherish the hope of being readmitted to the sanctuary:

> As a deer longs for fresh water,
>   so I long for you, O God!
> I thirst for God, the God who really lives.
> When shall I come, when may I appear before him?
>   (Ps. 42:1-2)

Still another troublesome question is the question of the real will of God. Which of the two prophets is correct: Hananiah, who advocates a reversal of foreign policy in favor of Israel (Jer. 28), or Jeremiah, who under commission by the same God is threatening utter destruction upon the nation of Judah (Jer. 27)? In a somewhat broader perspective, we can include here the struggle of men who are faithful to Yahweh against the belief in Baal which has been disseminated in the Israelite community. Which God is the real God of Israel? Which one shows himself to be the mightier? (Cf. 1 Kings 18; 22; and the prophets Hosea and Jeremiah.) Even the division between the

Samaritan and Jerusalem communities, which begins in the
Old Testment, goes back to profound differences of theological
opinion. What did God want as to the conduct of one's life,
worship, the locus of the cult? (Cf. Ezra 4; Neh. 3:33-38; 4.)
Since Old Testament times the will of God has often become
known only through struggle and pain. Those who suffer this
pain include true and false prophets as well as many who were
not aligned with either.

There is a fourth point at which there emerges in the Old
Testament a tendency leading to suffering that is rooted in the
theology and the structure of the community. After the
catastrophe of 587 B.C. Israel needed new coherent and
compelling ideas and forms of life if it was to continue to exist as
"God's people." In that time of distress Yahweh, the God of
Israel, acquired his universal dimensions. He became the sole
and exclusive creator and Lord of the world (this becomes most
readily evident in the book of Deutero-Isaiah, Isa. 40–55). At
the same time the doctrine of the will of God that had once been
revealed and now was found in written form in the Torah was
being firmly established (cf. Deut. 4:1-2; 2 Kings 23:3; Neh.
9:3). In these doctrinal opinions the Israelite community found
the adequate expression of its new form of organization.
Without the constraints of a state and monarchy of their own,
they came together into a "church" that was grounded in their
belonging to a people and in their confession. Even though this
development perhaps was necessary, still it also brought grave
distress to people. Any such policy of drawing boundaries of
distinction produces hardening on one side and embitterment
on the other. The Old Testament has several accounts of foreign
wives, in whom people saw a constant danger to their own faith
(cf. Gen. 3:1-6; 1 Kings 11:1-13), who were simply expelled—
losing their husbands and children, who certainly did not suffer
the loss lightly (Ezra 9, 10; Neh. 13:23-31; Num. 25:6-15): human
suffering caused for the sake of a national idea! In our texts, of
course, only the leaders of the people are grieved (cf. Ezra 9:3;
10:6), and the opposition to the inhuman measures was only very
timid (Ezra 10:15). Phinehas, who had stabbed an Israelite

and his Midianite wife to atone for the apostasy from Yahweh, was explicitly praised by God for his "zeal" (Num. 25:11).

The concern for keeping the community and the faith pure then also led—it is probable that this too first occurred in the exilic or postexilic period—to bloody persecution of sooth-sayers, conjurors, and many others of a different belief. It is true that we read already in the ancient law cited in Exod. 22:17, "You shall not allow witches to live." But this proscription could be aimed at "black magic" and sorcery that endangered the community, which is taboo in all cultures. It is in the deuteronomic law (Deut. 18:9-13; 2 Kings 21:6; 23:24) that the eradication of those who do not blamelessly adhere to the cult of Yahweh becomes a socio-political program: murder in the name of a utopian purity of the faith which will never be actualized? The same question must be posed with reference to the ideology of the so-called "holy war" in the Old Testament. That the land flowing with milk and honey had to be purged of all Canaanite elements by the immigrant Israelites is demon-strably only a later idea which coincides with the interests of the exilic community that was struggling for its existence and its re-formation. Therefore we need not—thank God!—take the laws and accounts of mass murder (cf. Deut. 20; Josh. 6:24; 8:24-29; 11:11) as historical reality. That which still remains is, however, bad enough. The theologians (or perhaps we would better say, the ideologues) of Israel's isolation from the world of the other peoples regarded the "others" as deserving of annihilation. Is not such a theological dogmatism, which turns into the hatred of outsiders, itself essentially a form of human suffering? The traces of this way of thinking can be followed through history. In the trials of the heretics and the burning of witches, in crusades and among "Christian" colonial masters, among racists and anticommunists, we often encounter Old Testament ways of thinking and arguing.

c) Conflicts with enemies

When there is an abundance of possibilities for suffering even in the structure of one's own nation and community, it is hardly surprising that conflicts with alien groups could intensify the suffering of people (cf. 2 Sam. 24:14). This holds true in the ancient Orient, particularly for encounters in battle, because all other forms of "cold war," or of economic or psychological terror, though not unknown, were subordinated to actual war. The way wars were conducted in Old Testament times was always gruesome on both sides, far removed from the almost sporting duel which still is suggested by some of the accounts (cf. 1 Sam. 17; 2 Sam. 2:12-16; 2 Kings 14:11).

As soon as Israel was settled in the land of Canaan, it had to suffer, like all inhabitants of arable land, under attacks by Bedouin tribes that camped in the desert, conducted their raids with swift camel-borne troops, and then disappeared again with their booty into the wasteland (cf. Judg. 6:1-6; 7; 1 Sam. 30). In the time of Moses, the Midianites were still the natural allies of Israelite tribes (Exod. 2:15 ff.; 18:1 ff.); to the Israelite farmers they were mortal enemies (cf. Num. 31:1-12; this story of the "revenge of Midian" certainly is told from the perspective of the later inhabitants of the arable land). The Amalekites, likewise nomads who used camels, followed the same strategy of attack (Deut. 25:17-18). Theft of the flocks and herds, destruction of harvests (Judg. 6:4), and carrying wives and children away into slavery (1 Sam 30:2) meant a fatal threat to the ancient Israelite farmers. In the last-cited account, the grief of those affected intensified into a boundless bitterness against David, the commandant of the city Ziklag that had been attacked: "David was in a dangerous plight; his people wanted to stone him, so embittered were they because they had lost sons and daughters" (1 Sam. 30:6).

From time to time Israel had no less trouble with the settled smaller neighboring peoples. The Canaanite cities that were already in the land were indeed to a large extent spared in the (predominantly peaceful) immigration of Israelite tribes and clans (Judg. 2:17-33); yet here and there conflicts of interests arose between the old settlers and the newcomers, and these led to bloody battles. Thus Shechem (Gen. 34),

Bethel (Judg. 2:22-25), and finally Jerusalem (2 Sam. 5:6-8) were conquered by the cunning of the weaker force. And once the northern tribes were even able at Megiddo to conquer a considerable contingent of war chariots (Judg. 4–5). In addition to the Canaanites, the other neighboring peoples in "their own" land were the natural enemies of Israel. The Philistines (cf. 1 Sam. 4), Edomites (cf. 2 Sam. 8:13-14; 1 Kings 11:15-16), Moabites (cf. 2 Sam. 8:2), Ammonites (cf. 2 Sam. 10; 12:26-31), Arameans (cf. 2 Sam. 8:3-8; 1 Kings 15:16-22), and Phoenicians (cf. Judg. 1:31; 1 Kings 9:11-13) were more or less equal to the nation of Israel in population and strength. The Egyptians, Assyrians, and Babylonians, on the other hand, and later the Persians, Greeks, and Romans, represented the world powers of that time, to which Israel was again and again subject. There was one thing these all had in common, as distinguished from the booty-hungry Bedouin tribes. When these waged war against Israel, or Israel against them, as a rule it was over the possession of the land of Canaan, or at least over the position of preeminent power in the contested region. Hence the wars among settled neighbors had a distinctive stamp all their own. The Israelites of the Old Testament times apparently regarded these wars of conquest and defense as unavoidable and necessary. In a land that formed a strategic bridge between great powers and which down to the present day is subject to especially sharp contention, such an attitude is not surprising. Yet we do not possess any theoretical utterances about the causes and uses of war. On the contrary, in the course of the centuries of Israelite history, there is an increase in the admonitions not to trust in horse and rider, sword and chariot, but in Yahweh's help (cf. Isa. 7:4; 30:15; Hos. 1:7; Jer. 38:17-18; 2 Chr. 20:1-30). Does this not reflect a weariness of war, which must have been the fruit of many bitter experiences? In Psalm 129, for example, the expansive phase of Israelite policy appears to have been long forgotten.

> From the very first they have fought against me—
> thus let Israel say—

> From the very first they have beset me,
>   but they have never destroyed me.
> Plowshares went up and down my back,
>   making long furrows back and forth.
>
> (vv. 1-3)

Israel ultimately found itself in its own special passion narrative
(cf. Isa. 42:18–43:5), at the end of which a special hope breaks
forth (cf. Hos. 2:20-25; Isa. 2:1-4; Ps. 46:8-11).

Let us turn once again to the concrete experiences of
suffering in the wars which Israel waged. First among these is
the struggle of men in open field combat, which brought death
and wounds to hundreds (cf. 1 Sam. 4:1-2; 11:11; 14:6-15;
23:1-5; 31:1-10; etc.), and the besieging of established towns
and cities. In case of continuing resistance, the situation of the
defenders became untenable, as one can see, for example, in
the frightful story in 2 Kings 6:24-31 (cf. also 2 Sam. 20:15-22; 2
Kings 25:2; Zech. 9:3-4). The worst thing, however, was
undoubtedly the treatment that the defeated person had to
expect from the conquerer. The list of outrages is lengthy:
dishonor to the fallen and refusal of burial (cf. 1 Sam. 31:9-10;
Jer. 19:7); slaying and mutilation of captured soldiers (cf. 2 Sam.
8:2; 1 Sam. 11:2); execution of the leaders (Josh. 10:24-27; 1
Sam. 15:32-33; 2 Kings 25:18-21); plundering and destruction of
the conquered cities (2 Sam. 12:30; 2 Kings 24:13; 25:9);
murdering of married women (2 Kings 8:12; Amos 1:13; 1 Sam.
27: 9, 11); slaughter of children (cf. Ps. 137:9; Jer. 31:15; Nah.
3:10); deportation and enslavement of the survivors (Jer. 48:7; 2
Kings 24:14-16; Judg. 5:30); compulsory labor for the new
masters (2 Sam. 12:31; Exod. 5:5-18); handing over or sale of
prisoners to a third party (Amos 1:6, 9). These and many other
Old Testament passages speak without a tone of moral
indignation at the suffering which men inflict on each other in
war, not even when the cruelties are clearly to be classified as
transgressions according to the standards of that time (cf. the
ripping up of pregnant women, 2 Kings 8:12; Amos 1:13; the
handing over of captives, Amos 1:6). Friends and foes are
equally capable of torturing the defeated. Israel only slightly

glosses over its own conduct (cf. Samuel's justification of the
murder of the Amalekite Agag, in 1 Sam. 15:33, and the utterly
neutral portrayal of David's deed, in 2 Sam. 8:2). Thus war and
the consequences of war are for the Israelite—with differences
in degree in the various epochs of Israel's history—the
regrettable other side of the necessary struggle for survival.

The many wars that touched Israel left behind them their
traces in the thought-world of the Old Testament. The prophets'
proclamation of disaster makes preferential use of ideas of war (cf.
Hos. 14:1; Jer. 4:23-28; Ezek. 6:1-7; Isa. 13; 24:1-13; Mic. 1:10-16;
Zeph. 1:16; 3:6-8), as well as of the apocalyptic vision of the great
catastrophe (Ezek. 38–39; Dan. 11). Images of war occur in prayer
texts, even outside the hymns of victory and national laments (cf.
Pss. 3:1; 7:12-13; 35:3; 57:4; 61:3; etc.), and the Lamentations of
Jeremiah are, like other prayers of lamentation and expiation of
the nation, an affecting testimony to the suffering that had come
upon Israel in consequence of involvement in war (cf. Lam. 1; 2;
4; 5; Pss. 44; 79; 83; 137; Neh. 9). The Old Testament theologians
could not help somehow connecting this suffering with Yahweh.
Thus Psalm 89 first cites the divine promises that had been made
to David (v. 1-37), and then continues:

> But you are angry with your chosen King;
>   you have deserted and rejected him.
> You have broken your covenant with your servant
>   and thrown his crown in the dirt.
> You have torn down the walls of his city
>   and left his forts in ruins.
> All who pass by steal his belongings;
>   all his neighbors laugh at him.
> You have given the victory to his enemies;
>   you have made them all happy.
> You have made his weapons useless
>   and let him be defeated in battle.
> You have taken away his royal scepter
>   and knocked his throne to the ground.
> You have made him old before his time
>   and covered him with disgrace.
>
>   (Ps. 89:38-45)

4. Fear

In the preceding section we considered suffering and its causes in the Old Testament predominantly in terms of interpersonal relationships. Now we must take into account also the sphere of superhuman powers. The Israelites certainly did not draw lines in this way between the human and the nonhuman realm. For them, as we have already said, the entire world sheltered a single household, of various kinds of corporeal and noncorporeal beings. For example, the "enemy," who in the Psalms causes the misfortune of the person uttering the prayer (cf. Pss. 13:2, 4; 22:12-13, 16; 31:8, 11, 15; 59:6-7), bears human, animal, and demonic features. It is utterly useless to try to describe him exclusively as one being or another. The hostile, life-threatening power can simply emerge anywhere in the reality of that time. It can alienate the person nearest and dearest to one and turn him into a ruthless persecutor (cf. Pss. 35; 55:12-15; 88:18), or it can attack one as a bloodthirsty monster (Gen. 32:25; Exod. 4:24; Ps. 91:5-6). Evil has many forms, and it is native to all the realms which we strive so painstakingly to distinguish. For our understanding, however, the suprasensual sphere presents something distinctive. We connect it with the deepest levels of the human soul, and the title "Fear," which stands at the head of the present section, is intended to indicate that the roots of all human experiences of suffering lie precisely in that transhuman realm.

a) Fear of demons

It is an old disputed question whether there are, after all, preserved in the Old Testament the remnants of an earlier belief in demons and spirits. Had not the clear claim of the one God, who had delivered and accompanied Israel, once and for all swept away the "lower" manifestations of human religiosity? (Cf. Exod. 20:2-6; Isa. 43:10-11; 44:6-20). In fact one can read the entire Old Testament as a kind of account of the struggle of the one, true, only powerful and merciful God against all possible alien deities and superstitious errors of his people

Israel. To put it in another way, in this respect the Old Testament is a single passion narrative of the chosen people and their God. But precisely therein is proved the fearful reality of the "other" gods and all the powers of mischief. For Yahweh, the God of Israel, does not become angry without reason. His people know and are practicing religious convictions of an alien kind. They are breaking the bond of faithfulness and are deliberately choosing other divine partners—thus the judgment of the prophets and the exilic authors. Indeed, the "official" theology strives to suppress every variant form of the "national religion" (we adopt this label even though the actual state of things was much more complex). In only a few places are elements of the belief in demons and the other deities incorporated in such an affirmative way that they are still clearly recognizable in the preserved texts as foreign objects (cf. Lev. 16:10: the sin-offering to the desert demon Azazel; Ps. 82:1: Yahweh assumes the chairmanship in the assembly of the gods). Old Testament faith is in the main set in sharp opposition to any recognition of other powers in addition to Yahweh. And precisely this drawing of the battlelines shows how ineradicably deep are the roots of such tendencies in man. A look at our own situation can only confirm this. Neither Christian preaching nor anti-Christian enlightenment has been able up till now to abolish even the rankest proliferation of superstition, the veneration of saints and spiritism.

Against the background of this painful and never-ending conflict between "official" monotheism and actual "polydae-monism" we must ask, How did the Israelite experience the assaults and persecutions that threatened him from the side of spirits and demons?

It was quite natural for people to attribute to these evil powers—insofar as they were identifiable in personal terms— certain "customs" of life. The Israelite had to be prepared for these if he wished to avoid trouble. Thus, the demons preferred to practice their mischief in the desert or in ruined places (Lev. 16:10; Isa. 13:21), often in the company of sinister creatures such as owls and jackals. The Hebrew collective concept for this category of demons could be translated literally as "the hairy ones" (Luther's Bible: *"Feldgeister"*; cf. Lev. 17:7; Isa. 34:14:

the "night monster" that is also mentioned here is the witch "Lilith," who is well known from ancient Oriental texts). The Israelites understood this term to include demons that took the form of goats. Watercourses (Gen. 32:23 ff.), wooded areas (cf. 2 Sam. 18:8), and probably wild mountainous regions also could harbor evil spirits. All of them attack men and where possible kill them; it usually remains an open question as to what motives prompt their aggression. Is it hunger, envy, sexual lust, or merely destructive rage? The demons do not merely dominate particular localities. They swarm out, invade the realm of human life, often in those times of the day that are most favorable to them.

> In the evenings they return, . . .
> they snarl like dogs
> and slink around the city.
>
> > (Ps. 59:6, 14)

Here, in a typical prayer of lamentation and supplication for an individual, the complex cause of suffering is specified. Human enemies (vv. 1-3, 12-13) in league with demons that are like dogs (vv. 6, 14-15) pursue the one who is praying. In Ps. 91:5-6 still other times of the day are mentioned in which demons become active. The "night-terror" and his colleagues prefer the darkness; in the daytime a witch discharges her arrows, and in the midday heat a fever-demon seizes men. Many other Old Testament passages indirectly testify to demonic activity. They speak, for example, of "trouble" (Num. 23:21; Ps. 55:10-11), "injury" (Isa. 59:4), "vanity" (1 Sam. 12:21; Ezek. 13:6; Hos. 12:11), "mischief" (Ps. 7:16), "evil" (Deut. 31:17; Jer. 1:14), "distress" (Gen. 42:21; Jer. 6:24), "destruction" (Isa. 59:7; Amos 5:9), "devastation" (Exod. 23:29; Lev. 26:33), "terror" (Jer. 20:10; Ps. 31:13), "horror" (Exod. 23:27-28; Ezek. 7:27), "delusion" (Isa. 44:20; Jer. 5:27), "shame" (Ezek. 5:15; Ps. 40:15), and "curse" (Deut. 28:45; 29:19; Isa. 24:6; Mal. 2:2). They speak of these in such a way that one frequently gains the impression that they are independent powers. Thus, occasionally, illnesses are hardly to be distinguished from the powers that cause them (cf. Lev. 26:16, 25; Deut. 28:20-44), and the "plagues of Egypt" are in principle subject to manipulation. The Egyptian "magicians" can keep up very well for a time, before they are compelled to acknowledge Yahweh's greater power (Exod. 7:11, 22; 8:3, 14). Above all, any malicious word, any curse, set in motion a reality that could no longer be controlled (Num. 5:22; Ps. 109:18). All this speaks clearly for the existence of a demonic world-perspective even within the Yahweh religion. It is true that the evil powers are (theoretically) restrained by Yahweh and to a certain extent are in his service, yet they still have enough capacity to exert injurious influence to cause men to be afraid. The oppressed Israelite may have thought along these lines: The great God is as far from me as is the government; he is more occupied with matters of state than with my personal fate. Hence it is up to me to deal with the powers that threaten my life. (The emancipation of the "official" religion from the everyday struggles of the individual is even down to the present time a major motive in the existence and growth of religious subcultures.) Because Saul could no longer endure God's silence, he sought out the witch of Endor (1 Sam. 28); because the Israelites were disappointed in Yahweh, they "attached themselves" to other deities (Num. 25; Jer. 44). And because the fertility cults promised better results in the harvest, people worshipped the Canaanite baalim (Hos. 2:7-10).

Now according to the theological judgment of the authors of the Old Testment, it is precisely this involvement with alien powers that brings unutterable suffering upon the individual and the entire nation. Even if we dissociate ourselves at this point from such an interpretation of Israel's history, still it may clearly be seen that the daily encounter with the powers of harm and calamity was certainly a burden for men. It called for constant watchfulness, and it quite certainly produced various anxieties and neuroses. Comparative studies of animistic and spiritistic groups and communities existing today can give us an impression of what the fear of demons and spirits can mean. The book and the film entitled *The Exorcist* are, even in their public impact, eloquent illustrations of a hankering after the sinister and a relishing of horror.

The Old Testament texts, like many other ancient Oriental documents as well, bear witness that the demons were not only malicious and bloodthirsty (cf. Exod. 4:24-26), but also lustful (cf. Gen. 6:2). Everything sexual therefore was regarded as dangerous in the highest degree. Thus the numerous Old Testament sexual taboos have their origin, not in some sort of prudery nor in ethical reflections, but wholly and simply in the fear of demons. The veiling of the bride (presupposed in Gen. 29:23, 25), purification rites after menstruation or emission of seed (Lev. 15), the prohibition of incest (Lev. 18), the prohibition of remarriage of a divorced woman (Deut. 24:4), and even the ancient law about the altar that is intended to prevent the exposure of the priest's genitals (Exod. 20:26): all these originally served to ward off evil spirits. The same may be presumed with respect to many other prescriptions and customs: dissimilar things might not be combined, whether wool and flax in a garment, ox and ass in a yoke, or several kinds of seed in a field (Lev. 19:19; Deut. 22:9-11). Women might not wear men's clothing, nor men wear women's clothing (Deut. 22:5). Various kinds of food could be dangerous, because apparently it was possible for a demon to enter the body through them (cf. Lev. 11; Deut. 14:3-20). Contact with dead animals or men (Lev. 11:39; 21:1-4; Hag. 2:13) and with various illnesses (Lev. 13:45-46; 2 Chr. 26:21) would render one unclean.

The specific reasons for such precautionary measures naturally passed into oblivion with the passage of time; many religious customs naturally were gradually, and in the course of a theological systematizing, given a basis in the faith in Yahweh. (One may compare the formula, "It is 'an abomination to Yahweh' "—Deut. 22:5; 24:4; Prov. 11:1—and the expression, "It is to be an abomination to you"—which may be interpreted, "It is dangerous to you"—Lev. 11:9, 10, 13, 20.) These developments, however, by no means signal the end of the fear of demons in the Israelite's life of faith. Demonology rather becomes a respectable theological theme in the extra-canonical writings; and this is not owing exclusively to the particularly large numbers of foreign influences that were felt in Israel in the postexilic period. It appears to me that demonism was always present and could no longer be overlooked even by Old Testament theology. An example: The apocryphal book of Tobit tells as a quite natural thing that a demon named Asmodaeus killed in succession seven husbands of on woman on their respective wedding nights (Tob. 3:8). Numerous finds of amulets from Israelite cities (e.g., Megiddo) provide sufficient proof that the fear of demons in Israel was a harsh reality in all periods.

We possess a superabundance of Old Testament texts that reflect either directly or indirectly the feelings of the person tormented by overpowering beings. The laments of the individual in the Old Testament Psalter contain, at least in figurative allusions, portrayals of the condition of anxiety which is the consequence of being under demonic threat.

> Many enemies surround me like bulls;
>   they are all around me,
>   like fierce bulls from the land of Bashan.
> They open their mouths like lions.
>   roaring and tearing at me.
>
> My strength is gone,
>   gone like water spilled on the ground.
> All my bones are out of joint;
>   my heart is like melted wax.
> My throat is as dry as dust,
>   and my tongue sticks to the roof of my mouth.
> You have left me for dead in the dust.
>
> A gang of evil men is around me;
>   like a pack of dogs they close in on me.
>   (Ps. 22:12-16 TEV)

Here we have the same mixture of human and demonic features that we have already observed in Psalm 59! There is also the accusing lament addressed to Yahweh: "You have left me for dead in the dust" (vv. 15c). The animal symbolism and the symptoms of illness alluded to, however, make it likely that this prayer formulary was also intended for cases of demonic attack (cf. Pss. 7:12-16; 10:7-11; 57:4; 58:3-5; 140:1-3.)

In the book of Job the fear of the spirit world perhaps is expressed even more clearly. For example, Eliphaz speaks of things that appear in dreams, which in antiquity were considered to have a very definite connection with reality (Job 4:13): "Then dreadful fear seized me," and "My hair stood on end" (v. 15). Even the preliminary encounter with the pernicious power of demons evokes terror. This is all the more true when one renounces God and thus automatically falls into the hands of the evil one. Bildad, the second of Job's comforters, sketches the following picture, among others, of the unhappy person:

> All around him terror is awaiting;
>   it follows him at every step.
> He used to be rich, but now he goes hungry;
>   disaster stands and waits at his side.
> A deadly disease spreads over his body
>   and causes his arms and legs to rot.
> He is torn from the tent where he lived secure,
>   and is dragged off to face King Death.
> Now anyone may live in his tent—
>   after sulfur is sprinkled to disinfect it!
>   (Job 18:11-15 TEV)

It is clear that here the suffering one is being hounded by evil spirits. The text itself in fact mentions by name only one member of the hellish pack (v. 14), the "King Death," literally "king of terrors." This title also appears elsewhere in the ancient Orient to identify the god of death and the underworld. From this it follows that "terror," "disaster," and "rot" in verses 11-12 also are demonic powers. The Hebrew letters in verse 15, which Luther's text renders as "which does not belong to him" can read, with only a slight emendation, as "Lilith," the nocturnal specter that is already familiar to us. And what does the hellish swarm do? It devours the unfortunate one, as it were (v. 13), and dispatches him to the underworld (v. 14).

b) Fear of God and of one's own guilt

Demons, malicious powers, and rival foreign deities were realities of the Israelite faith in every period. But they were embedded in, and in part even blended with, the comprehensive confession of the one God of Israel, who alone was able to give succor (Exod. 15:21; 20:2-6; Deut. 26:7-9; Isa. 46:9). We can hardly any longer discern how the Israelite harmonized these two levels of belief. Perhaps the "lower belief in God," on the one hand, and the "higher belief in God," on the other hand, actually correspond to specific strata of human existence or forms of social organization respectively, so that a harmonizing of the two is never accomplished. In any case it appears certain that Yahweh, the God of Israel—and thus by his very nature the tribal and national deity—also assumed the role of the patriarchal deities. Yahweh also became personal God, family God, clan God. The prayers that are preserved in the Old Testament are all addressed, in their present form, to Yahweh, even though in many of them this proper name is missing and has been replaced by the general form of address "God" (thus, for example, predominantly in Pss. 42–83). This means that Israel expected and received primarily from Yahweh its weal and woe.

How is this to be understood? Can Israel's God then also be responsible for the suffering of man? The Old Testament witnesses would answer this question in the affirmative; not, however, in the sense of an elaborated theological system according to which the Almighty simply must be responsible for everything. No, they would take historical experience as their point of departure. Yahweh has entered into a relationship of patronage with Israel (Exod. 3:6 ff.; 24:11); it is counted among his possessions. He saves and blesses his people. And any disruption of the relationship of trust, any turning away of Yahweh from his people, is equivalent in meaning to suffering and decline.

But we must not think that suffering, which means "Godforsakenness," is, in the Old Testament, in principle transparent in its meaning, subject to calculation. Certainly, in looking back it was and is easy to sort out and interpret suffering that has been endured; and a great many Old Testament texts speak from a considerable historical distance from the events. Thus the "Deuteronomist," who wrote during the Exile, could very summarily treat the history of Israel according to a theological scheme that is remarkably influential in church and theology even down to the present day: Yahweh leads his people into the promised land; Israel becomes unfaithful and falls away from him; Yahweh becomes angry and imposes severe punishment; the suffering drives the apostates to repentance; Yahweh has mercy and gives a new season of blessing (cf. Deut. 1:34–3:11; Judg. 2:6–3:5; 1 Sam. 12:6-15; 2 Kings 17:7-23; Pss. 78; 106). One must simply realize the manner of expression in which God's turning away—always as a reaction to repeated breaches of loyalty on the part of his people—is here described. Yahweh's "wrath blazes forth," his people become "an abomination to him," he "casts them away," his "wrath comes upon Israel," he "removes them from his sight," he "delivers them into the hands of plunderers," "sells" them, and so forth (Pss. 106:40; 78:21; 59; 2 Kings 17:18-20; 1 Sam. 12:9; Judg. 2:14-15; Deut. 1:34). All this is the language of historical results that are complete. Human guilt has provoked God's judgment. But the suffering lies at least as far back in the past as the catastrophes of the two World Wars are for us.

When we seek for the fresh experiences of suffering on the part of the Israelite people, therefore, we must once again read between the lines of the historical texts and listen to other voices of the Old Testament which speak immediately of the remoteness of God and of misfortune. For at least this much is clear, in case of acute distress, there cannot be a handy explanatory scheme lying ready at hand, whereby suffering is interpreted and its sharpness removed. We have already spoken about this in connection with the illness of the individual. Present distress is a sign that God's protection and blessing have become ineffective. This by itself is reason enough to be shocked and to do one's utmost to identify the cause of God's turning away (cf. above, II.2.c). It is much the same story in the case of national emergency. God's absence or his inactivity, which is manifest in suffering or misfortune, or simply in God's silence, is the major reason for concern. Thus ancient bits of tradition of the history of Saul tell that in a critical situation the king was unable to get any answer from Yahweh (1 Sam. 14:37; 28:6). What is meant is that even the repeated use of casting lots to seek an oracle provided no information about how Israel should conduct itself in the struggle against its enemies. Yahweh, Israel's patron, was silent—the security of the people of God is lost. The same thing is true in different circumstances, when the communication with Yahweh through the prophetic word is broken off (Ps. 74:9; Ezek. 8:1; 14:1 ff.; 20:1 ff.) or when the burden created by failures, defeats, and catastrophes of every kind becomes so great that the conclusion can no longer be avoided: Yahweh has turned away from us! (cf. Josh. 7:2 ff.; 2 Sam. 21:1 ff.). It is true that in some of the accounts cited a search for "the guilty party" is undertaken as the obvious thing to do (1 Sam. 14:38 ff.; Josh. 7:7-8), but the unfolding of the narratives makes it clear in any case that this is a second step. Moreover, it is shaped by the narrator who already knows the outcome of the story. A number of prayers and songs used in worship, such as Psalms 44, 74, and 89, show, moreover, with full clarity, how little the present suffering was to be explained by a simple reference to the worshiper's own failure or guilt. Instead, it held true in like manner for individual and national experience. The certainty that God's presence and protection had been lost signified a profound shaking of life itself. It drove the Israelite to prayers of lamentation and supplication which always led to the despairing question, "My God, my God, why hast thou forsaken me?" (Ps. 22:1). "Why dost thou rage against the sheep of thy pasture?" (Ps. 74:1). "Why hast thou broken down the protective wall (of thy vineyard)?" (Ps. 80:12). "Why dost thou withdraw thy hand?" (Ps. 74:11). "Why wilt thou forget us forever?" (Lam. 5:20). "Why dost thou behave like an alien in

the land, like a wanderer who tarries only for a night? Why art
thou so weak, like a warrior who can no longer give help?" (Jer.
14:8-9). "Why should the foreigners say, Where is their God?"
(Pss. 79:10; 115:2; Joel 2:17). "Why dost thou sleep, O
Lord? . . . Why dost thou hide thy face? Why dost thou
disregard our affliction?" (Ps. 44:23-24). We detect that this
language does not stem from theological reflection that is
having to work through the problem of trouble in the past. It
bears the warmth of immediate contact with suffering. And yet
it is already liturgically structured; that is, all the examples
cited belong to the prayers used in public worship.

We do not need to retract any of what has been said when
we now state that in the Old Testament, God's turning away
naturally is often understood as the consequence of human
misconduct. Therefore "sin" had to play a significant role in
Israel's theology and day-to-day life. It would take us too far
afield here to attempt an investigation of the rise, scope, and
ramifications of the "consciousness of sin" in ancient Israel. It
may suffice to say this much. At that time "sin" was not, as in the
remnants of language that still use this word today, a moral affair
or a matter of fashion and of self-control; instead, it consisted of
some misconduct of man, of whatever kind or whatever ethical
level, that affected his God. "Sin" was to be displeasing to God.
This could occur through a wrong sacrifice (Gen. 4:3-4; Num.
16; 1 Sam. 15:25; Amos 5:22), or by violation of God's sanctuary,
as it were his energy-charged private sphere (Exod. 3:5;
19:12-13; 2 Sam. 6:7; Isa. 6:5), through faithlessness (1 Kings 18;
22; Hos. 8; Ezek. 16), or through transgression of fixed cultic,
social, or legal norms (Lev. 1–7; Deut. 27:11-26; Pss. 15; 50;
Hos. 4). In this perspective it is understandable that any sort of
misconduct in relation to God could become, for the individual
as well as for the people as a whole, a major source of danger and
suffering. The conjunction of misconduct—divine wrath—
punishment then was also a possible conceptual model, which
after appropriate investigations could be adduced to account for
the suffering that was being experienced. Quite apart from this
secondary utilization of the consciousness of sin, however, the

"fear of sin" represented a very real torment that affected body and spirit in suffering in equal measure. One prayer-text portrays the suffering under unforgiven sin thus:

> When I tried to remain silent (about my guilt),
> I became grievously ill.
> I groaned the whole day long.
> Thou hast left me no rest, day or night.
> My strength disappeared,
> I was dried up, as by the heat of the summer.
>
> (Ps. 32:3-4)

Although as a rule they are rather reserved in their portrayal of suffering, the prayers of penitence in the historical works convey a similar picture of being harried and exhausted (cf. e.g., Exod. 32:11-14; 32:31-32; Ezra 9; Neh. 9; Dan. 9). Human guilt is a destructive force. This basic insight is the foundation of the entirety of the prophets' proclamation of disaster (cf. e.g., Isa. 3; Jer. 2; Mic. 1–3), the teaching of the teachers of wisdom (cf. e.g., Prov. 11:19; 14:34; 21:8; 22:8; 28:20), and the announcement of a fearful end of the world by late apocalyptists (Ezek. 38–39; Zech. 13–14; Dan. 11–12). No doubt Israel compressed, in all these diverse strata of its tradition, its own painful historical experiences into testimonies against human nature. Actually the amazing thing is only that basic theological judgments about the corruption and irredeemable lostness of man in the Old Testament are relatively rare; cf. Gen. 3–11, with the verse that was so important later on, "The imagination of man's heart is evil from his youth" (Gen. 8:21 RSV), and Psalm 14, with the statement which is no less programmatically understood in Christian theology, "They are corrupt, they do abominable deeds, there is none that does good" (Ps. 14:1 RSV). The Old Testament as a whole simply does not take sin as the cause of suffering with undue seriousness. It does lay it to man's charge that he brings trouble upon himself because he does not understand how to live aright. But along with this the Old Testament recognizes all sorts of superhuman, uncontrollable powers as the cause of suffering, and it wrestles with the view that Yahweh himself causes suffering without any recognizable reason.

c) Fear of God's arbitrariness (Job)

God inflicts suffering, even without any perceptible reason. How does this experience harmonize with the belief that Yahweh is absolutely just and is the powerful protector of Israel? The same question is still current among us today and has allowed many to break up and to become cold and cynical. How can God allow all that happens on earth? For the Israelite it was in some ways easier, and in some ways more difficult, to pose this question. A strict doctrine of God, with its absolute affirmations about God's purity, goodness, and righteousness, had not yet, as happened later in the Christian tradition, suppressed the vital, lively perspective of his personal activity. On the other hand, the totality of Israel's faith was indeed based precisely on Yahweh's personal dependability. In short, the witnesses in the Old Testament posed the problem. They did not solve it in what would have been a thoroughly obvious and easy way; they could very well have put all the responsibility for evil upon demons and devils. No, Yahweh remains, in the Old Testament, the one who has life and death in his hand and bestows them as he wills (1 Sam. 2:6-8; Amos 3:6; Isa. 40:15-17). The theological debate is kindled and existential suffering is enflamed by the contradiction with the innumerable promises of Yahweh that have been given since the days of the patriarchs. Had not Yahweh as it were "made himself available" to his people (cf. Exod. 3:6-10)? And yet he remains (ultimately in harmony with the then-prevailing views of lordship and the obligation of protection) the free Lord of Israel, who is accountable to no one!

The painful experience of Yahweh's incalculability has at least two sides in the Old Testament. On the one hand, the devout person observes that "the godless prosper" (cf. Pss. 10; 49; 73; Eccles. 4:1-3). This is a severe trial for his faith, for his own security, which results from a well-ordered relationship with God, is thereby called into question.

> But as for me, my feet had almost stumbled,
> my steps had well-nigh slipped.
> For I was envious of the arrogant,
> when I saw the prosperity of the wicked.
> (Ps. 73:2-3 RSV)

Ironically—and the biblical text is full of fine, profound irony directed against the dominant religion of law—even the prophet Jonah suffers such torments. He regards the clemency shown to Nineveh as unjustified and is gravely angry at Yahweh (Jonah 4). Yahweh's favoring of rivals impels Saul to murderous attacks (1 Sam. 19:9-10), Cain to fratricide (Gen. 4:5-8), and Israel's enemies occasionally to despair (Num. 24:10-19; 1 Kings 20:23-30; 2 Kings 19; Ps. 2). The idea of being "chosen," which had developed in Israel from a "normal," group-egoistic feeling of superiority into a theologically grounded system with wide ramifications, inevitably included the suffering of those who did not enjoy the favored position. Thus Esau/Edom was bound to get the worst of it in the context with his brother Jacob/Israel, because God (and the mother, Rebekah) supported the younger brother (Gen. 27). In the perspective of the narrative, he was simply defrauded of his inheritance.

On the other hand, we hear in the Old Testament the voices of those who feel themselves persecuted and smitten by God without having given sufficient occasion for such treatment. We think first of all of the Psalms with their declarations of innocence and of the book of Job. The sufferings of the men of God and prophets belong to a similar category, but we shall concern ourselves with these later in a separate treatment.

How did an Israelite, in the face of his own suffering, which had to signal for him God's turning away from him, maintain his "I am innocent" against this wrathful God? (In the Hebrew this was often expressed in positive terms: I am "perfect," or "blameless"—Pss. 26:1, 11; Job 9:21). One may compare the similar expressions, "guiltless" (2 Sam. 3:28), "righteous" (Pss. 7:8; 18:20-26), "upright" (1 Sam. 29:6). Where does a defeated

nation get the courage to assert (in the worship liturgy!) such as
the following?

> All this has come upon us,
>   though we have not forgotten thee,
>   or been false to thy covenant.
> Our heart has not turned back,
>   nor have our steps departed from thy way,
> that thou shouldst have broken us in the place of jackals,
>   and covered us with deep darkness.
>
>
> If we had forgotten the name of our God,
>   or spread forth our hands to a strange god,
>   would not God discover this?
>   For he knows the secrets of the heart.
> Nay, for thy sake we are slain all the day long,
>   and accounted as sheep for the slaughter.
> (Ps. 44:17-22 RSV)

In a cultural context where it was quite natural to make man
himself responsible for his misfortune, and where the prayer,
"Who knows how often he has sinned? Forgive me my secret
faults" (Ps. 19:12), seems to have been the general clue to all
suffering, the protestation of innocence must be a monstrosity,
and putting the blame on God must be a blasphemy. Psalm 44 is
not an isolated instance in the Old Testament; there is a similar
argument on behalf of the individual in distress in Psalms 7, 17,
and 26, and for the defeated nation in Psalms 74, 80, 83, and 89.
Has the mind here been thrown into confusion by despair?
Have these prayers gone beyond being petitions for help, and
become renunciations of God? They obviously border on the
language and the conduct of the godless (cf. Ps. 10:2-13; Job
15:20-35). We do not have any satisfactory answer. It is likely
that the question of "guilt" or "innocence" was determined, in
cases of illness as well as in cases of national catastrophe, by a
divinely sanctioned judicial decision (cf. Num. 5:11-31; Josh.
7:2-26), before one could utter a prayer of supplication. This
assumption would reduce the foolhardiness of the person

uttering this Old Testament prayer to human dimensions.

The book of Job undoubtedly portrays an extreme case of innocent suffering, and at the same time it represents a climactic point in the literary treatment of this theme. At the beginning we referred to the two introductory chapters of the book, which tell of Job's being plunged into misery. Now it is our task to understand Job's struggle against his three sophisticated friends, who are arguing from the perspective of "the true faith," as well as against God (Job 3–42). It may be said here by way of a statement of principle: The attempts at understanding that are presented here naturally are only a small selection from the abundant variety of scholarly opinion. Reasons of space prohibit our engaging here in a discussion with other interpreters of the Bible. Consequently this limited presentation must suffice to attract the reader to a confrontation with the biblical texts.

What kind of work is the book of Job? What is its aim? Here we are hardly dealing with a cultic-liturgical text, as in the case of Israel's prayers in the Psalms. On the other hand, however, the book is not a private outpouring, comparable to a modern-day diary or confession. Job's dialogue appears rather to be comparable to a theological didactic poem, which interweaves experience and theological reflection with unprecedented intensity. It probably arose in Israel very late, probably in the fourth or third century B.C., and thus is among the latest writings of the Old Testament, which were composed during the time of the declining Persian and the rising Greek hegemony. To be sure, the subject of "the righteous man who suffers" has ancient Oriental forerunners which we can trace all the way back to the Sumerian era around 2000 B.C.

For Job, the world has collapsed. His pain is unutterable (2:13). Nevertheless he, the sufferer, begins the conversation. But the only thing he can bring forth is a curse on the day of his birth (3:2 ff.). His suffering has destroyed his will to live. Only rarely do we encounter such situations in the Old Testament (cf. 1 Sam. 31:4; 1 Kings 19:4; Jer. 20:14-18; Ps. 90:10). It seems that longing for death, like every other form of introversion or psychic instability, was quite alien to the Israelite. Hence this first utterance of Job is all the more surprising. It is already on the far side of lament and supplication. It indicates hopelessness and self-abandonment. In his despair Job renounces life and chooses death. A comparison with the prayers of lamentation from the Psalter is instructive: There the person praying—perhaps with the exception of Psalm 88—still has hope of escaping the underworld (cf. Ps. 6; 13; 31; 69; 102).

It is only the countering of the men who intend to give comfort to Job that sets the debate in course. These friends and counselors eloquently adduce all the arguments for the righteousness of God that can be raised by the school-theologians even down to the present day. For example, "you are already all right; your suffering is only a gracious course of education provided by your God. Only have courage, it will soon be better" (cf. Job 4; 5; 8). "God knows better than you do why you must suffer so. Every man has enough faults fully to justify harsh instruction" (cf. Job 11). "Even if there is no other fault in you, there is at least this, you are doubting God's righteousness and are rebelling against his leading" (cf. Job 15). "You certainly are among the ungodly; so repent of your wrongdoing" (cf. Job 18). "All experience teaches that your pride, which persuades you to claim innocence, will soon come to a fall" (cf. Job 20). "Do not be so stubborn! Acknowledge that before God man is always in the wrong" (cf. Job 22; 25). "Just use the possibilities that are at hand—cultus, prayer, supplication—to be reconciled with God" (cf. Job 33). The arguments overlap and are repetitive, and they are occasionally elaborated. They come from the arsenal of a theology that is interested in the *doctrine* of God and in the preservation of social and civil institutions, a theology that must be at cross purposes with the innocent sufferer. "God never does anything unjust" (34:12). "How could a man be right against God?" (25:4). For the sufferer these are at best statistical truths that are far wide of the mark as far as his fate is concerned. He cannot integrate his personal suffering into that larger context in which perhaps human conduct and the human situation can be reckoned up in relation to each other. The upright man still must ask, "Why me? People who are worse than I am are prospering!" (cf. Job 24). Thus the finely calculated theological admonitions of his friends are salt in the wounds (a typical failing of official theology, by the way!).

Therefore Job's responses to his comforters become ever more vigorous and more bitter. His cry is increasingly directed against God, who is denying him his rights.

> I can be in the right, but I am not allowed to speak.
> I must ask for mercy from the one who is persecuting me.
> I can call to him, but he will not answer me.
> No, I do not believe that he will listen to me.
> He seizes me with fearful power
> and smites me with new wounds without cause.
> He takes away my breath
> and fills me with misfortune.
> If it is a matter of strength, then he is there.
> If it is a matter of right, (he says), "I will not be
>   summoned."
>
> I am innocent! But he pronounces me guilty.
> No one can charge me with wrong, but he condemns me.
> I am innocent! I concede nothing about myself.
> I hate this life.
> Now it is all the same to me. I say aloud,
> He destroys both the guilty and the innocent.
> When misfortune demands a victim,
> he amuses himself at the suffering of the innocent.
>   (Job 9:15-23)

To the innocent sufferer, the "official" God becomes a sadistic tyrant. He is exposed to indescribable torments; the certainty that he is suffering injustice makes every pain and every fear even more profound. The former trust in God of the person suffering misfortune is turned into nameless terror.

> I was completely innocent. Then he attacked me.
> He seized me by the neck and flung me to the ground.
> He uses me as a target;
> his arrows surround me.
> He unmercifully crushes my body,

so that my gall is poured out on the ground.
Heavily armed, he rages against me
and smites me in pieces.

I have clothed myself in garments of mourning
and bowed myself low in the dust.
My face is inflamed with weeping,
my eyes have lost their brilliance.
But I still have done nothing wrong!
My prayers have always been pure.

(Job 16:12-17)

Therefore I am terrified now in God's presence.
When I think of him, terror seizes me.
Indeed, God has crushed me inwardly;
he, the Almighty, drives me insane.

(Job 23:15-16)

God alone has Job's tortures on his conscience. Job's
expressions of grief are only powerless reflex actions of a man
who knows that he is undone and who yet cannot help but cry
out at the injustice he is suffering. Just as in the process he
occasionally accuses his friends directly (e.g., 13:4; 16:1-6;
19:1-5), so also he repeatedly strives to bring God himself to
account (e.g., 7:11-21; 9:27-31; 10:2-22; 13:3, 18 ff.; 23:3-9;
31:35-37). Near the end of the first round of speeches we find
the following prayer "out of the depths" (cf. Ps. 130:1).

Catastrophes have befallen me;
my courage to live is gone.
My happiness has dissolved into nothingness.
My vital strength is broken.
Misery has seized me.
It racks my bones,
it gnaws on me and gives me no rest.

God seizes me violently,
he binds me in as with a straitjacket.
He casts me in the mire;

I am worth no more than dust and ashes.

I cry to thee for help; thou dost not answer me.
I stand, but thou dost not heed me.
Thou hast become my most cruel enemy;
thou dost play thy strength against me.
Thou liftest me up and lettest me go;
thou lettest me be smashed in a hurricane.
I know that thou wilt bring me down to death,
where all life endeth.

(Job 30:15-23)

Job's words speak for themselves. Psychologically considered, they show a suffering person in that borderland between death and life in which all values are relativized or are inverted. It is only quite recently that modern science has begun anew to concern itself with this last phase of life and has sought to understand the outbreaks of the fear of life and longing for death, the interplay between the last rebellion against "undeserved" death and submission to the necessity of dying. However, so far as I can see, the problem of "innocent suffering" in the narrower sense has not been taken up by psychology, but only by the social and political sciences—always in terms of the interlocking of systems with respect to suffering. So then it remains a task for theology (and we should wish that theology were ready and capable for that task) to accompany the suffering individual to the point where life becomes meaningless because in the fearful discrepancy between one's conduct of his life and his present condition the "brutality" of God becomes visible. In such situations dogmatic comfort is no longer of any use. We should learn this from the example of Job's friends and from the encounter with our contemporaries who suffer unending exploitation. Here only unconditional solidarity can be of help; and the Bible has a lot to say about this matter.

5. Failure

Oddly, the life-affirming Old Testament speaks frequently of "being put to shame" (cf. Isa. 37:27; Ps. 31:17), "having to be ashamed" (cf. Isa. 1:29; Jer. 31:19; Ezek. 36:32; Ps. 35:26), "stumbling" and "falling" (cf. Ps. 73:2; Lev. 26:36-37; Isa. 31:3), of "being turned back," "refraining" (cf. Isa. 50:5, Ps. 40:15; Job 32:1; Ruth 1:11-13), of being "broken" or "defeated" (cf. Isa. 61:1; Josh. 1:9; Isa. 8:9-10), and of manifold failures and inabilities in human life (cf. Gen. 11:8; Deut. 28:29; 1 Kings 15:21; Exod. 8:14; 18:18; Judg. 2:14; 2 Kings 3:26; Ezek. 7:19; Lam. 1:14). The passages cited form only a minute sample (only a concordance can document the abundance of expressions that belong in this category); they stem from the most widely diverse categories of texts and spheres of life. But we should not be deceived: even when "frustration" and "failure" are wished away, blamed on the enemy, or only symbolically understood, still behind such forms of expression there are very real and, for Israel, typical experiences of life. Like every other cultural group, the ancient Near East—and Israel as a part of it—developed certain ideas of values in relation to life and established these as norms. And when a person either as an exceptional occurrence or as a regular practice did not achieve the norm that was applicable to him, then he suffered more or less total shipwreck. He knew that he had not fulfilled expectations; he felt useless and at the end considered his whole life as no longer meaningful.

What, more precisely, lies behind the Old Testament ideas of the failure of a man? According to the Israelite wish-fantasy, a man is to find his satisfaction in all his functions, in work, love, battle, or celebration. He is to fulfill his obligation to God and man in the role in society and community that has been assigned to him. And he is to be, both for himself and for his Creator, a signpost; he is to stimulate admiration, to be famed (cf. Ps. 8:4-5). "He who pursues righteousness and faithfulness will find life and honor" (Prov. 21:21). What is interesting about this maxim is not only the pairing of the substantives, but also the counsel to strive with all one's powers for the highest goods, to "pursue" them (this is a literal translation of the word). To the theological thinkers of the Old Testament it is clear that man should reflect the nature of God (cf. Gen. 2:26-27; Lev. 19:2). Therewith there are planted at once, in Old Testament anthropology, several seeds of a striving for achievement, the blessed and fearful consequences of which we are able to measure only today for the first time. It may be added that not only do the fulfillment of existence and the striving after honor and glory determine the life of the individual, but they are also the guiding principle for groups and nations, and indeed in a certain sense even for God and the gods. How else are we to understand the fact that not only does Israel bring honor to Yahweh (cf. Pss. 29:2, 9; 66:2), but that God himself defends his honor against the false gods (cf. Isa. 41:8; 44:6-7)?

It is against this background that the Israelite had his experience of reality. He experienced failure and rejection. The Old Testament shows how deeply he must have been disturbed by the fact that he often failed to achieve his goals. We shall select a few forms in which this particular suffering appeared, without at all going into the experiences of loss, fear, and guilt that are touched upon thereby.

a) Failure of the individual

A man can unexpectedly find his way blocked. He sets his mind on something, but his intention cannot be carried through; his self-confidence is shaken. King Ahab by no means originally intended to commit murder. Instead, he intended to compensate Naboth generously for his vineyard (1 Kings 21:2). The rejection of this well-intentioned offer leaves him cold. He lies upon his bed, does not want to see or hear anyone, and refuses to take nourishment (1 Kings 21:4). Pantomime will serve better than an abundance of words to portray the helpless rage that besets one who sees his plans go awry (cf. Gen. 4:5; 2 Sam. 13:2; Jonah 4:1, 5). When a man is frustrated in his intention, when he must acknowledge his powerlessness on a sensitive point, then he suffers. It is a part of the wisdom of the wise person to acquiesce without murmuring in such situations (Prov. 16:9).

It is far worse when a person appears to be a chronic

failure. The Old Testament collections of proverbs, which reflect with extraordinary compactness the life-experiences of Israel, are intensively concerned with this problem. They declare that stupidity, laziness, drunkenness, arrogance, greed, envy, sexual debauchery, and unrighteousness are the major causes of human suffering (cf. Prov. 5:1-14; 11:2-11; 16:18-23; 19:8-11; 23:1-8, 29-35; 24:1-2, 30-34).

> Who has woe? Who has sorrow?
>   Who has strife? Who has complaining?
> Who has wounds without cause?   .
>   Who has redness of eyes?
> (Prov. 23:29 RSV)

The drinker brings such calamities upon himself (v. 30)! And how do such "turns" and "defects" come about, that cause a man to ruin himself? Israel's teachers of wisdom can no more give an answer to this question than can the other writers of the Old Testament. The evil that can frustrate even the noblest strivings of a man is simply there; like a built-in explosive device or latent infection, it is constantly present. Israel's teachers of wisdom content themselves with describing the ways of conduct that arouse the evil, that cause it to discharge—with all its painful consequences for man and society. The Old Testament proverbs are outstanding witnesses to this pedagogical process by which the young man in particular is supposed to be guided to a fulfilled and successful life.

In the question as to the source of evil in man, Genesis 3 offers essentially the same picture as does the wisdom of the proverbs, only the great primeval story of man's fall deals even more intensively and fundamentally with the actual faith of man. Prescisely for this reason the narrator projects his current knowledge of man back into the time of beginnings. What he wishes to say thereby gains the status of what is unconditionally applicable. The conflict between man and God is placed back in the creation. Man receives a certain administrative authority which is based on his being in God's image (Gen. 1:26-28; 2:15). But his knowledge, and his power, are meant to remain limited

(Gen. 2:16-17). Incomprehensibly, man believes the insinuation that he can actually find himself only if he attains the highest level of power. Therefore he breaks through the barrier which to him is the essence of dependence, of frustrated and unfulfilled existence. He wants to be like God (Gen. 3:5), to develop into his purported greatness, which however is also somehow placed within him. And after his revolutionary breakthrough he only discovers his own wretchedness (Gen. 3:7). Dream and reality are grossly divergent. The "sentences of judgment" upon woman (Gen. 3:16) and man (Gen. 3:17-19) place a seal upon the collapse of human striving to be high and mighty. But further, this story is not played out in the past alone; it is as it were the model for a scenario according to which our life proceeds even today. Every human activity is in itself burdened with danger and futility. This holds true particularly for "gainful employment" (Gen. 3:17-19). The Old Testament narrator can, in the context of his world-view, freely make use of mythological language. A curse is placed upon the cultivated ground; it prevents the full ripening of the dreams of the human urge to undertake and achieve. To put it in nonmythical language, the results of labor are always equivocal. They insure man's existence and progress, they confirm him in the role of doer, and they proclaim his fame. At the same time, man is producing the means and the circumstances for his own downfall; one need only think of the achievements of the industrial era. Of course the Israelites did not constantly and exclusively express profound ideas about work. There are in the Old Testament also sufficiently unstrained positive voices; these honor the success of human deeds and divine blessing (cf. Prov. 12:27; 14:23; Pss. 65:9-13; 104:13-15, 23, 27). Yet it is not only significant for our topic that here and there some texts carry further the line of the story of the fall and represent labor from the perspective of its vanity and fruitlessness (cf. Pss. 90:13, 17; 127:1-2; Eccles. 2:4-11).

We return once again to the more general question. What role did failure play as an experience of suffering for the Israelite? Two Old Testament figures of losers and winners may render the matter·clearly evident.

The greatest stories of success in the Old Testament are those of Joseph and of David (Gen. 37-50; 1 Sam. 16–2 Sam. 5). Now we disregard the fact that in them the happy outcome gives to the suffering a certain value. Joseph is the pampered favorite son of an aging father (Gen. 37:3); his arrogance (37:5-11) is punished with a fearful vengeance (37:12-36). Pride goes before a fall! (Prov. 16:18). But Joseph's pathway of suffering is not at an end. The Hebrew is indeed favored by his God (Gen. 39:2, 23), but he must nevertheless spend painful years in Pharaoh's prison. Indeed, his hope of getting out appears for a time to be vanishing (Gen. 40:14, 23). Good fortune and misery are, as in this story, inextricably and deliberately interwoven. Joseph's grievous experiences are, both in style and in content, as much a part of the narrative as the hero's silent acceptance of all his suffering. But behind this lies the experience of life, no happiness without suffering! This is pedagogically presented in the sense of Israel's wisdom literature (cf. Prov. 3:11-12; 29:17).

The case of David is somewhat different. The narrator is not so strictly bound to the patterns of the wisdom literature. Instead, he introduces into his account genuinely biographical elements. After the meteoric rise of the shepherd youth (1 Sam. 16–17), there comes a period of grave setbacks (1 Sam. 19–29). The hero is surrounded by an entire historically constructed ensemble. In addition to his adversary Saul there appear all sorts of major actors such as Jonathan, Michal, Samuel, Abiathar, Doeg, Achish, and numerous members of the populace, priests, mercenaries, and Philistines. As Saul's mortal political enemy David is hunted, denounced, and suspected, and has to endure the most difficult situations (cf. 1 Sam. 19:9-10, 12; 21:4 ff., 13-14; 22:2; 23:2-3, 7 ff., 15, 19 ff.; 24:5 ff.; 26:1 ff.; 29:3 ff.). The individual scenes of David's suffering certainly have diverse motivations and emphases in the total context; but as a rule they exhibit a closer proximity to life than the corresponding parts of the story of Joseph. The reader of the story of David notes that a man of this kind must go through severe testing. The opposition that he encounters can only strengthen him—if it does not break him. The experience of life and history stands in the background of the emergence of this story of David.

Again, the experience of suffering has a different look in the cases of two Old Testament losers. Samson is afflicted by wives and by enemies (Judg. 14–16). His immense strength that was bestowed on him by Yahweh breaks through several times, it is true, but on the whole things go downhill for him. At the end, however, already blinded and enslaved, he is able to celebrate a victory in a violent rebellious moment. "He thought, 'I will die with the Philistines.' He bowed himself with all his might, and the house fell in upon the lords and all the people who were there. And by his death he killed even more enemies than during his lifetime" (Judg. 16:30). The final downfall is likewise his greatest victory.

The same cannot be said of Saul. Israel's first king has continued to be known to the tradition primarily as a negative figure. After losing a battle he ends his life in suicide (1 Sam. 31:4). He is an unconditional failure, and if one leaves out of account the solemnities of his burial (1 Sam. 31:11-13; 2 Sam. 1:17 ff.), he remains without the slightest conciliatory notice. In this respect his end is almost like the death of enemy rulers (cf. Abimelech, in Judg. 9:52 ff.; Sisera, in Judg. 4:17-22; both suffered the still greater indignity of being done to death by women). An obscure and inglorious death, celebrated by one's enemies, is another variation of human failure as the Old Testament sees it.

In Israel the individual's experiences of suffering were frequently transferred to societal entities and nations. This in itself is not at all surprising. We too speak of "juristic persons," meaning by this term those groups and associations to which we wish to attribute, for functional reasons, certain human qualities. Ancient man liked emotional comparisons. Israel could be described, for example, as an unfaithful wife (Hos. 2:4), a she-camel in heat (Jer. 2:23), a ravenous wolf (Gen. 49:27), or a patient servant (Isa. 44:21). Thus also in the case of the failure of collective plans. The songs of lamentation and ruin, which make the city or the nation a personified subject or object (cf. Lam. 1; 2; 4; Isa. 13; 15; 17; 19; 23; Ezek. 27:32), bewail not only material losses but also frustrated greatness. And the collective pain is in any case a summing up of the individuals' experiences of suffering (cf., for example, Isa. 15:2-3; 19:8-10; Ezek. 32:24-25).

b) The meaninglessness of life

It is not only occasionally or in the performance of work for his daily bread that man comes up against painful boundaries. Bruised and battered by what he observes and what he encounters in everyday life, through simple reflection he can arrive at profoundly disturbing conclusions about his position in the world. Life, even at its best, remains incomplete and unsure. Death is a grim and forbidding boundary, and the inexorable passage of time calls everything that is accomplished into question. This thought of perishability prompts one to reflect whether the whole of life then has any meaning after all. It is the same question that can also arise out of the pressure of suffering and the sense of God's injustice. Here it is born out of skeptical reflection. It will be best for us to listen to some selected texts; they will speak for themselves, and they touch a nerve of our own times.

> Let me know, Yahweh, whether I must die!
> How many days are meted out to me?
> Why am I so perishable?
> Behold, thou hast given me a mere handbreadth of life.
> That is nothing in comparison to thee.
> How wretched is man!
> He is an insubstantial shadow,
> a breath, and yet he makes great turmoil.
> He accumulates what he can, and does not know
>   who will inherit it all.
>
> (Ps. 39:4-6)

It is possible that seriously ill persons may have prayed thus in the face of death. The psalm however deliberately speaks in quite general terms of the constantly experienced mortality which in contrast to God's "eternity" becomes a tormenting thing.

> Thou dost sow men like seed, year after year;
> they grow up like flowers in the meadow:
> In the morning they flourish,
> and by evening they are already withered. . . .
>
> (Ps. 90:5-6)
>
> Thy wrath is a burden on our lives,
> therefore they are as fleeting as a sigh.
> We live perhaps seventy years
> or even eighty.
> But what do these years bring us? Trouble and woe!
> How quickly is everything past and gone, and
> we are no longer there.
>
> (Ps. 90:9-10)

The words of Deutero-Isaiah appear to be reminiscent of these: "All flesh is as grass . . ." (Isa. 40:6). The motif of guilt in the psalm (Ps. 90:7-9), which is missing in Isaiah, changes nothing as far as the problem itself is concerned: In the perspective of the universe and of eternity (ps. 90:1-4), man is nothing but straw.

> For there is hope for a tree,
>   if it be cut down, that it will sprout again,
>   and that its shoots will not cease.
> Though its root grow old in the earth,
>   and its stump die in the ground,
> yet at the scent of water it will bud
>   and put forth branches like a young plant.
> But man dies, and is laid low;
>   man breathes his last, and where is he?
> As waters fail from a lake,
>   and a river wastes away and dries up,
> so man lies down and rises not again;
>   till the heavens are no more he will not awake,
>   or be roused out of his sleep.
>
> (Job 14:7-12 RSV)

In the case of Job, irony and bitterness are mixed into the meditation. Even a look downward, into the plant-world, confirms the grotesque perversity of human existence. What remains of man's self-estimate as the crown of creation?

Before we go a step further, we must ask whether such gloomy reflections arise only in times of personal or cultural crisis, or whether they belong to the normal inventory of spiritual and intellectual life. To put it more precisely, is the universal agitation in the face of his mortality a symptom of illness on man's part? The Old Testament data may not be interpreted in this way. Indeed, there are cultures in which the fate of death is accepted as obvious or even beneficial, as an integral part of the eternal cycle that leads to universal perfection (Hinduism, Buddhism). Suffering in the Old Testament under the impact of the personal fate of death, therefore, is a culture-specific thing. This theme of death was the general property of the ancient Orient. A single example, in the Sumerian-Accadian Gilgamesh epic the hero searches for the plant of life in order to be able to revive his deceased friend Enkidu. But the miraculous instrument is stolen from him by the serpent, and death remains unconquered. The concern that the necessity of dying can render life utterly meaningless is typical of the ancient Near East. We do not need to reconstruct any special times of crisis in order to explain this experience of suffering. This does not exclude the possibility that in periods of profound agitation the skeptical ideas may come to the fore more prominently than at other times.

Here now we must speak of the book of Ecclesiastes. It must have been written in the later Old Testament times (the third century B.C.). What appears in it is not so much a current mood of crisis and collapse as rather a certain weariness, the resignation that can befall a person when the traditional values and structures no longer suffice for the mastery of life. The main motto of the Preacher is "All is to no purpose" (Luther: "vain"; cf. Eccles. 1:2, 14; 2:1, 11, 15; 4:16; 6:9; 8:14). Nothing in the world has stability, nothing can be depended upon. And even the highest goods of the spirit or of the world—it is not worthwhile to concern oneself with them. Money, possessions, wife? (cf. Eccles. 2:1-11; 5:9-16). "All nothing, a striving after the wind; there is utterly no profit in them!" (2:11b). Man still must die, and he can take nothing with him (5:14). Wisdom, virtue, righteousness? (cf. 2:12-17; 3:16-17; 4:1-3; 8:10, 14-15). The good man can perish, and the bad man live a long time (7:15; 6:14; 9:2). "Where there is much wisdom, there also is much suffering. To increase knowledge is to multiply pains" (1:18). Labor and striving, social position, reflection, or rebellion, all are worth nothing; they lead only to intolerable burdens (2:23; 3:9, 11; 4:4; 5:7; 8:17). The only commendable attitude is to let things run their course, to use the favor of the moment as a gift of God, and to rejoice in the brief span of life, for what it is worth (3:12-13, 22; 5:17-19; 9:7-10).

In Ecclesiastes suffering is directly connected with the patterns of life which in the Old Testament tradition, and especially in the wisdom literature, were regarded as exemplary. The Preacher appears on the basis of a fatalistic belief in providence to turn the traditional values upside down. Human zeal for knowledge and achievement produces suffering; the way out is a passive attitude of a consumer. It may be evident how very closely such analyses correspond to the mood of the times which we encounter nowadays in the super-civilized western cultures. Of course Christian theologians often refuse to affirm the actual frame of mind of men today. On that point one need only listen to or read contemporary funeral discourses. A pale, insipid belief in the hereafter, which is far removed from the explosive power of the early Christian Easter message, is supposed to whitewash the suffering over mortality and anxiety over the meaninglessness of all life. No, the declarations of Ecclesiastes, even to the very formulations, are up-to-date; they reflect the genuine agony of (western) man.

c) The suffering of the commissioned person

Although the two sections that now follow likewise treat the subject of failure in one's "calling" and in the face of lofty aims, they deserve a separate treatment. What is involved here is the fact that according to the Old Testament, people called into service by God almost unavoidably suffer failure in the exercise of their commission. How can we understand this? We shall first examine the fate of the individual, and in the next section the way of the Old Testament people of God.

Anyone who hears of the suffering of the "commissioned ones" in the Old Testament probably thinks at once of the prophets. They also are actually exemplary representatives of those involuntary sufferers or martyrs. But suffering for God's sake does not affect them alone. There are some testimonies of a more general kind in the Old Testament, perhaps a kind of prelude to prophetic suffering, and there are troubles and distresses beyond the work of the prophets which the "service of God" imposes directly.

> For it is for thy sake that I have borne reproach,
>   that shame has covered my face.
> I have become a stranger to my brethren,
>   an alien to my mother's sons.
>
> For zeal for thy house has consumed me,
>   and the insults of those who insult thee
>   have fallen on me.
>
> (Ps. 69:7-9 RSV)

If we are not entirely mistaken, we have here a general prayer of lamentation and supplication, such as could have been uttered by innumerable "sufferers." What then is meant by the "for thy sake" in the lamentation? Certainly not "for the sake of thy commission," and not at all "for thee, in thy place." Probably the meaning is simply, as in the parallel passage Psalm 44:22: "Thou, Yahweh, hast willed it so!" "Thou art responsible for my misfortune!" The continuation, however, goes a bit further in the direction of the prophetic conflict. The person praying has taken his stand for Yahweh, for his temple, however one may conceive of this in specific terms. And the scorn of his fellowmen is his reward! How is something like this possible? Why must suffering be the lot of the person who consciously takes the side of God? (cf. Gen. 4:3-8; 20:11; 1 Kings 13:11-32).

Here a parenthetical observation is appropriate. The painful experience that a man who apparently is acting for God suffers a harsh fate became a major theological theme in the period of the Exile. The people of Israel themselves were to blame for the catastrophe of 587 B.C.—thus the historical construction of the theologians of the Exile. The people had repeatedly rebelled against Yahweh, had fallen away from him, although the God of Israel had continued to send his preachers of repentance (Judg. 2:16-19; 1 Kings 17:13-14; Neh. 9:26). The malignity of the people naturally was also directed against Yahweh's emissaries; they became Israel's whipping boys. Beginning with the sixth century at least some prophetic figures of the Old Testament tradition were vigorously repainted with features provided by this highly schematic view of history. Moses became the forefather of all the prophets (cf. Deut. 18:15; Exod. 33:11): he utterly wore himself out in his service as mediator between Yahweh and the people (cf. Exod. 32:30-33). Elijah was zealous for the worship of Yahweh alone and had to endure persecution (1 Kings 18-19). In the case of Jeremiah perhaps the original picture and the retouching can most readily be distinguished. Jeremiah 26 and 36 appear to fit quite well into the schematic theology of history of the exilic theologians, while Jeremiah 20, 37–39, and 43 are significantly closer to actuality. All of this means that we must take very careful note of who is presenting the sufferings of the prophets, and from what perspective. The summary judgment of the later time that a prophet must suffer because the refractory people rebel against his message reflects the sting of conscience of the exilic community and is not a direct testimony to the actual situation of the preexilic prophets.

Yet even after we make this allowance, we still can find in the Old Testament sufficient indications that the conflict between prophet, seer, or man of God and the authority of the state was always a very real possibility and that it was almost always (cf. the legendary exception 2 Kings 1:9-16) decided against the messengers of Yahweh. Micaiah ben Imlah dared, as the only one against four hundred prophets of Baal (this feature is perhaps a later retouching), to announce to the kings

Jehoshaphat and Ahab a catastrophic defeat. He was beaten for
his trouble (1 Kings 22:24). Amos aroused the displeasure of the
high priest by his preaching in Bethel; he was expelled (Amos
7:10-13). Hosea and Micah are confronted—as is shown by their
words of disputation, which occasionally preserve traces of
verbal attacks against them—by a hostile audience (cf. Hos. 9:7;
Micah 3:5-8). Isaiah apparently had to experience the ridiculing
of his message. Those whom he addressed drunkenly tried to
mimic him, "Zawlazaw, cawlacaw" (Isa. 28:10, 13), as though he
were demented. It may be that the familiar saying, "Is Saul also
among the prophets?" (1 Sam. 10:11) has the same mocking
undertone. Because of his often ecstatic conduct the prophet
was halfway counted among the madmen. Finally, in the book
of Jeremiah people have found an entire passion narrative. Let
us leave aside for the moment the exilic additions (these
include, in my opinion, the so-called "Confessions" of
Jeremiah, lengthy prayers of lamentation that are supposed to
show the personal distresses of the prophet: Jer. 11:18-23;
12:1-6; 15:10-21; 17:12-18; 18:18-23; 20:7-18). Jeremiah was
whipped (20:2), threatened (29:26-27), arrested and held
prisoner on suspicion of favoring the enemy (37:11-13), thrown
into a slimy cistern (38:6), and dragged away to Egypt by
insurgents (43:5-7). And even these are only scattered episodes
from the life of an emissary whose task it was to deliver
predominantly bad news. Various other indications could be
found for all the Old Testament prophets that their lot was a
harsh one. The structure and the content of the prophetic
words of impending doom, the "symbolic actions" (e.g., Hos. 1,
3; Isa. 8:1-3; 20:3; Jer. 13:1-7; 27:2; Ezek. 4), reactions of fright
to visions and verbal revelations (e.g., Amos 7:2, 5; Isa. 6:5; Jer.
1:6), etc. The life-story of those commissioned by Yahweh was a
kind of passion narrative.

This becomes even clearer in at least one passage of the
exilic literature of the Old Testament. When the power of the
state was extinguished, the preexilic confrontation of prophet
and king obviously disappeared. Yet the tensions in relation to
the nation and its new stratum of leadership continued under
different circumstances (cf. Ezek. 13-14; Hag. 1:2 ff.; 2:14;

Zech. 5:1-4; 7:5-6; Mal. 1:6 ff.; 2:1 ff.). In addition, there developed during the Exile something new out of the prophetic, messianic, and priestly traditions. The figure of the suffering servant of God in Deutero-Isaiah. This figure still continues to provide riddles for scholars. Is it symbolically intended? Is it supposed to represent the suffering nation of Israel? Does the anonymous prophet of the Exile speak of himself or of someone else? (cf. Acts 8:34). It is clear that suffering beyond measure is heaped upon the "servant" and that he vicariously bears this suffering for many others. He himself says:

> I gave my back to the smiters,
>   and my cheeks to those who pulled out the beard;
> I hid not my face
>   from shame and spitting.
>
> (Isa. 50:6 RSV)

And others say of him:

> He was put to shame, hardly still a man;
> disfigured by pain, full of disease,
> and people turned away from him in horror.
> He was despised, and we wanted nothing to do with him.
> But it was our sickness that he took upon himself;
> he endured our pains.
> And we thought that he had been smitten by God,
> that God had punished and afflicted him.
> No, he was wounded because of our sin,
> bruised for our guilt.
> The punishment for our wrongdoing lay upon him,
> He was injured and we were healed.
>
> (Isa. 53:3-5)

Suffering for others? Although there are suggestions of such an attitude in the Old Testament (cf. e.g., Lev. 19:18; Judg. 19:24; Ps. 35:13-14; Prov. 17:17), the idea in this form is unprecedented. Unfortunately we cannot say what specific sufferings compensate for what "sins," or how the reckoning takes place. Nevertheless this substitution in suffering remains important, not least of all because it comes to have an influence in the New Testament that could not be foreseen in the Babylonian exile.

If we survey the experiences of suffering of Yahweh's commissioned ones, we may see that the prophetic figures of the Old Testament underwent double suffering. They came face to face with the reality of Yahweh, discerned the claim of the absolute, and sensed their own wretchedness. When they attempted to represent Yahweh's claim and consolation in the community and society, they promptly encountered rejection, which evoked new pain. Phenomenologically considered, the prophetic figures of the Old Testament stand with one foot outside the orders of society. They are genuine critics of the system, who nevertheless do not go underground but, still suffering, identify with their contemporaries in solidarity.

d) Failure of the people of God

The failure of the people of God is a theme of the Old Testament in the same measure as is their election. The two aspects belong together in an indissoluble unity. But since we know how little the relationship of Israel to its God was a dogmatic truth and how much it was rather actuality and history, we shall guard against treating all the expressions of the Old Testament alike.

In the early period, before nationhood, as we have already noted, Israel must have understood its call altogether similarly to any human group that develops a natural feeling of its own worth and of superiority in relation to others. Victories were celebrated (Exod. 15:21; Judg. 5:2-31; Ps. 68) and defeats were lamented with just as much ceremony (Judg. 20:23, 26; 1 Sam. 11:1-4; 13:5-8, 19-23; 30:1-6; 31). In the period of the monarchy there arose a distinctive, religiously grounded national consciousness. It had its center of gravity in the trust in Yahweh's presence on Mount Zion (cf. Ps. 46; 48). This city was holy and therefore had to be impregnable. The Davidic king who ruled there as viceroy and son of God (2 Sam. 7:8-16; Pss. 2;

110) cherished a (utopian!) claim to world-dominion (cf. Pss. 2;
110). But woe when such an exaggerated belief began to waver!
When the Assyrians attacked, near the end of the eighth
century B.C., Hezekiah had to ransom the city by payment of a
heavy tribute (2 Kings 18:13-16). To later theologians this
version is an insult to the holy city. They thoroughly discussed
the theological backgrounds of the delicate situation (2 Kings
18:17–19:34) and then invoked an angel of God, who in a great
bloodbath liberated the Judeans (2 Kings 19:35).

But then in 587 B.C. the inconceivable became a reality.
Jerusalem fell into the hands of the Babylonians, and the
Davidic dynasty lost the ruling power after having existed for
some four hundred years. This event can only be compared
with the gravest cases of collapse of nations and cultures in the
course of world history. In the range of our experience,
analogies are suggested to the end of the German Kaiser's reign
in 1918 or the capitulation in 1945. For Israel, however, the fall
of Jerusalem signified even more directly and more totally the
most profound shaking of belief in God (cf. Lam. 1; 2; 4; Ezek.
16; 19; etc.). Certainly, the prophets had long before then
spoken of the fall of the partial states Israel and Judah, but they
obviously had left no traces in the general consciousness. The
prophetic announcement of impending disaster can prompt a
certain discomfort and uneasiness. In this respect it is like the
warnings that are being uttered nowadays by guardians of the
environment, futurologists, and far-sighted politicians. But it
will not have the power to shake a nation, so that it will
undertake the necessary labor of repentance even before the
catastrophe. Or, said in another way, national or general human
suffering cannot be anticipated; it can—unfortunately—only be
repeatedly experienced in catastrophes. Or still again, we have
good reason to doubt that humanity is capable of learning from
history.

The continuation of Israel's history, insofar as it is
discernible in the Old Testament, confirms our fears. In 587
B.C. Israel had come to grief in its belief that through and with
Yahweh it could occupy a unique position in the world. The fall
of the temple, the royal house, and the nation, however, had

amazingly strengthened the consciousness of being elect (see above, II.3.b). Deutero-Isaiah is not only a witness to an incipient universalism in Israel's faith, but he is also the authority for boundless particularist expectations (cf. Isa. 43:3-4; 45:14-17; or even the Jerusalem-centrism of Trito-Isaiah, Isa. 56–66). With its isolation from its environment which we have already mentioned, Israel helped to lay the groundwork for the way in which it would miss its goal in the following period. The books of Daniel and Esther and the later apocryphal literature tell of fearful persecutions to which the Jews were exposed because of their religion (cf. Dan. 3; 6; Esther 3). The immediate occasion is, in the three cases cited, always the same. The Jews refuse to show religious reverence to any authority other than Yahweh. The strict adherence to the first and second commandments in conjunction with the claim of special status in the pagan environment set off the pogroms. This in no way means that the blame for antisemitism is to be placed on the Jews. It would be criminal to accuse the many millions of victims and to acquit their murderers. But both Jews and Christians (!) again and again in the course of history have prepared the way, through their peculiar faith and their peculiar manner of life, for the specific forms of their own downfall.

e) God's suffering

The Japanese theologian, K. Kitamori, has written a book with the title, *The Theology of the Pain of God*. In this book he tries to show that God, as we can recognize him in the Bible, is most intimately involved in the world and even shares "in his own body" in its experience of perversion and destruction. This is a fundamental biblical truth. God does not seclude himself somewhere in a "hereafter" or other remote place, whether in heaven or in holy places. Certainly there are also these conceptions of the "remote" God (cf. 1 Kings 8:27; Ps. 2:4). But wherever he may "dwell," he comes to the rebellious, zealous, or suffering men of his choice (Gen. 11:5; 18:21; Exod. 25:8; 2 Sam. 5:24; Ps. 12:5). He wills to be with men in bad times as well as good (Exod. 3:7-8; 33:14-15; Num. 10:35-36). Even the most sophisticated theologians of the Old Testament, who would have preferred to make Yahweh unapproachable and unreachable, still let him be present in the theater of human history in the form of words (Deut. 30:11-14), of an angel (Exod. 23:20-23), of a pillar of fire and cloud (Lev. 9:23-24; Exod. 13:21), in the storm (Job 38:1), or in an earthquake (Ps. 68:7-8). The nearness of God is the real concern of the Old Testament; his loftiness and exaltation are actualized in his nearness to man. Consequently, God even participates in the misery of man. His pain for the world is never the wailing sympathy of an uninvolved onlooker, but the genuine pain of one who is directly affected, the suffering of a comrade, who takes upon himself a part of the burden.

This should now be explored in the various strata of the Old Testament tradition. However, we shall be able to select only a few specific points of view.

The Old Testament writers attribute to Yahweh qualities and responses that already contain within themselves the element of pain. God can "contend" with men and things, and he can even be "jealous" (Exod. 20:5; Josh. 24:13; Nah. 1:2). In such cases the punishment of the nation is done out of a sense of injured honor (Ezek. 5:13; Zeph. 3:8). He is "angry" and "enraged" (Exod. 4:14; Num. 11:1, 10, 33; Ps. 79:5), and he feels "compassion" and "remorse" (Gen. 6:5-6; Exod. 32:14; Judg. 2:18; 1 Sam. 15:11), he "cries out" and "roars" in excitement and pain (Isa. 42:13-14; Amos 1:2). In these and other passages one can detect how far the Old Testament is from reluctance to understand the motions of God's mind by the analogy of human emotions. The Israelite is far from the calm, the superiority, and the eternity of the Greek belief in God; instead, he takes God as his partner and even ascribes to him the capacity to suffer—for the Greek thinkers this is blasphemy! All such affirmations in the Old Testament are deeply rooted in the emotional language of human suffering. "Pity" (e.g., Hos. 2:23) is a new turning toward a beloved person that is rooted in keen anxiety; "regret" (e.g., Gen. 6:6) is the painful concession to have failed in one's plan. Thus for the Israelite God's suffering is, strange as it may sound, precisely like human suffering, a bitter experience that injures body and spirit. Further, we certainly may interpret the Old Testament to indicate that God's suffering results from the coinciding of human and divine actions. God is not a melancholy being who could find within himself the occasion for being dissatisfied or bitter. His pain is the consequence of human misconduct. In principle it also holds true for most forms of human suffering that they arise out of the interaction of partners and the colliding of interests. If what we have said earlier from time to time about guilt and innocence in suffering and about God's "arbitrariness" is valid, we must now conclude that according to the Old Testament perspective, Yahweh can truly participate in the suffering of the world, not only as the one who causes it, but also as a victim.

The matter becomes still clearer when we lift out of the Old Testament texts the roles that Yahweh plays in the painful confrontations with men.

It is conceded that Yahweh is frequently the accuser and judge of superhuman dimensions, who only has his pronouncements of judgment communicated (Amos 1:3 ff.; Hos. 4:1-3; Isa. 5:25-30; Jer. 5:15-17; Ezek. 7:1-4). But to absolutize the expressions would be to render the Old Testament view of God grotesque. In all the prophetic books other tendencies come to the fore. Yahweh's spokesmen begin to argue; Yahweh no longer appears as an autonomous tyrant, but as the strict educator (Amos 4:6-11; Hos. 6:4-6). Or again, Yahweh feels abandoned by Israel like a husband who is abandoned by his wayward wife (Hos. 2:4-5; Jer. 2:2; 3:1-5; Ezek. 16:23). Indeed, he appears as the one injured, offended, and even accused, who must defend himself against his people in a judicial process.

> Thus says Yahweh:
> What fault did your fathers find with me,
>   that they should forsake me?
> They went after nothingness
>   and in so doing themselves became nothing.

> They no longer asked, "Where is Yahweh?
> He brought us out of Egypt,
>   he led us in the wilderness,
>   in the terrible desert land."
>   (Jer. 2:5-6)

Jeremiah 2:4-37 is a typical defense speech; the accused person cites everything that can serve to acquit him, and he strives to expose the guilt of his accusers. Further, there is lacking neither the lamenting, accusatory tone (vv. 10-13), nor the reference to the present wretched condition of the accusing party (vv. 14-16), nor the summons to impartial witnesses (v. 12). We should note that Yahweh summons third parties against Israel; they are to bear witness against his people.

> Hear, you heavens,
>   you earth, give heed!
>   Yahweh wants to speak!
> "I have brought up children,
>   but they have rebelled against me.
> An ox knows his owner,
>   and an ass knows where his stall is.
> But Israel has no awareness,
>   my people have no spark of understanding."
>   (Isa. 1:2-3)

Here is the same form of the summoning of witnesses before the court, only with even stronger stressing of the accusation! Yahweh as a party in a judicial proceeding against Israel is not merely a figure of speech; it is bitter reality, a part of the suffering of God (cf. Deut. 31:28; 32:1, 4-6; Micah 1:2; 6:1-5; Ps. 50:4).

   After all this has been said it cannot be surprising that outcries of grief and lamentation in the name of Yahweh also have been handed down in the tradition. In them the God of Israel, as it were, assumes the function of the closest friend who does penance in sackcloth and ashes for his suffering friend (Ps. 35:13).

> Is not Ephraim my darling son?
> Is he not a splendid child?
> Even when I speak against him,
>   he still is on my heart.
> And then my heart breaks because of him,
>   I must have pity on him, says Yahweh.
> (Jer. 31:20)

> My anguish, my anguish! I writhe in pain!
>   Oh, the walls of my heart!
> My heart is beating wildly;
>   I cannot keep silent;
> for I hear the sound of the trumpet,
>   the alarm of war.
> Disaster follows hard on disaster,
>   the whole land is laid waste.
> Suddenly my tents are destroyed,
>   my curtains in a moment.
> How long must I see the standard,
>   and hear the sound of the trumpet?
> "For my people are foolish,
>   they know me not;
> they are stupid children,
>   they have no understanding.
> They are skilled in doing evil,
>   but how to do good they know not."
> (Jer. 4:19-22 RSV)

Tones of lamentation also emerge in other prophetic utterances (cf. Hos. 4:6; 5:11; 6:4; 11:8; Amos 4:6-11; 5:16-17; Ezek. 6:11; 13:18). God suffers with his people? Indeed! According to the Old Testament perspective it could not be otherwise. Yahweh is related to Israel in kinship or in covenant. He is directly affected by the misfortune and failure of this people. From this perspective the problem of suffering must be given a new accent. It is astounding that within the Old Testament the awareness of God's actually suffering with his people never is explicitly employed for the solution of the problem. Did Job and Ecclesiastes simply overlook this possibility? Or did the absurdity of the idea of encountering God himself in suffering have a repelling effect?

III. Does suffering have meaning?

Two things actually must have become evident from the preceding. The compulsion to fit his suffering and the suffering of others into the structure of the world in a meaningful way is a part of man's striving for knowledge. And the interpretations of suffering cannot be uniform, because it appears in many different forms and because it poses riddles that are too difficult. The why-question is posed in the Old Testament with unrelenting doggedness, especially in the prayer texts (cf. Pss. 10:1, 13; 22:1; 42:9; 44:23-24; 74:1, 11; Jer. 15:18; 20:18; Job 3:20; 9:29; 13:24; 19:22). Anyone who raises the question thus cannot stop with a mere description of the suffering. He must inquire into causes and intentions that surround it and thus make it rational. What is the source of the evil that produces suffering? How is suffering related to the applicable system of values and norms? What effect does suffering have upon the individual and upon society? Can it be prevented or cured? Pain is an important occasion for man to reflect upon God and the world. And we really are speaking about human suffering only when this process of thought and interpretation has been set in motion.

1. Animal suffering

Altogether in contrast to our fine theory of the consciousness of human suffering, we must of course declare that there has been and is an infinite amount of suffering that is simply accepted or before which the sufferer has already capitulated. The traditions that he has received or the outward circumstances cause him to fall silent and in mute resignation to await his fate. Just as an animal in its hiding place licks its wound and endures the pain until either its condition improves or it dies, so also man can suffer like an animal, unquestioningly, unthinkingly, without resisting. It may be an instinctive attitude that prevails against the consciousness, when there is no longer any prospect of a change in the situation.

The Old Testament characteristically says very little about such "suffering without complaining." And yet it was known in Israel just as it is today (it is a characteristic mark of this animal type of suffering that one speaks of it as little as possible!). Mephibosheth—one of a host of crippled, blind, and chronically ill—was a cripple from his fifth year onward. The narrator tells this four different times (2 Sam. 4:4; 9:3; 13; 19:27), but what sort of great fuss is one to make of it? God has made both the rich and the poor (Prov. 22:2). So what then? Acquired conduct related to specific roles frequently is not seen as especially distressing, even when it brings with it pain, privation, and sacrifice (cf. Gen. 22:6-8). And the embittered response of the Preacher still sounds in our ears, "All is vanity!"

Of course it often is difficult to determine, in regard to the Old Testament texts, how much is restraint in interpreting suffering and how much is resignation as a consequence of profound trust in God. For example, where is the focus, the center of gravity, in Job 1:21, "The Lord giveth, and the Lord taketh away" (the passage often is quoted only to this point)? How are we to understand "becoming dumb" or "falling silent," a stance that is recommended to or forced upon the sufferer (cf. Pss. 37:7; 38:13-14; 39:2 Luther: "I must consume my pain within me"; 42:5, 11; 43:5; Job 40:4; 42:2-6). Although it is nowhere stated in the Old Testament, the hosts of the wretched and the poor (Pss.3:10; 82:3; 109:16; Jer. 22:16), the broken and the depressed (Pss. 34:18; 51:17; Isa. 57:15; 61:1), in all likelihood did not all together have the courage or the opportunity to articulate their suffering. It is not without reason that special declarations of deliverance apply to them. Yahweh must undertake to transform their hopeless destiny (Pss. 12:5; 76:9; Isa. 11:4; 49:13). There certainly are only traces to be found in the Old Testament, and amazingly faint traces at that;

but every religion appears also to contain forces within it that
seek to minimize or to glorify suffering in such a way that the
critical consciousness of the sufferer is blocked out. Still the
"quiet in the land" (Ps. 35:20) were, in a very dreary epoch of
Israelite history, something like an ideal picture. Normally the
trust in God of the devout person of the Old Testament is
supported by remarkable activity (cf. Pss. 23; 31; 62).

2. The curse of the evil deed

In the Israelite's active coming to grips with suffering we
find a seemingly original attitude which we are able only with
difficulty to identify by a name. If we eliminate the element of
malicious relish from our saying, "he got what was coming to
him," then what remains is similar to the ancient Oriental
"curse of the evil deed." Anyone who engages in evil infects
himself in the process, he "digs his own grave" (Prov. 26:27), for
evil automatically rebounds on the doer. This view still leaves
God altogether out of the picture. It is also doubtful whether it
reckons with particular powers or forces that could be executive
organs of immanent justice. It rather appears as though evil is
conceived of indeed as an animated power, but not in a specific
personal form. Faithfulness, righteousness, peace, and the like
also frequently appear as independent entities (cf. Ps.
85:10-11); they are, on their own part, rewards and fruits of
human good conduct.

There is a parallel between the refraining from any
interpretation of suffering and the assumption that suffering is
the automatic consequence of the evil deed. In both cases a
certain natural inevitability is conceded to it. Suffering
develops—like plants and fruit—from the seed (Prov. 22:8;
Hos. 8:7; 10:13). Hence nothing about it can be changed. Only
this, according to the theory of the boomerang effect of evil
action, man literally holds in his hand what he proposes to sow.
If he suffers, then he himself has given the impetus to this
suffering. The evil that he does is immediately and directly the
evil that he must suffer (Prov. 29:6; Pss. 7:16; 141:10), in which

he is ensnared or caught (Pss. 9:16; 57:6; Job 18:8-10). Hence one can curse the evildoer simply by wishing his own baseness back upon his own head (Judg. 9:20, 57; 1 Kings 21:19; 22:38; Ps. 28:4-5). Hence the blood of one who is slain has a voice of its own and can be avenged (Gen. 4:10; Lev. 20:9; Jer. 26:15; Hos. 12:15). Therefore, in an ancient judicial system every misdeed is imitated with exactly the same punishment, an eye for an eye, a tooth for a tooth (Exod. 21:23-25). According to this view, the equating of the evil deed and the consequential suffering goes so far that a single word can be used to denote both. "His crime (murder, injustice, etc.) comes upon him" (Lev. 20:9; Ps. 7:16) simply means that the harm caused wholly corresponds to that which is suffered in return.

> He loved to curse; let curses come on him!
> He did not like blessing; may it be far from him!
> He clothed himself with cursing as his coat,
>   may it soak into his body like water,
>   like oil into his bones!
> May it be like a garment which he wraps round him,
>   like a belt with which he daily girds himself!
>   (Ps. 109:17-19 RSV)

The evildoer gets what he wants. Is all suffering explainable in these terms? Hardly. The simple balancing up of deeds and condition of life is preeminently suited for the evaluation of the suffering of someone else. This is demonstrated by the speeches of Job's comforters. But for the person who is himself affected, it may very well be difficult to classify himself in this way. In a more mathematical form the belief in the correspondence between deeds and the condition of one's life has remained familiar in the western industrial societies. Here people like to say that every man is the artisan of his own fortune and consequently is himself responsible for his own misfortune. More or less closely woven networks of social security then cannot prevent one's wearing oneself out in the competitive struggle or feeling abandoned and deserted in suffering.

3. Suffering as expiation *to make atonement for*

In the Old Testament (and certainly in many other cultures), suffering can be regarded as a means of expiation. A deity has been injured through human misconduct. He becomes angry, strikes back, and brings disaster upon the culprit and his community. But because the deity in principle stands in a friendly, and even a familiar, relationship to the sufferer, the suffering will soften the wrath of God. God cannot bear to see his own people in misery; his justifiable indignation is transformed into compassion.

This is, in broad features, the scheme of things in which suffering can assume an expiatory, atoning function. Now the Old Testament speaks throughout of a God who is united with man, who—against his better knowledge—accepts even corrupt humanity. He cares for the disobedient (Gen. 3:20-21), protects the guilty (4:13-15), and even gives to his admittedly corrupt creatures a chance at life (8:21-22). He shows mercy to the apostates (Num. 14:10-20; Isa. 4:3-4). For his wrath often blazes forth (Exod. 32:10; Num. 11:1; 25:3; Isa. 9:11), but at the sight of suffering his rage is stilled (Judg. 2:18; Jer. 8:21).

This process of softening can be very easily discerned from the prayers of lamentation. These prayers contain portrayals of suffering that obviously are meant to touch and move God. The ancient Sumerians of Mesopotamia were already familiar with a "heart-soothing lament" to the patron deity. The Israelite person offering prayer also understands his lament in this sense. He sketches a melancholy picture: His illness is destroying him (Pss. 22:14-17; 31:10; 38:2-4; 102:3-7). Friend and foe alike treat him as an outcast (Pss. 22:6-8; 35:7, 11-12, 15-16; 41:5-7; 56:1-2, 5-6; 64:3-6; 69:19-21). The suppliant explicitly speaks of his weeping, crying, pondering, and anguish (Pss. 6:6; 77:1-3, 6-10; 88:1, 9, 13; Isa. 38:13-14). Hostile armies have caused fearful destruction, and they slander and ridicule (Pss. 74:3-8; 83:2-8; Lam. 2:16). Thus, suffering here is not hidden, but is presented, in what to our taste often is a strong, obtrusive way, to the one who has caused it, or who is responsible for the wellbeing of those who worship him.

For the Old Testament historical writers and prophets, moreover, the nation of Israel itself becomes a prime example of how suffering and privation again and again move God and thereby modify their harsh fate.

> He who sows with tears can harvest with joy.
> We went forth weeping and scattered the seed;
> we return with rejoicing and gather our sheaves.
>   (Ps. 126:5-6)

This is a summary of the bitter experiences of the Exile, as the grievous experiences of the collapse and of foreign domination were repeatedly thought through in that very time. In looking back at their history, people could see that Yahweh had untiringly been unconcerned for the misery of his people (Exod. 3:7; Deut. 26:7; Judg. 2:18; 1 Sam. 9:16; 2 Sam. 24:16; 2 Kings 13:4; 14:26). And although in their announcement of judgment the prophets often were uncompromisingly harsh, or seemed to be so, in their educational efforts toward the conversion of their people (cf. Amos 4:6-11; Hag. 1:5-6; 2:15-19), the promises of deliverance have a significantly different tone. In the latter case there is hardly any more setting forth of conditions; the measure of Israel's suffering appears to be full, so that Yahweh in his compassionate concern must intervene (cf. Isa. 40:1-2; 41:14, 17; 42:13-16, 22; 43:1-5; Jer. 30-31; Ezek. 36-37). The suffering of the people has reached its intended aim. We saw earlier how at last in the discourses of the suffering servant of God the view of expiation comes to a theologically thought-out formulation (cf. Isa. 42:1-4; 49:4; 50:6; 52:13–53:12). The Israelite sacrificial system with its manifold expiatory actions became a substitute here and there for human suffering and dying. Such an understanding becomes obvious, for example, in the ransoming of the human sacrifice of the firstborn (Gen. 22:12-13); Exod. 13:13; 22:28).

4. Punishment from God

The idea that suffering can be a punishment from God is not far removed from the conception of expiation. It presupposes the idea of a functioning legal system; a society that is familiar with the administration of justice and the condemnation of offenses will also seek to understand human suffering as punishment for transgressions. The sufferer has failed to observe the existing norms, whether of a cultic, a social, or an ethical nature. The misfortune is his punishment which, corresponding to the human legal stipulations, can have compensatory and educational functions. The Old Testament's declarations of punishment indicate both aims (Exod. 21:18—22:16, with the exception of 21:23-25; Deut. 17:13; 19:20; 21:21).

In this perspective, any suffering can be a result of the violation of norms; we spoke about this in our discussion of the various kinds of suffering. Yahweh is in the last analysis the supreme judge (Pss. 7:8-11; 58:10-11; 82:1-4; Prov. 16:10-11). He apportions to everyone his destiny according to his merits (Deut. 32:35, 41; Ps. 62:12; Prov. 19:17; Mic. 4:3); a man can take his suffering to Yahweh as if it were a judicial proceeding (Ps. 35:1). All the ancient Oriental cultures had a god or goddess who was responsible in a special way for justice. This concern very definitely included aid for the poor, the weak, and the unfortunate (Exod. 23:6, 11; 1 Sam. 2:2-8; Ps. 35:10; Isa. 25:4).

Suffering as punishment: To a certain degree the misfortune is capable of being calculated. Not that this first became true only in late Judaism, when there were collections of rules for conduct contained in the Mishna and the Talmud. In the Old Testament the individual knew from the very first his rights and his obligations in society and in the cultic community (Amos 5:14-15; Mic. 6:8). Man lived in a network of unwritten ordinances, and he might not transgress these rules with impunity. Misfortune that was experienced might possibly be a reminder of a misdeed or an omission. If this proved true, then the suffering could be localized and perhaps could be limited. The sufferer could simply endure the punishment, as did Michal (2 Sam. 6:16, 23), Moses (Num. 27:12-14; Deut. 34:4-5), or Samson (Judg. 16:17, 21), or he could attempt to have the sentence revised, as we read in the story of Cain (Gen. 4:13-14; cf. Is. 38; Ps. 35).

5. Divine discipline

A favorite interpretation of suffering in the Old Testament is aimed at comprehending pain and misfortune as a means of discipline employed by God. This suggests a meaning in suffering that does not necessarily issue from human misconduct, and that possibly admits of a constructive handling of the suffering.

Every serious observer of human behavior knows that communication of knowledge alone to a child does not suffice. The child must develop in close encounter with his environment. This includes the experience of discovering his own limits. According to the Israelite view, however, it is only through his own pain that man learns to stay within his limits and thereby to provide a basis for his happiness. The child easily becomes immune to words (cf. Prov. 10:1; 28:7; 29:19; Isa. 1:2), and therefore the educator must use the rod (Prov. 13:24; 19:18; 20:30). We are much too strongly set in the Jewish-western tradition to be able entirely to suppress an approving nod at this point. Yet we should be given pause by reports that describe many so-called primitive peoples. There are cultures in which the infliction of pain in the educational process is unknown. Even there the child certainly learns to know his limits through painful experience, but the educator does not intensify the frustrations of the pupil by use of the rod. This prompts the question whether the adoption of the idea of discipline in this sense into theology is unavoidable.

Nevertheless, the Old Testament has applied to Yahweh and his relationship to Israel the harsh ideals of education of its own society. We have already remarked how under God's leading, Joseph, David, and Jonah became mature men. The examples of Yahweh's "educational labors" (Isa. 43:24) could be multiplied ad infinitum. Job's comforters, for example, like to go into this standard theme of Israel's everyday faith. God sends

evil presentiments and illnesses, and consequently man
perceives his error, is saved, and is rewarded all the more (Job
33:14-30). The sufferer should consider himself fortunate when
God subjects him to harsh discipline. For no matter how fierce
the tests may be, at the last, the one who has been tested is
splendidly blessed (Job 5:17-26). And the prophets and the
psalms make abundant use of the figurative language of
educational punishment (cf. Hos. 2–3; Jer. 3:6-20; Isa. 48;
Ezek. 16).

What does this classifying of suffering signify for the
sufferer? If he accepts the interpretation as the psalmist
does—"Do not reprove me in wrath" (6:1)—then he has the
opportunity, even in his misfortune, to mobilize confidence
and strength that will prove useful in his restoration.

6. Special educational aims; apocalyptic

In individual cases in the Old Testament there are
envisioned specific educational aims that are supposed to be
attained through the fiery test of suffering. In the story of
Joseph the way leads to the highest office of the state that the
kingdom of the Pharaoh has to offer, an unprecedented career
for the shepherd youth from Israel. Psalm 73 pictures the
torments of the person who must suffer unjustly and who sees
others, less righteous than himself, flourishing. He learns
through his suffering that nevertheless at the last righteous
judgment will prevail (Ps. 73:16 ff.). The narrator of the story of
Job has his hero at last doubly and triply compensated (Job
42:10-17). The suppliant in the Old Testament awaits a
restoration of his earlier happiness after the time of suffering
(Ps. 118:17 ff.).

In the later period of Old Testament times, in the outlook
for all Israel, the expectation of a good outcome of the way of
suffering was solidified into a glowing portrayal of the future
glory. The sufferings of their history, particularly of the period
of the Exile, were the occasion for this. Prophets of that period
whose names we do not know, but whose utterances and

discourses have been preserved in the books of earlier
colleagues already considered authoritative, emphatically
announced the restoration of Jerusalem and its temple (Isa.
62; Zech. 8; Hag. 2; Ezek. 40–48) and the recovery of political
independence, indeed, of preeminence in the world (Isa.
49:22-23; 60:1-7; Jer. 33:7-9, 15; Ezek. 36:33-36; Joel 4; Mich.
4:1-5; Zech. 3). The range of vision frequently is expanded to
include the renewal of the entire creation (Isa. 11:1-9;
65:17-25). The time of suffering that precedes this renewal
becomes a transitional stage which, if it does not become devoid
of significance, nevertheless is easier to endure because of the
anticipated joy. The sufferings of Israel are like momentary
pangs that are quickly followed by the joy over the birth (Isa.
66:7-10). Flood and fire can hardly find any vulnerable spot in
the elect (Isa. 43:2). Israel can survive the storm of wrath in a
hiding place (Isa. 26:20), for even in the time of distress Yahweh
is, contrary to all appearance, its protector (Isa. 25:4). He
comforts his people in their suffering (Jer. 31:16). Indeed, even
for his own sake God puts an end to the shame and misery of
Israel (Ezek. 36:3, 6; 22-23). The punishment of Israel is only
slight in comparison to what God will mete out to its enemies
(Zech. 1:14-15). God carefully takes note of the despair of the
community, that does not know what to make of his promises
(Mal. 3:14-16). The final judgment signifies, all in all, the
purification of Israel (Mal. 3:3; Zech. 13:9), an idea that
emerges in the Old Testament in various versions, particularly
in the figure of the refining of metal (cf. Isa. 48:10; Jer. 6:27-30;
Ps. 66:10).

The later apocalyptic way of viewing history took up,
systematized, and expanded this interpretation of Israel's
sufferings with ever-increasing vigor (cf. Ezek. 38:9, 19-23;
Dan. 11:33-35; 12:1, 10). God becomes the educator of the
human race, a director of the world, who step by step brings
about the end, in such a way that the dross of evil is burned out
of the world. It is obvious that such an interpretation of
suffering in universal terms functions in an extreme fashion to
fit pain and misfortune of the individual into a superdimen-
sional system of coordinates. And the elevation of the suffering

into a comprehensive context of meaning actually can be redemptive for the individual; but of course it can also deform him into an insensitive nonhuman. One may think of those who in fanatical blindness press forward to become sacrifices for fatherland, race, or ideology.

7. The satanic counterthrust

Suffering is always ambiguous. The interpretations that have been offered up to this point do not suffice to give meaning to suffering. In any case, we seek, exactly as did the ancient Israelites, for still other possibilities. All the attempts of Old Testament thinkers mentioned above are grounded in the assumption that Israel's one God is ultimately responsible for the weal and woe of his people. They have the further presupposition that in some way or another the sufferer himself has given impetus to his suffering. Of course man likes to seek for the causes of suffering in a third place, outside the range of responsibility of both God and the sufferer. From this perspective then, suffering acquires such labels as "injustice," "violence," "slander," and "malice." If the source of suffering in "enemy territory" is certain, then a different interpretation, and particularly a new pattern of conduct for the sufferer, can result.

As we have seen at several points, the idea of "the enemy" is not foreign to the Old Testament, precisely in connection with the experiences of suffering. In a world that teems with spirits there are the most widely diverse powers and entities that can be dangerous for man, regardless of how stoutly one believes in the one, sole God. The Old Testament demons, powers of mischief, and enemies are all characterized by their common cunning with which they lie in wait for man (cf. Pss. 5:9-19; 7:12-14; 10:1-9, etc.). In the process they keep their essential form hidden; the Old Testament texts only contain expressions about their pernicious machinations. Sometimes the mythical beings that still functioned in Israel's environment as genuine gods emerge as adversaries of God and man in the Old

Testament: death (Pss. 16:10; 18:4-5; 49:14-15), the floods
(Gen. 1:2; 7:11; Ps. 77:16), sea monsters (Pss. 74:13-14; 89:10;
Isa. 27:1), all possess, under the overlordship of Yahweh, their
own power; but even this power is not more specifically
defined. Only in the latest strata of the Old Testament do the
contours of a divine adversary more clearly emerge. The Old
Testament calls him Satan (Greek: *diabolos* = "slanderer,
accuser, destroyer"; hence "devil") and sees him originally as a
celestial prosecuting attorney (Ps. 109:6; Job 1:6 ff.; Zech.
3:1-2; 1 Chr. 21:1). Only this figure has survived the centuries
and still today claims a certain reality even in official
declarations of the church. On the national level there may be
added to the figures in the Old Testament that cause suffering
the sinister foreign nations (Jer. 4:6-7) and the superdimen-
sional enemy kings (Dan. 11; Ezek. 39).

What meaning can suffering have when it issues from hostile
powers? Various arrangements are conceivable. Suffering can
also be provoked, in this case, by the sufferer himself, just as it
can also serve a good end under the higher leading of God. At
any rate, this is the way Joseph interprets his own history of
suffering (Gen. 50:20). Possibly the unfortunate one attains a
different distance from his suffering if a third party is held
responsible for the misfortune. The evil influences from
without that make life bitter for him now are actually "the work
of the devil," which one must shake off or drive out. There is no
longer the necessity to identify wholly or partially with the pain
or to find oneself in suffering. The sufferer can commit all his
energies against the one who is causing the distress and for the
overcoming of his own weakened condition. For the teachers of
wisdom the causes of suffering were in part of an external kind.
They recommended the avoidance of evil (Job 28:28; Prov.
1:10; 4:14-15; 5:8-10). It is not uncommon for Old Testament
texts to urge a struggle against evil. The king is obligated to such
a struggle by virtue of his office (2 Sam. 23:6-7; Ps. 72:4), and the
exilic community as a whole seeks to keep itself pure (Lev. 19;
Deut. 21:21). In the next chapter we shall discuss still further
combative reactions to suffering.

Thus, in our cultural context, to regard suffering as some

sort of devilish influence from without is a normal human
tendency. It arises out of a certain sense of self-worth and in
extreme cases leads to a division of the world into one realm of
light and another of darkness. It is important to note that in the
Old Testament such a separation—it was the basic principle of
the ancient Persian religion—was not practiced. Hence the
struggle against evil remains undecided; Old Testament faith
tends more toward the overcoming of suffering than toward
separation from the corrupt world.

8. The inscrutable purpose of God

In many Old Testament passages it is clearly evident that
the problem of suffering simply eludes any valid interpretation
within human history. It cannot be said with certainty why a
particular man or a nation has to endure this fate. At the last the
one who is affected remains alone with his suffering, and he
himself cannot fathom it (Prov. 14:10; Job). If one wants to avoid
falling into an apathetic fatalism, almost the only way out is to
explain his suffering, together with its causes and its aims, as
God's secret. This is what the Preacher in Ecclesiastes does,
and he stands very close to the boundaries of fatalism. Other
Old Testament witnesses leave more room for man. Man
proposes and God disposes! (cf. Prov. 16:9, 19:21; Jer.
10:23-24). The Lord shapes the course of life; he has the right
plan for the world of nations (Isa. 4:27-31; 55:8-9; Pss. 31:15;
92:5-6; 139:16). Suffering has a value in the thought of God that
is known only to him; it is not necessarily to be understood as a
means of discipline or as a punishment (cf. Ps. 23:4). It is
enough for the sufferer to know that even the dark and obscure
ways are watched over by God.

I know what kind of thoughts I have concerning you, says the Lord:
thoughts of peace and not of mischief, that I shall give to you the
end that you await.

(Jer. 29:11, following Luther's translation)

Thus reads an utterance of God in the book of Jeremiah. The
response of the suppliant is found in the numerous expressions

of trust in the Psalter (cf. Pss. 62:1-2, 5–8; 71:1, 7). Here
suffering is in no way fitted into a rational scheme. The meaning
of suffering remains hidden, and the distress is entrusted to the
one who is mightier. Thus the Old Testament suppliant
frequently conducts himself as is recommended in the First
Epistle of Peter: "Cast all your care on him, for he cares for you"
(5:7).

There is no unitary meaning of suffering to be drawn from
the Old Testament. We maintain that the various discernible
attempts at interpretation (disregarding the renunciation of any
ascription of meaning) are typically human, culturally conditioned efforts to distance oneself from suffering and to gain
some clarity concerning it. They oscillate in the Old Testament
between the ascription of pain to the devil and the glorification
of it, and they exhibit a great deal of modesty and a sense of
reality. Man has only a handful of possibilities for deriving any
meaning from suffering. He will try out his hypotheses in
succession and intermingled with each other, whenever the
floodwaters rise to the level of his chin. And he will not get a bit
further when he lacks a basic attitude of trust. Because the Old
Testament still has practically no belief in a resurrection, Old
Testament theology cannot construct any hope of the hereafter
as a counterbalance to suffering. From this fact, and from the
unique trust in the God of Israel, there grew the immense
burden of the devout Israelite and Jewish person.

IV. Reactions to suffering

To draw some meaning from suffering in reflecting upon it from
a distance and to bear the suffering in one's own body are two
quite different things. The best theories about misfortune can
fail in the crucial moment and leave the believing thinker as a
moaning heap of misery. Conversely, it has often happened
that in the midst of the most extreme distress, ideas have

proved valid that the sufferer only a little while earlier would have rejected. Now we shall inquire as to kinds of behavior, actually discernible in the Old Testament, which were practiced by men who were smitten by suffering. And we shall attempt here, as in the preceding chapter, with a summary presentation of the most important points, to supplement the foregoing detailed analysis of Israel's experiences of suffering and to illumine this form from a different perspective.

1. Flight

Regardless of the form of the theoretical attitudes of Israel, flight from threatening evil is among the kinds of conduct most frequently mentioned in the Old Testament. We can check this in terms of the opposite possibility. There are only a few texts that speak of voluntary suffering (cf. Isa. 50:6; 53:4, 7). No one strives to be placed in danger. It is true that the three young men whom Nebuchadnezzar condemned to a fiery death go into the furnace with legendary composure (Dan. 4:16-18, 23, 25); we have also spoken of the fact that people in Israel also certainly bore many burdens with equanimity and that patience was highly esteemed (cf. Lam. 3:26-27). But all this is far removed from any longing for martyrdom. In the Old Testament, when avoidable suffering threatens, it is almost a prevailing slogan, "Save yourself if you can!" The reflex action of flight from danger even prevails against many an obligation of solidarity, as when the teacher of wisdom urgently counsels against standing surety for another (Prov. 6:1-5; 11:15; 17:18; 20:16). It appears that only very strong, vital interests can outweigh the tendency to avoid pain and suffering (cf. Gen. 4:23-24; 2 Sam. 2:18-19, 23). Another fact is significant here. The Old Testament contains relatively few hero stories that celebrate personal courage (cf. Judg. 14-16; 1 Sam. 14). On the other hand, there are quite a good many stories of flight. Many famous figures of Old Testament history are portrayed at some point in their career as refugees: Jacob (Gen. 27:41 ff.;

31); Moses (Exod. 2:11 ff.); Jotham (Judg. 9:21); Jephthah (Judg. 11:3); David (1 Sam. 19–21; 2 Sam. 15–19); Jeroboam I (1 Kings 11:40); Elijah (1 Kings 19:3-4); Zedekiah (2 Kings 25:4); and Jonah (Jonah 1:3, 10). And this in spite of the fact that even before Isaiah the principle may have been familiar, "He who believes will not flee" (Isa. 28:16). The Old Testament man obviously followed his natural inclination to avoid suffering. The Old Testament contains all sorts of counsels to take flight (Ps. 11:1; Jer. 4:6; 50:8; Zech. 2:10-11), and it occasionally gives expression to laments over possibilities of flight that have been obstructed (Gen. 16:7-8; Josh. 10:16, 26; 1 Sam. 15:8, 32; 1 Kings 19:4; Ps. 139:7; cf. Jonah 2:12). In the rarest cases the move to withdraw was calmly planned, as in the case of David's escape from Jerusalem (2 Sam. 15:13-17). Normally, however, the decision to flee was an emotional decision, carried out in precipitate haste (Exod. 12:11; 1 Sam. 4:10; 2 Kings 7:7). In the Old Testament, flight from suffering is not in principle injurious to honor; it is a normal, recognized reaction to danger.

2. Immobility in affliction

According to the Old Testament, affliction, or even just the announcement of the necessity of suffering, can have such a shock effect that a person dies inwardly, becomes apathetic, incapable of rational or emotional defense. He can even collapse physically. Eli, the old priest at the shrine of Shiloh, had had great troubles with his sons, according to the narratives that have been preserved (1 Sam. 2:22-25). When he was ninety-eight years old, he learned of Israel's defeat in battle against the Philistines, heard the dreadful news of the death of his sons and the loss of the ark of the covenant, and fell dead from his seat (1 Sam. 4:12-18). Another story sets forth even more graphically the effect of bad news. Nabal, a large landowner in the area where David was ranging as a guerilla fighter, suffered a kind of stroke when his wife disclosed to him the danger in which he had been just a day earlier(!). "Then his heart stopped beating, and became like a stone. And about ten

days later Yahweh slew Nabal" (1 Sam. 25:37-38). Of course
these are extreme cases; yet pain and terror always tend to
cripple the one who suffers. Crying out and other usual
expressions of suffering are suppressed (Gen. 34:5; Amos 6:10;
Deut. 2:25; Judg. 4:15; 1 Sam. 28:20; Prov. 3:25; Jer. 4:9). Fear
causes a man utterly to melt (Isa. 8:6), to quake (Job 4:14), to
tremble (Deut. 28:65-67), and to cower (1 Kings 20:30). Since
every society makes certain expressions of distress conven-
tional, but this becoming immobilized in such distress tends to
frustrate the appropriate reaction, it is not surprising that the
Old Testament regards the condition of paralysis and confusion
as particularly grave and injurious.

3. Immediate resistance

Suffering can prompt instinctive reflexes of flight and
uncontrollable signs of paralysis in the sufferer. At the same
time, in the normal case there are aroused in him the forces of
resistance. The person affected more or less consciously
assumes a stance of combat against the calamity and its causes
(or the agents causing it). Of course it is here that reflection
must begin. Does resistance have any prospect of success? May
one fight against his calamity when it has been initiated by his
own guilt or by the will of God? Yet the combative drive for
self-preservation usually is stronger than any possible misgiv-
ings. Spontaneous acts of resistance consist primarily of the
sufferer's cries of pain and pleas for aid, and of measures of
defense that are still available to him in his affliction.

The Old Testament writings exhibit no reluctance to
picture man as crying out. Just as the audible outburst of joy is
regarded as natural (Exod. 32:18; Ps. 126:2; 2 Chr. 20:19, 21,
28), so also the weeping and moaning of the sufferer are not only
socially acceptable but even necessary, for example, because of
their communicative function. They are indications of physical
or psychic pain, and they have the same effect upon others as an
explicit cry for help (Gen. 27:34; Isa. 33:7; 2 Sam. 19:1, 5). The
cries of the woman in birthpangs (Isa. 26:17; Jer. 4:31), the cry

for help of one who has been attacked (Jer. 20:8; Job 19:7), the wailing of one who is sorrowing (Isa. 14:31; 65:14; Joel 1:8), and crying aloud in prayer (Neh. 9:4; Pss. 22:1; 32:3), all these are established conceptions in the Old Testament which in part have been formulated into fixed forms of expression. Even the oppressed mediator betwen Yahweh and Israel cries out in his distress to God (Num. 12:13; Ezek. 11:13), and after catastrophes the lamentation of an entire nation is raised (Amos 5:16-17; Jer. 9:16-20; Ezek. 27:30-32). Moreover, the loudness of the cry in these manifestations of suffering is not the sole measure. The sighing, moaning, and groaning of the persons in distress is often a signal to those around that is equal to an outcry (Ezek. 21:11-12; 24:15-24; Prov. 5:11; Pss. 79:11; 102:20).

It is more than psychologically interesting that the Old Testament also speaks of the "indignation" that brews in the sufferer and presses for release of the pressure (Exod. 11:8; 1 Sam. 20:34; 1 Kings 21:4). If a person is weak, he hardly has any recourse other than verbal ways: complaints, laments, and protests (cf. Exod. 2:23; 5:15-16). One who still has power will under some circumstances strike back brutally. Lamech boasts of having exacted revenge sevenfold (Gen. 4:23-24). The practice of blood-revenge as a whole, the age-old law of the desert, is based upon this spontaneous urge for retribution that is not softened by any legal proceeding (Ps. 94:1-2). Finally, one who has superhuman powers at his disposal will have the injury that he has suffered avenged by having fire fall from heaven or bears come out of the forest to rend the evildoers (2 Kings 1:9-12; 2:13-14). According to the Old Testament, suffering thus sometimes evokes spontaneous, less structured defensive reactions that range all the way from outcries of pain and calls for help to physical countermeasures.

4. The rational life

We have occasionally referred to the fact that the wisdom literature warns against evil. "Avoid the evil and you will avoid suffering." That could be the motto of this part of the pedagogy of this literature (cf. Prov. 23:29-35). But the wisdom-teaching also has a complementary, affirmative aspect. "He who lives rationally will be happy, and no suffering will touch him" (cf. Prov. 2:1-9; 3:1-4, 13-26; 4:2-19). The constructive fashioning of what makes life precious will prevent misfortune. Or, stated the other way around, personal suffering is as a rule a consequence of deviation from the right way, which is indicated by morality and belief. Man remains on the right track as long as he follows the rules for life that have been handed down. In these rules, rationality and the fear of God alike are expressed. The main figure is the "righteousness" that keeps the whole world in order and in balance (Prov. 10:3, 6,7, 11, 16, etc.). The opposite pole is the "godless," "evil," or "senseless" person who does not heed the rules of the game of life and who brings himself into misfortune (Prov. 10:16, 20-21, 23-25, 27-28, 30-32).

It is obvious that here we have to do with a program of instruction that, as such, does not represent a spontaneous reaction to suffering. Enough distance to allow for reflection is necessary for one to arrive at such universal truths. Thus this "program" actually belongs to the interpretations of suffering that we have discussed earlier. We have gone into it again here because, first of all, the wisdom of the Old Testament exhibits a strong element of praxis, and in the second place, the doctrinal opinions certainly corresponded to active attitudes in real life as well. Unfortunately, there is hardly any "sage in action" to be observed in the Old Testament. Job corresponds to the ideal conceptions of wise caution and the fear of God (Job 1:1-5). The devout figures in the book of Daniel and in the story of Esther come close to them, but yet they apparently are already in the sphere of influence of the written law. Otherwise, in the Old Testament we encounter, from Moses to Jeremiah, and even to Ezra and Nehemiah, the impulsive characters to whom we can hardly attribute a calm, reflective response to suffering.

This does not mean that the wisdom-concept of the finding of happiness and the avoidance of suffering was inoperative in Israel. From the existence of the "program of instruction" we may in this case infer the practical application in life. And the

borrowing by the prophets and rabbis from the teachers of
wisdom strengthens the impression that "seek the good and
avoid the evil" did not remain mere theory (cf. Amos 5:14-15;
Jer. 7:3-7; Ezek. 18:5-7; Lev. 19; Pss. 1; 119).

5. Ritual defense

When we read the Old Testament testimonies against
their socio-cultural background, it becomes evident that the
real bulwark against calamity consisted at times in an
appropriate warding-off action of a ritual nature, which as a rule
required the collaboration of persons other than the sufferer
himself. We have already dealt with this fact now and then, for
example, in connection with the treatment of illness and the
fear of demons. Now our concern is to gain a comprehensive
overview of the diversity of ritual actions that, according to the
Old Testament perspective, were suited for combatting
calamity. The fact that in the evaluation of the rituals of defense,
official religion and popular belief utilized different standards
and therefore frequently came into conflict will not concern us
in our present context.

If we leave aside the fact that every spontaneous reaction of
fear contains certain elements of cultural structuring (indeed,
one *learns* even the forms of spontaneous expression of fear!),
then the diverse gestures of defense and cries of distress are the
first "ordinary" reactions of the person smitten or threatened by
calamity. In any case, these are standardized and ritualized
expressions, even when they appear to us unlikely ones.
Shaking the head (2 Kings 19:21; Pss. 22:7; 109:25; Job 16:4),
throwing dust in the air (Job 2:12; Josh. 7:6), rending one's
garments (Gen. 37:29, 34; 44:13), clapping one's hands (Num.
24:10; Lam. 2:15), hissing at someone or something (1 Kings
9:8; Jer. 19:8; Zeph. 2:15), putting on sackcloth (2 Sam. 3:31; 1
Kings 21:27; 2 Kings 6:30), and similar actions certainly were
originally intended to drive away the evil spirits. In the
Yahweh-faith they may have gradually lost their original
intention, but in any case they continued to be socially

recognized manifestations of the person who was suffering or was under threat. Precisely the same thing is true of the "prescribed" verbal expressions. We find in the Old Testament, directed to various intended audiences, ejaculatory prayers (Judg. 15:18; Ps. 107:6, 13, 19, 28), imprecations (Gen. 9:25; Jer. 20:14-15), protests and lamentations (Exod. 2:23; 1 Sam. 15:32), petitions (2 Kings 6:26; 8:3), and vows (2 Sam. 15:7-8). If the sufferer wished to apply to some agency, whether secular, religious, or divine, from whom he expected aid, then he had to employ definite forms, in gesture and in the choice of words. This holds true even for the first request for help, the spontaneous outcry in distress. To cite only one example—the sentences that are formed with the Hebrew word "help me" (hosi'eni; the shout of jubilation, "Hosanna," later developed out of this) have a very similar structure, although they are scattered throughout many biblical books and over a long period of Old Testament history (Josh. 10:6; 2 Sam. 3:18; 14:4; 2 Kings 6:26; 16:7; 19:19; Isa. 37:20; Jer. 2:17; 17:14; Pss. 3:7; 6:4; 7:1; 12:1; 22:21; 28:9; 31:16; 54:2; 59:2; 60:5; 69:1; 71:2; 86:2, 16; 106:47; 108:6; 109:26; 118:25; 119:94, 146; 1 Chr. 16:35). Another example—if a person who is suffering or imperiled seeks the help of someone else, then he must observe the established forms, adopt a submissive stance, and correctly form his words. Abigail, the wife of the large landowner Nabal, provides us with a perfect example of the proper suppliant attitude and behavior (1 Sam. 25:18-31). Similar accounts are given of other suppliants, both men and women (cf. 1 Kings 3:17-21; 20:30-32; 2 Kings 4:1, 27-28; Jer. 37:18-20).

If it is important in interpersonal relationships for the sufferer to react properly, it is all the more crucial in the relationship of the person seeking help with God. We have already spoken in some detail about the story of Hezekiah's illness (Isa. 38) and the prayer of the sick in Psalm 38. Unfortunately, the Old Testament lacks any more detailed portrayals of the treatment of the sick in Israel (cf. 1 Kings 17:17-24; 2 Kings 5). Yet it may be assumed that the prophet or the priest led in a service of prayer for the sufferer, probably in the presence of the family. The most essential elements of the ritual were—after the inquiry of Yahweh for the purpose of diagnosis—the following: the rites of sacrifice and purification (cf. Pss. 5:3; 26:6), the prayer of the sufferer (cf. Pss. 3–7; 11–13; 17; 22; etc.), and the liturgist's pronouncement of healing (cf. Pss. 12:5; 91:3-13). We can assume that, 2 Chr. 16:12 notwithstanding, the medical treatment of the sick (perhaps except for the simple treatment of wounds) was set within a ritual context. In any case, in addition to Hezekiah's prayer of supplication, Isaiah has a plaster of figs laid upon Hezekiah's boil (Isa. 38:21). The liturgy on behalf of the sufferer must have been varied from case to case, according to the nature of the situation. We are unable to discern details; but in the individual prayers of lamentation preserved in the Psalter, the emphasis apparently sometimes is placed upon the declaration of innocence (cf. Ps. 26) or conversely upon the confession of sin (cf. Ps. 51) and then again on the description of the symptoms of the illness (cf. Ps. 38) or the persecution by enemies (cf. Ps. 102). Psalm 59 could have been used primarily for cases where there was the threat of demons, and Psalm 71 for older men who were in distress.

Official actions on behalf of the individual sufferer were not the only rituals for combatting calamity that Israel produced. It is true that the Old Testment testimonies are incomplete in this regard, yet frequently enough we find indications of extensive mourning customs when death occurred (Gen. 50:1-3, 7, 10; 2 Sam. 1:17-27; 3:31-35; Jer. 16:5-7) and of lamentations after the destruction and loss of a city (cf. Ezek. 27; Isa. 23; Jer. 50). For those who were left behind and the other survivors the situations were occasions of deep distress, and it is hard to see why these sufferings should not have been treated in Israel in religious gatherings, and thus before Yahweh. The frequently cited argument that Yahweh has nothing to do with death does not hold, for the rites for overcoming grief and desolation certainly served in part for the survivors and not exclusively for the deceased. But be that as it may, in the book of Lamentations we probably have before us some poems that were composed after the fall of Jerusalem in 587 B.C. and were used in public observances of penitence and lamentation. There is still more documentation to be found in the Old Testament of the rituals for the conquest of calamity (cf. Deut. 21:1-9; Lev. 16; Neh. 9). The texts that we have cited will suffice to allow us to affirm that life in Israel was secured against evil and its effects by a whole network of social, magical, and religious rituals.

6. Transformation of suffering

We must take into account the fact that the ritual conquest of calamity in Israel was not exclusively exorcistic in function. That would hardly comport with the belief in God of the Old Testament witnesses, a belief that remarkably attributes the origination or at least a part of the responsibility for suffering to its own God. While the belief in the demons or the devil can easily serve as a theoretical foundation for the sharp, even exorcistic combatting of suffering, the derivation of suffering from Yahweh possibly had as its consequence a different confrontation with the darker aspect of human life.

The radical forming of a battleline against evil and those responsible for it naturally comes to view in the Old Testament. One might translate Psalm 6:8 as "Get out, you scoundrels!" What are meant here are the figures of the enemy, projected into the supra-individual and typical level, that are responsible for the suffering of the suppliant. Still other passages in the Psalms show the suffering petitioner who, in the midst of prayer in the context of worship, directly addresses his adversaries as though they were present (Pss. 4:2-5; 55:13; 62:3). The challenge probably is aimed at the anonymous powers and their human accomplices who are seeking the suppliant's life. There are only a few psalms of lamentation that do not in some way or another join issue with these sources of suffering, usually in the form of imprecations (cf. Pss. 109:6 ff.; 137:7-9; 139:19-24; Jer. 20:10-11).

Because the question of the significance of the Old Testament psalms of imprecation and revenge is repeatedly raised in the Christian community, a few explanatory comments may be permitted. We must note that the curses uttered against the enemy (a) arise in a situation of suffering (not out of a position of strength!), that they (b) are aimed at the anonymous guilty party, who (c) nevertheless is infected with his evil deed, and that they (d) can only be executed by God (no private justice!). From the perspective of our contemporary knowledge we can add: These curses correspond precisely to the ineradicable human pattern of thinking in terms of friends and enemies. The problem is not how such thinking can be eliminated, but only how it can be integrated into social conduct that is marked by solidarity and love. Psychology and group therapy, altogether in harmony with the Old Testament psalms of imprecation, advise against simply repressing the wish to fly at the "enemy's" throat. The feeling of hatred that is bottled up in the sufferer must be expressed, and if necessary must be screamed out. Only in this way is there liberation from the calamity or assimilation of that which threatens to destroy life.

Although the Old Testament to a large extent regards suffering as harassing fire from without, as an incursion of evil that is to be checked, we should keep our eyes open to the question whether the assumption that Yahweh has his hand in the event has left its traces. There are, first of all, once again the psalms of lamentation. Some of them do not mention the enemy at all. Is this a sign of a nobler attitude? or of an enlightened, spiritualized faith? It is rather the sober insight that in this case the misery comes directly from God himself and has its justification from him:

> . . . though you have crushed me and broken me,
> I will be happy once again.
> Close your eyes to my sins
>   and wipe out all my evil.
>
> (Ps. 51:8-9)

One may compare similar prayers, as for example in Hosea 6:1-3, Jeremiah 14:7-9, and Joel 1:2-2:17. The numerous expressions of trust that appear in the prayers of lamentation point in the same direction (cf. Pss. 22:1-3; 23; 31:1-4; 62; 63). Because everything comes from Yahweh's hand (Ps. 31:15), suffering is an intermediate station on the way to a more intensive fellowship with him. The same testimony is borne by the songs of thanksgiving that were presented in a special worship service of thanksgiving after the deliverance. They once more take up, in a lively report, the calamity that has been overcome, and thereby they show that the trouble is not forgotten, but is recognized as a precondition for God's coming to save (cf. Pss. 30; 40; 118; Jonah 2; 1 Sam. 2:1-10; Isa. 38:10-20). When a sufferer in the midst of his pain and uncertainty can sigh as does the suppliant of Psalms 42 and 43, he has really overcome the suffering (Pss. 42:5, 11; 43:5); it has not been repelled or amputated, but the sufferer has assimilated it to himself and thereby has become more mature.

The testimonies from the prayer formulas must be supplemented from presentations offered by narrative texts, because for the authors of the Old Testament the narrative is at least as important a means of expression as abstract definition is for us. We said earlier that in the Old Testament no one chooses suffering voluntarily. This is only one side of the coin. Under the pressure of circumstances, that is, moved by the right motivations, the Israelites of the Old Testament exhibit a great readiness to suffer. Moses is willing—for the sake of his office as mediator—to bear the punishment of his people (Exod. 32:32); Abigail takes upon herself the responsibility for the foolish behavior of her husband (1 Sam. 25:24); Ruth insists on sharing the fate of her mother-in-law Naomi (Ruth 1:16-17): familial loyalty to the death! Faithfulness is quite similarly demonstrated by Jonathan (1 Sam. 18–20), Ittai (2 Sam. 15:19-21), and Ebed-Melech (Jer. 38:7-13). In three of the cases cited, we have to do with a foreigner who maintains loyalty to an Israelite. Further; the king intercedes for his people (2 Sam. 24:17; 2 Kings 6:30), Abraham for his nephew Lot (Gen. 18:16-33), Joab for Absalom (2 Sam. 14:1-24), and the people for Jonathan (1 Sam. 14:45). In each case there is a great risk of being brought down to destruction with the other person. The prophets

Prophets

assume their task more or less reluctantly (Amos 7:14-15; Isa. 6:5, 8; Jer. 1:6; 20:9), but at the last with full personal commitment, in spite of the difficulties that await them. We can go a step further. It is not also a sign of readiness to suffer when a person, for the sake of a higher value, refrains from something? David forgoes the possibility of taking revenge (1 Sam. 24; 26), and the prophets all apparently renounce an "ordinary" existence. Of Jeremiah it is specifically said that he was not permitted to establish a family (Jer. 16:1), and of Isaiah that by the names he gave his children and by his occasionally going naked (Isa. 7:3; 8:3; 20:2-4) he made himself a laughingstock. We have already spoken of the sacrificial readiness of Samson (Judg. 16:28-30), of Daniel (Dan. 6), and of the young men in the fiery furnace (Dan. 3). In short, there is no lack of documentation to show that suffering was constructively assimilated in Israel. A high point in the readiness to suffer certainly is attained where the solidarity with another person becomes so strong (cf. Lev. 19:18, 34; Prov. 17:17) that one is willing and ready to suffer for the other (Isa. 50:6; 53:4-5).

7. Reshaping of the world

Still another aspect of the conquest of suffering must be considered. The obvious aim of all conscious reactions to painful experiences is the restoration of the earlier condition in which no suffering was present. Health, social status, possessions, inner equanimity, honor, pleasure, etc., need to be regained. But this holds true not only in the narrow sense for the special and isolated situations of suffering, but the laments and accusations that are evoked in the Old Testament by suffering frequently betray a broader interest. The person who sees the ungodly flourishing not only feels that he himself is being defrauded, but he imagines the entire world-order to be in danger (cf. Pss. 37; 49; 73). Anyone who becomes frustrated in his own life very readily sees "everything under the sun" (Ecclesiastes) as meaningless. Anyone who observes some cases of social injustice will easily discover the structural weakness of a system (Amos 2:6-8; 5:14-15, 21-24). The suffering that is experienced in individual, specific moments can be symptomatic. Hence, it would not be surprising if reactions to a particular calamity oftentimes aim beyond the specific occasion, aiming at a reshaping of the circumstances that produce the sufferings. Why not attack evil at its root and get rid of it once and for all?

We cannot here explore the question to what extent this applies in detail in the measures that appear in the Old Testament. Rituals for the overcoming of calamity naturally have a certain universal validity; they are used, with minimal variations, for many persons. On the other hand, we may conjecture a tendency to construct each individual ceremony in the first instance for a specific "case." Thus, for example, the Lamentations offer features of the individual that clearly point beyond the individual case. If the religious service of supplication for the sufferer is observed in a small group, then the thanksgiving celebration after the deliverance or healing belongs in the "great congregation" (Pss. 22:22 ff.; 69:30 ff.). God's act has an exemplary value for the entire community. The portrayal of evil frequently assumes such general features and is set in contrast to a community in such a way that even here a collective dimension of suffering becomes visible (Pss. 55:9; 59:6-7). Yahweh has in view ultimately, not merely the individual, but those who are in distress in general (Pss. 11:4 ff.; 12:5). The prophetic proclamation is, by its very nature, aimed more at the entirety of the nation of Israel. Thus, when calamity is mentioned in their utterances, it is in its social dimension, which frequently includes problems of structure as well (Amos 4:6-11; Hos. 5:8-14; Ezek. 34). In the assurances of deliverance of later times the suffering of the many is often the immediate occasion for Yahweh's intervention (Isa. 59; Jer. 30; Zech. 11:4-17). We can say that in the Old Testament, calamity is often seen in its social, national, and even cosmic dimensions. On the very same scale, then, there follow the human and divine reactions to the necessity of suffering as well.

V. Hope in suffering

1. Suffering today

Sorrow and joy are, like love and hate, basic elements of human life. An existence free of trouble occurs only in our dreams and programs for the future, not in our reality. The idea of a paradisiac condition is a powerful aggregate of stimuli for human action; on the other hand, according to all our experience, suffering remains a necessary sign of the finitude of all that we do. Anyone who wants to reflect upon trouble and calamity must in any case begin with the reality that is permeated with suffering, not in some nonhistorical before or after.

Where and how do people suffer today? It is difficult to evaluate one's own times, perhaps even more difficult than to arrive at an evaluation of alien cultures. The analyses of critics of the present also range from blooming optimism (frequently in those regions of the earth where the greatest need prevails) to utter frustration (frequently where wealth is concentrated). How are things with suffering man in actuality? A few facts call for consideration.

The contemporary structures of the economy and of society establish the conditions under which people suffer today. Where technical civilization is lacking, millions of people, in the "developing countries" often 50 to 90 percent of the population, are reduced to intensifying poverty. If industrialization has taken hold in a country, then a "lowest level" of people, perhaps 1 to 10 percent (the sick, the addicts, the chronically unemployed, etc.), sinks into wretchedness and misery. Thus, we can calculate that at least half of the four billion people on earth are living below the standard that we would regard as compatible with human dignity. And statistically speaking, there is not the slightest prospect that their fate will improve. For the population is increasing, and this means more undernourishment and unemployment, illiteracy and illness. And the gulf separating the rich and the poor is becoming greater year by year. Wealth grows like a bacterial culture, and poverty eats away like a cancerous sore. More bluntly put, wealth increases at the expense of poverty. Still more pointedly, anyone who writes or reads books probably belongs to the company of those who share in prosperity. Books do not reach the majority, who are vegetating in poverty and exploitation. This is why most of the suffering of humanity, which results from the structurally conditioned unequal distribution of goods, is so easily forgotten.

The industrial society itself, which is composed predominantly of prosperous white people, produces its own sufferings. The dissolution and restructuring of the forms of social organization leads to insecurity; the continual competitive struggle and the pressure for achievement in their western and eastern variations shatter the nervous system. The unitary view of the world is lost; the explosion of knowledge and growing specialization heighten the disorientation. Man adapts himself, in labor and leisure, to a technicized environment; he becomes a robot. In addition to this, there are all sorts of injurious consequences and attendant phenomena connected with the process of industrialization: the squandering of raw materials, the disruption of the environment, misuse of drugs and medicines, the polarizing of interest groups and power groups, armaments races among the nations, bad planning and bad investments, and so on.

How does man live and suffer under these modern conditions? He is as sick as ever, persecuted, humiliated, exploited, hungry, despairing. The personal experiences of suffering are altogether comparable with those of the ancient Israelites. And it would be extremely difficult to weigh them against each other, either quantitatively or qualitatively. It is true that the suffering of the individual and of the many occurs today in a different cultural context. The question is whether the reflections that may be discerned from the Old Testament times, about the causes, aims, and conquest of suffering, can still contribute something for the present day.

2. Are the Old Testament answers usable?

We are seeking a confrontation with the biblical utterances. In our case the starting point is the comparability of the
experiences of suffering then and now. The consideration of the
different cultural contexts then brings to light questions that
can be extremely important for the problem of suffering in our
time.

a) The Old Testament writers recognize a multiplicity of
experiences, causes, and interpretations of suffering. But they
do not systematize their discoveries. They appear to take each
calamity individually and to react to it in the way that seems
appropriate to them. A thoroughly pragmatic attitude! Does
not this attitude disregard the fact that in theory we must
distinguish between self-incurred calamity and that caused by
someone or something else? And between avoidable and
inescapable suffering? And particularly, it seems to us,
between the calamity that is caused by society itself, through its
structure, and the accidental misfortune? Why does the Old
Testament not succeed in finding an unequivocal answer to the
question of how we are to think of the relationship of the one
God of Israel to suffering? We shall have to attribute to the Old
Testament witnesses a certain indifference toward problems of
theory and structure. They were still unacquainted with many
things that influence our thinking and inquiring. Philosophical
and theological doctrinal constructions, scientific investigation
of social connections, and of campaigns of exploitation and
annihilation that belong to the industrial age still lay beyond the
horizons of their experience. Hence, we can say that the
classifying of suffering in the Old Testament does not
correspond to our desires; nevertheless, we can find analogies
in the Old Testament for the major types of modern suffering.
Even the blind spots of that time and our own time correspond.
Animal suffering and anonymous suffering, the suffering of the
enemy, of the outcast, and of the lowly frequently gains no
attention. This really may no longer be possible since the
coming of Christ, who made the suffering of all his own
suffering.

b) The Old Testament exhibits a surprising tendency to bring the calamity of individuals, as well as of entire groups, out into the open. The technical civilization would like to suppress calamity, and as much as possible consigns it to the individual (one may compare the death scene in Genesis 49 with dying in a modern hospital). The sufferer is indeed even at best a good consumer of medicines. Of course the Old Testament also is acquainted with the isolation of people who are suffering from dangerous illnesses, the possessed, and those marked by God. But before society withdraws from the sufferer, it strives, by means of its rituals, to rehabilitate the unfortunate one. These rituals are intended to articulate laments and to alter the consciousness, and in part the circumstances, in such a way that deliverance and healing become possible. It is true that the industrial societies spend immense amounts to develop systems for the treatment and counseling of the sufferers. However, these systems function only imperfectly, because they are deficient in the human dimension (in spite of the unselfish devotion of many employed in these systems), and the sufferer is left alone with himself. The Old Testament (like many agrarian societies today) knows a social dimension of suffering which has been lost to the atomized industrial society.

c) This is certainly related to the changed understanding of existence. In the Old Testament we encounter a thoroughly personal world view, while today the mechanistic interpretation of the world holds the favored position. Calamity is no longer caused by decisions of the will of divine beings, but by agents, processes, and developments that can be determined with scientific exactness. (The structurally affected calamity is, in this connection, often suppressed and silenced because it calls in question the investigator's own position.) Here arise the most difficult problems for us. Must we return to a demonistic and theistic understanding of the world? Or go forward to a more consistent and more humane "mechanism"? In the final analysis, one's personal understanding of God is at stake here. We frequently remark how inadequate is the explanation of calamity in terms of the will of our God. But we need personal security. Our assembly-line civilization does not provide it for us. Does God remain only as the exalted Father, who indeed no longer breaks into the mechanical routine of our everyday life, but stands ready as our comforter? The Old Testament constitutes a vigorous challenge to our contemporary technical-scientific world view. We certainly cannot simply adopt the view of the ancient Israelites, but we can allow the question to be addressed to ourselves. How do you stand in your personal existence, especially in suffering?

d) The responsibility for calamity has been shifted since Old Testament times. If one arbitrarily attributes the causes of suffering in the ancient world, one half to men and the other half to superhuman forces, the corresponding proportions today perhaps would be 90 percent and 10 percent respectively. That is to say, to a remarkable degree man has taken into his own hands the responsibility for his fate. Would anyone like to assert that things are better for mankind as a whole as a result of this change? Who is responsible now for traffic accidents, the undernourishment of children, wars, broken marriages, shattered existences, criminality? What remains to be blamed on nonhuman forces? Earthquakes and natural catastrophes? Even these only in part, for man is already engaged in manipulating the weather. This new relationship of man to power, which also produces suffering, must have its reciprocal impact, then, upon the assessment and the combatting of evil. Criminal trials occasionally disclose the fact that the crime can be a product of developments in society (e.g., during the Eichmann trial in Jerusalem insightful commentators spoke about the "Eichmann in us"). This means that the whole of society must feel partially responsible for the evil that occurs. This holds true for all the calamity that is caused by man. Such a view of things was still hidden from the people of the Old Testament.

e) Suffering can (if it does not utterly destroy or irreparably cripple, stultify, or paralyze) acquire an ultimate aim for the person who suffers. The Old Testament says that suffering can prepare the way for something better; it can purify, educate, or stabilize the person affected, and so on. Suffering can contribute to one's being human. In light of individual experience, we shall confirm this positive evaluation of a severe fate. Now the Old Testament makes such assertions with the limitation to the earthly life. Resurrection and eternal glory come into view only at the extreme periphery of the Old Testament. Is the Old Testament testimony rendered out-of-date, made unusable, or relativized by the Christian belief in the resurrection? I believe that the internal confrontation with suffering retains its own importance. Regardless of how one conceives of the future of the cosmos and the coming of the kingdom of God, man needs a "short-term" solution to the problem of suffering, or at least the attempt to fit suffering into the span of time that one can comprehend and survey. In this sense the Old Testament continues, even down to the present day, to be a counterbalance to the New Testament's eschatologizing and spiritualizing of suffering.

f) No one today will want to claim that we are living in the most just of all possible worlds. The burden of distress is too heavy on this globe for one to be able to ignore it or to argue it away. It cries out to the heavens, but the heavens do not answer. How can one bear up in such a world? Must we not be driven into madness by any thought of the totality of suffering that is occurring in any single moment? The Old Testament timidly suggests the idea that God is not far removed from the arena of suffering, but is very close at hand, and that he is not there as a spectator, but as one who is affected, as one who suffers. God suffers with the men who must suffer. This thought can give hope. In the New Testament it becomes a central theme. God is not God in the aura of glory, but in the form of the one tortured and put to death. Anyone who wishes to seek God should not fret over the fact that in this world things do not go right and justice is not done. He should look for the unrighteousness in himself and should seek God among those who are suffering under this unrighteousness.

B.
SUFFERING
IN THE
NEW TESTAMENT

Introduction

The fact that, according to the New Testament, suffering and the readiness to suffer belong to Christian existence is nowadays sometimes discredited as a glorification of pain and suffering. Indeed, some regard the New Testament theology of the cross as a Christian form of sado-masochism and as a sanctioning of oppression. It must be readily admitted that the Christian understanding of suffering has often been misused to maintain the status quo and to justify affliction. It must also be conceded that on the basis of the New Testament, one can fully sympathize with the fact that neither man nor God is willing simply to be reconciled to the misery of this world. But on the other hand, in what U. Hedinger calls the "Christian revolt—even against the justifications of suffering found in the Scriptures," people frequently go too far and indeed too one-sidedly tie the New Testament to the recommendation that suffering merely be accepted. In contrast to this perspective, J. B. Metz has represented the *memoria passionis* itself as an insistent and liberating challenge which must be placed as an antihistory in opposition to the usual historical Darwinism that represents history as the story of those who have prevailed, succeeded, and arrived. In a time that is marked by a phobia concerning suffering and that to some extent takes refuge in the illusion of a safe and sound world that is utterly free of calamity, such a reminder can contribute to our own assimilation of suffering and our ability to endure it, but it also can serve to make us sensitive to the sufferings of others.

In the second part of such *memoria* we shall concentrate our attention on what the New Testament calls to mind. Of course here the question immediately is raised once again as to the relationship of Christian suffering then and Christian suffering today. Nevertheless, it must be recognized at once that with all the uniqueness of the respective conditions and modes of suffering, there are certain motifs that are constant. There is a modern ignorance, and indeed arrogance, that supposes that the variety, intensity, and depth of modern experiences of suffering have never been felt before. Others have thought, conversely, that the measure of suffering, when compared to earlier experiences, has been diminished, when one thinks of modern possibilities of healing through medicine and the like. However, it does not make much sense to measure troubles and calculate them in relation to each other, or even to ask whether ancient crucifixion was more painful than modern gassing, or whether the thirty-nine stripes that Paul had to endure five times were more painful than the blows and the electric shocks in modern torture chambers. Of course all this does not lie on the same plane. It is obvious that in many respects suffering nowadays is experienced, assessed, and overcome in ways different from those of that time. For example, when Paul cites physical labor in one of his catalogs of afflictions, alongside hunger and thirst, beatings and homelessness, this appears hardly to be reconcilable and comparable with the long-dominant romantic interpretation of labor. On the other hand, depending on the nature and the harshness of the labor and the excessive demands that often are connected with it, perhaps there are many nowadays who could once again find some sympathy with Paul's view, even though in a time of unemployment there are others who would see it differently. Moreover, we should not allow ourselves to be too greatly irritated by the outdated conceptions of the world (e.g., demons as agents that cause illnesses) or antiquated practices (for example, obscure methods of treatment in the healing of illnesses). It is obvious that we cannot adopt the demonological or "medicinal" views of the New Testament accounts of healing. But this does not at all mean the devaluation of the real message of these narratives, that is, the battle against suffering, which began with Jesus, is and remains up to the present day a task of Christians that does not and cannot go out of date.

We must not exaggerate even the motif of subjectivity that is always in operation. Hunger is hunger, and thirst is thirst.

Certainly in our latitudes nowadays, there is more suffering of
the overnourished as a consequence of their overindulgence
than of hungry people from undernourishment, as of course
everyone after all suffers in some way or another. But in the
New Testament the distress that may be suffered by the rich
man (Luke 16:19 ff.) or by those who "wear soft raiment and
dwell in kings' houses" (Matt. 11:8) does not hold the same
interest as does that of the poor and hungry Lazarus. This fact
must not be blunted, and it remains as reality that is disturbing
for all Christians, one that calls for their solidarity and
imagination, particularly in relation to the hunger that is in the
world. The conquest of hunger and the provision of
superabundance will not bring happiness and end all suffering,
but can instead create new kinds of suffering. But this
awareness certainly should not ease anyone's conscience to
allow others still to go hungry and to defend the status quo. It
also forbids us to regard the hungry as the only ones who are
suffering. The New Testament is a book for all those who suffer,
even for those who are the source of their own suffering.
Therefore what the New Testament says about illness and
oppression, homelessness or the denial of just wages to the
workers in the harvest, and the like, is, in spite of all the
differences, altogether comparable to modern experiences.
This similarity also applies with reference to the causes,
interpretations, and even the conquest of suffering.

Of course, there are distinctions to be noted even within
the New Testament itself, but that will be done here only
implicitly, without our making an intensive study of issues in
the history of traditions and the like. The reader himself will
note, for example, that in the section dealing with the
interpretations of suffering, the Jesus-tradition of the Gospels is
almost totally left aside, while on the other hand, in the section
dealing with the overcoming of suffering, it is strongly
represented. From this it certainly may be concluded that Jesus
himself was less engaged in interpreting suffering than he was
in actively working to overcome it. Similarly, the suffering
Christ as an example plays a major role only in certain writings;

in contrast to these, in the writings of Paul this role is much less prominent, if it is not lacking altogether. However, we shall speak of these different accents only indirectly, particularly since one may not forthwith make them into contradictions. Even the person whose primary concern is not to reflect upon the meaning and the cause of suffering, but to strive to overcome it, as is obviously the case with Jesus, has at least implicitly expressed himself on the subject now and then (cf. below, on the connection between the forgiveness of sins and the healing of the sick). And anyone who, like Paul, considers (and experiences!) suffering primarily in the context of Christology is by no means content with that, but attempts to relieve suffering by rendering aid, as through offerings and the like. Anyone who nowadays proposes that we stop asking about the meaning of suffering and only devote ourselves to mobilizing the resistance to affliction will have to allow the question, on the one hand, whether he is not thereby advancing an irrational happy-ending theology and a naive *homo-faber* ideology, indeed, whether he is not abandoning the hapless sufferers and dismissing their fate, which in fact becomes all the more painful because of the loss of meaning of their suffering in absurdity and fatalism. On the other hand, he will be obliged to tell how he proposes to deal responsibly with the New Testament, which attempts not only to contend against suffering, but also to comprehend it.

I. Experiences of suffering

1. The voice of suffering in the Old Testament

The manifold experiences of suffering within the New Testament need only to be set forth in broad outline, since in large measure they coincide with those of the Old Testament, but in part have also remained constant through the centuries.

It is practically self-evident that the Old Testament legacy itself served to preserve primitive Christianity from minimizing its sufferings and pains in Stoic apathy, speculatively reinterpreting it in gnostic indifference, or even soaring above it in fanaticism. The unmistakable voices of suffering in the Old Testament rather helped to give unvarnished expression to affliction and to avoid two wrong courses. The first of these is the Stoic way of rendering affliction harmless, by treating it as actually no evil at all, but only a product of the imagination, and saying that in the final analysis man only torments himself in it (cf. Epictetus, *Discourses* I.25.28; Seneca, *Epistle* 71.26). The other of these wrong courses in the gnostic assumption, according to which the "grave affliction in those worlds of darkness" (Ginza 152) is identical with coreality, which can be traced back to an evil original principle ("Woe is me in this corporeal garment," Ginza 461), from which corporeal state one can escape by means of gnosis and ecstasy (this perhaps is also the thesis of the false teachers in 2 Cor.). The way of modern men to regard discussion of affliction as taboo and to fall silent before it (cf., e.g., the admonition "Learn to suffer without complaining") was all the more foreign to primitive Christianity, for it was obviously aware that, like Job, the Old Testament does not "hold its tongue," but in suffering "speaks and laments" (Job 2:11). On the other hand, as a consequence of the Old Testament belief in creation it was equally impossible to regard the earth in an apocalyptic way as a solitary vale of tears or to make suffering the central theme, as is done in Buddhism. The real meaning and sense in referring back to the Old Testament, however, lies in the fact that primitive Christianity was guided by it to derive meaning from its own destiny of suffering and above all to understand the career of Jesus and his passion in the light of the Old Testament promise. How strongly the Old Testament language, its conceptual world, and its experience of suffering also determine the representation and the interpretation of the phenomenon of suffering within the New Testament is demonstrated from the first to the last, though with varying intensity.

a) Jesus' career in the light of the Old Testament

It begins in Matthew with the slaughter of the infants in Bethlehem, interpreted by means of an Old Testament quotation from Jeremiah 31:15, which is treated in terms of fulfillment or reflection:

Then was fulfilled what was spoken by the prophet Jeremiah:
"A voice was heard in Ramah,
wailing and loud lamentation,
Rachel weeping for her children;
she refused to be consoled,
because they were no more."
(Matt. 2:17-18 RSV)

According to the passage in Jeremiah, Rachel, who as the mother of the tribes of Joseph and Benjamin (cf. Gen. 35:16, 24) represents all Israelite mothers, sits in Ramah and bewails bitterly and inconsolably the loss of her sons, who through the fall of Israel have been taken away into exile. Matthew sees in this a prefiguring of the lamentations of the mothers of Bethlehem. The historicity of this slaughter of the innocents indeed is questionable, even though Herod was proverbially cruel and, out of fear of the loss of his power, even had his three oldest sons killed. But it is true, and historically accurate, that the Messiah does not appear in an idyllic world, but in a world that is dominated by the powerful, who, disregarding the tears of the innocent, do not shrink from any act of violence and, by means of their murderous commands, take great pains to liquidate the one who, as the advocate of those who are abused and oppressed, could call their rule into question. It is true also that in the context of the story of Jesus' infancy Matthew was concerned primarily with showing the parallel to the fate of the Moses who liberated Israel from Egypt; according to an ancient Moses-legend, Pharaoah so feared his birth that he sought to kill all the Israelite children (cf. Exod. 1:22), and in this instance also, the deliverer who has been sent by God escapes the murderous attack of men. Nevertheless, it is clear that from the

very beginning Jesus' career is seen in the light of the
experiences of suffering in the Old Testament. His history does
not become a "passion narrative" only at its end, but Jesus is
from the very first the one whose life was being sought (Matt.
2:20), and this was prefigured in the Old Testament.

Still another example may illustrate how strong was the
perception and undertanding of Jesus' career elsewhere as well
in the light of the psalms of tribulation and other texts of the Old
Testament that pertained to suffering. Matthew interprets
Jesus' healing of the sick with the words of the song of the
suffering servant of God: "He took our infirmities and bore our
diseases" (8:17 RSV; cf. Isa. 53:4; cf. also Matt. 12:9 ff.). But of
course Jesus' own fate of suffering is understood with special
emphasis in terms of the Old Testament story of suffering.
Thus, for example, even the terminology of the so-called
predictions of the passion indicates that Jesus is to suffer the fate
of the suffering prophets and righteous ones (cf. Mark 10:33-34
and par.), who bore ridicule, derision, and shame. The parable
of the wicked tenants (Mark 12:1 ff.) offers an allegorical
portrayal of the persecution and passion of those who are sent
by God into his "vineyard" (cf. Isa. 5:1), beaten, shamefully
treated, and slain. Then when at the last even the "beloved son"
and "heir" is seized, killed, and cast out of the vineyard, Jesus'
passion stands in continuity with the sufferings of others of
God's emissaries, into whose line he is set as the final and
decisive victim. It is possible that Jesus himself expected to
come to a violent end as a false prophet or a blasphemer and to
fail, to suffer, and to die in the line of the prophets (cf. e.g.,
Luke 13:32-33; Matt. 23:37).

Above all the *passion narrative* of Jesus (Mark 14–15 and
par.) becomes understandable only when one sees how heavily
the Old Testament is used again and again, even to the very
details, to give expression to Jesus' sufferings and to interpret
them. It is not only stated as a matter of principle that "the Son
of man goes as it is written of him" (Mark 14:21 RSV), and "the
Scriptures must be fulfilled" (Mark 14:49), but the attempt is
made to confirm this by means of various explicit quotations and
allusions within the narrative. In these passages, the formulas

of quotation ("for it stands written," and the like) are usually
lacking (not, however, in Matt. 27:9; Luke 22:37; John 15:25;
19:24), but it must be assumed that even so the Old Testament
references were recognized and understood. Jesus' saying in
Gethsemane, "My soul is deeply troubled, even unto death"
(Mark 14:34 and par.), for example, is reminiscent of Pss. 42:5,
11 and 43:5. His last words on the cross are words from the
Psalter: in Mark and Matthew, "My God, my God, why hast
thou forsaken me?" (Mark 15:34 and par. = Ps. 22:1; on this, cf.
II.1.b), and in Luke, "Father, into thy hands I commend my
spirit" (Luke 23:46 = Ps. 31:5). Even though the events often
are related only with individual Old Testament phrases (the
dividing of the garments in Mark 15:24, cf. Ps. 22:18; the
wagging of heads in Mark 15:29, cf. Ps. 22:7; the drink of
vinegar in Mark 15:36, cf. Ps. 69:21), still there stands behind
these the conviction that what we have in the passion of Jesus is
not a meaningless failure, but an actualization of God's plan,
and that his passion is in harmony with the events of suffering in
the Old Testament.

A special significance belongs above all to the Old
Testament psalms of suffering (Pss. 22 and 69), which treat of
the suffering of the righteous, whose lot of hardship is set forth
also in the book of Wisdom (cf. 2:1 ff. and the allusion to 2:17-18
in the scene where Jesus is being derided in Mark 15:31-32).
The Jews' words of ridicule with their echo of Ps. 22:8 (cf. also
Wisd. 2:17 ff.) are likewise suggestive of the suffering righteous
ones ("He has trusted in God. Now let God save him, if he wants
him," Matt. 27:43), as are Jesus words in John 19:28 ("I thirst"
= Ps. 22:15). Perhaps primitive Christianity saw in the fate of
these innocent sufferers, whom God promised to lift up out of
their humiliation (cf. Wisd. 5:1-5), the type of their suffering
Lord (cf. also the title, "the Righteous One," for the suffering
Christ in Acts 3:14; 7:52). It is amazing, on the other hand, that
as far as explicit utterances are concerned, the Deutero-Isaian
servant of God (Isa. 53) plays only a minor role in the
interpretation of Jesus'; suffering and dying (Luke 22:37; Acts
8:32-33; 1 Pet. 2:22, 24). Yet even here we must take note of
indirect influence, as in Jesus' silence before the Sanhedrin and

Pilate (Mark 14:61; 15:5; cf. Isa. 53:7), or in the words of the last supper (Mark 14:24 and par.; cf. Isa. 53:11-12), and outside the passion narrative perhaps in Mark 10:45 or in ancient Christological formulas such as Rom. 4:25, 1 Cor. 15:3, et passim (cf. Isa. 53:5, 7). In an atomistic use of the Old Testament, of course, such allusions do not also immediately signify that people saw in Jesus the suffering servant of God. What is of crucial significance are neither such christological identifications nor the often arbitrarily adduced details, but the belief that the *entire* passion of Jesus corresponds to the plan of salvation that is attested in the Old Testament. "*All* of this happened in order that the writings of the prophets might be fulfilled" (Matt. 26:56; cf. Luke 24:44).

Of course this "all," which can only be postulated and indeed only here and there finds fragmentary support in the Old Testament, is already an indication that Jesus' suffering and dying were not interpreted solely from the perspective of the Old Testament (cf. further II.1.c). "The stone that was rejected by the builders" (Ps. 118:22) is no longer, as in the Old Testament, the Israel that was rejected by the great powers of the Near East, but the Messiah (Mark 12:10-11; 1 Pet. 2:4 ff.). And a suffering Messiah could not be derived from the scripture, any more than a suffering and dying of the Son of man. In Judaism the features of suffering from Isaiah 53 are never given a messianic interpretation. And although Mark 9:12-13, for example, says that it is written concerning the Son of man that "he must suffer many things and be treated scornfully," just as also people did whatever they pleased to Elijah, who had come in the person of John the Baptist, this is nowhere "written" *expressis verbis*, which is probably why Matthew left out this statement. The statement that the prophets had already inquired as to the time of the "suffering" and the "glory" of Jesus (1 Pet. 1:11) is an *a posteriori* declaration and must not be allowed to gloss over the fact that the meaning of Jesus' suffering and dying came to the disciples only "afterward" (cf. John 13:7; Luke 24:27, 45-46), and people sensed an agreement and harmony with the Old Testament without, and even against, individual scriptural documentation. That the story of suffering in the Old Testament leads into that of the New Covenant thus is, in the last analysis, not a statement of the exegesis of the Old Testament but of the primitive Christian faith, which of course sought confirmation in the Old Testament.

b) Old Testament examples for the sufferings of Christians

But even apart from the history and person of Jesus, references to the Old Testament are always likewise references to the history of Israel's suffering. It is precisely the distressing experiences of their own present time that prompt the Christians to refer back to the Old Testament writings. Entire catalogs of experiences of suffering can thus be adduced. In the long chain of witnesses of faith from the Old Testament, which the author of the book of Hebrews understands as paradigmatic, it is said at the conclusion concerning the prophets and martyrs of the Old Testament—Jewish history:

> Others were tortured, not accepting release, so that they might attain a better resurrection. Others had to suffer mocking and scourging, and fetters and imprisonment as well. They were stoned, burned (?), sawn asunder, killed with the sword. They wandered about in sheepskins and goatskins, deprived, afflicted, tormented. These, of whom the world is not worthy, wandered in deserts and mountains, in dens and caves in the earth.
>
> (Heb. 11:36-38)

Some of this can be documented from the Old Testament: stoning (2 Chr. 24:21), killing with the sword (1 Kings 19:10; Jer. 26:23), imprisonment (1 Kings 22:27), mocking (Jer. 20:7-8), and living in caves (1 Kings 18:4). For other parts, there are only Jewish parallels: burning (2 Macc. 6:11), torture (2 Macc. 7), sawing asunder (Ascension of Isaiah 5:1), flight into the mountains and deserts (1 Macc. 2:28 ff.; 2 Macc. 5:27), and abuse (Ecclus. 49:7). In any case such a "cloud of witnesses" (of suffering; Heb. 12:1) of the "fathers" (cf. Heb. 11:2) could be set in view alongside the suffering Christ (cf. Heb. 12:2 et passim) as comforting and hortatory examples of suffering faith even for the readers' own present time. The long series of experiences of suffering is preceded by a list of deeds of faith that exhibit the conquering power of faith and the preserving power of grace. This shows that here suffering is not regarded as the only reality and is not made the subject as such, but is regarded as a mode of faith. Nevertheless it is characteristic that the history of faith in the Old Testament leads to suffering, and what is stressed is not victory and strength, but sacrifice and affliction. In this way, Christian faith can infer from the Old Testament that this faith itself, as a life of peregrination in this world, has to do with persecution and privation, expulsion from society, wandering about in hiding places, and the like. Indeed, faith also knows that the Old Testament martyrs' experiences of suffering did not yet bring with them the fulfillment of the promise, because God had in store "something better" (vv. 39-40); but on the other hand it can see, for example, in the sufferings of Moses a typological prefiguring of the sufferings of Christ (cf. Heb. 11:26). But in any case, the book of Hebrews itself admonishes the readers in the community's situations of suffering not to "forget the promise" (Heb. 12:5) and the interpretation of suffering contained within the promise, but to actualize this promise anew, although even according to the book of Hebrews it does not suffice simply to set the story of their own sufferings in the light of the Old Testament.

Particularly in Jewish Christian communities, it was possible elsewhere also to refer quite naturally to Old Testament experiences of suffering. Matthew, for example, saw in the history of Israel a long succession of martyrs from Abel to Zachariah, in whose train also are those who are sent forth by Jesus (Matt. 23:31-35). In Matt. 5:11-12 and Luke 6:22-23 the Old Testament idea of the suffering of the righteous is combined with that of the violent fate of the prophets and applied to the disciples. In Stephen's discourse in his own defense, Moses in particular plays a major role as prototype of the suffering and rejected emissary of God (Acts 7:17 ff.). And

the author of the epistle of James adduces the prophets and Job
as well-known ("you have heard") examples from whom one can
learn patient endurance in suffering, which apparently does not
at all need to be explicated in detail:

> As an example of endurance in suffering and of patience in
> waiting, my brothers, take the prophets, who spoke in the
> name of the Lord. Behold, we call those blessed who have
> remained steadfast. You have heard of the steadfastness of
> Job, and you are acquainted with the end that the Lord
> (wrought), for the Lord is full of mercy and compassion.
>   (James 5:10-11)

While the exemplary significance of the prophets as martyrs
was also well-known elsewhere in primitive Christianity (cf.
Matt. 5:12; 23:29 ff.; Acts 7:52), the example of suffering Job is
nowhere else mentioned. The Epistle of James is interested in
him not only because of his readiness to suffer, but also because
of the "end" that the Lord wrought. What is meant by this is
disputed. It is not entirely impossible that we are also to think of
the favorable conclusion of Job's life, his deliverance from his
own suffering and the restoration of his prosperity (cf. 42:10,
12-13), but the sharp criticism of wealth in the Epistle of James
makes it unlikely that the blessings of this life alone are what the
author had in mind. Hence it probably is the "eternal" outcome
of Job's time of suffering that is in view, which the Christians are
to remember when they are suffering (cf. also the Testament of
Benjamin 4:1; Testament of Asher 6:4).

Finally, for Paul, too, the significance of the Old
Testament texts about suffering is found not only within his
Christology, but also in utterances about the community's lot of
suffering (cf. e.g., Rom. 15:3 = Ps. 69:9, where Christ's
suffering blasphemies is understood as a paradigm). In Rom.
8:36 Paul quotes from the national lament in Psalm 44, which
traces Israel's martyrdoms to their belonging to Yahweh, in
order thus to comprehend the Christians' fate of suffering in the
light of the Old Testament: "For thy sake we are given over to
death the whole day long, we are regarded as sheep for

slaughtering." This is meant to provide documentation that the previously enumerated sufferings (v. 35) have been announced to the community by God and are in accordance with his will. Of course, the Christology ("for thy sake" now refers to Christ) radicalizes it still further (cf. the modified quotation of Ps. 118:18 in 2 Cor. 6:19, and further, II.2.a), but at the same time it is also placed in the context of the eschatological hope. Israel too will participate in that hope. Paul indeed quotes the lament of Elijah, "Lord, they have killed thy prophets and torn down thine altars, and I alone am left, and they are seeking my life" (Rom. 11:3; cf. 1 Kings 19:10, 14): However, God's answer to Elijah is for Paul the assurance that God has not cast off his people, but a remnant has remained which serves as a guarantee for the eschatological deliverance of Israel (Rom. 11:4; cf. 1 Kings 19:18). For the rest, it must be remembered that even without any explicit reference there can exist unspoken interconnections, as, for example, with the prophets' fate of suffering, particularly that of Jeremiah (cf. Jer. 11:18-19; 15:15 ff.; 20:1 ff.; 26:7 ff.; 37:1 ff.; 38:1 ff.), to be found in Paul's assessment of apostolic sufferings.

c) Old Testament guidance in the conquest of suffering

Finally, the Old Testament is also claimed as an example and an argument for the avoidance, the alleviating, or the conquest of suffering. This is done first of all by the quoting of words of wisdom on how one can avoid calamity: He who would love life and see good days, let him keep his tongue from evil and his lips from speaking deception. Let him turn away from evil and do good, let him seek peace and pursue it (1 Pet. 3:10-11). Even if the author of 1 Peter does not understand the "good days" to have a this-worldly reference but intends instead the life eternal, still this quotation from Psalm 34 is intended to say that by steering clear of sins of the tongue and aiming at the good, one can avoid conflict with one's environment and with the authorities (cf. 2:15-16; 3:13). The author himself indicates in other passages (2:19-20; 3:9, 16) that this is not an entirely realistic rule of prudence; yet it is intended not only that one should gain courage for suffering obedience but also that unnecessary confrontations should be

a cause of great distress

avoided. The author is well aware that sufferings are not unknown even in a life that is well lived. But where one can help man to avoid any avoidable calamity, this should be done.

Indeed, precisely from the Old Testament perspective it becomes legitimate and urgent to alleviate or to overcome suffering. Matt. 8:17 shows (cf. I.1.a.) that the struggle against suffering and illness is not illuminated and explained in terms of a general idea of humanity, but in terms of the scripture, whose eschatological fulfillment is dawning with Jesus' words and deeds. Further documentation is found in the "dispute" in Mark 2:23 ff., a conflict over the Sabbath that arose over the disciples' plucking ears of grain, which according to the Jewish view was not permitted on the Sabbath. Jesus counters the opponents' criticism of his disciples' conduct with a counter question, in which he argues making use of a "scriptural proof" from the Old Testament, and points to the example of David and his conduct with respect to the shewbread (1 Sam. 21:2 ff.). Even if this reference to David's transgressing the law probably was only later inserted, and moreover is not entirely convincing and compelling, it is intended by the narrator to provide documentation that David's conduct in satisfying his hunger makes it clear that the purpose of religious laws is not to let men suffer (v. 25). Of course it is only in Matthew that the disciples' breach of the Sabbath is explicitly attributed to their hunger (Matt. 12:1).

The reference to Isa. 61:1 in the so-called "inaugural discourse" of Jesus in Nazareth (Luke 4:17-19) gives a far more extensive and utterly programmatic expression to the salvation prophetically announced in the Old Testament with its dimensions of the overcoming of suffering (cf. also the references to Isa. 29:18-19, 35:6, and 61:1 in Matt. 11:5 and Luke 7:22-23). Jesus is to bring to mankind, by fulfilling the Old Testament promise, the end of poverty, imprisonment, and humiliation. He is sent by God "to bring good news to the poor, to proclaim liberation to the captives and the opening of the eyes of the blind, to set free those who are broken, and to announce the acceptable year of the Lord" (Luke 4:18). This may not only be understood figuratively. The proclamation of the good news belongs together with the healing of broken hearts just as much as it does with the fulness of salvation, understood in the Old Testament sense, in the real and earthly sense (cf. e.g., the physical healing of the blind, and vv. 26-27), and indeed "today" (v. 21). Under God's commission Jesus is to bring to an end the sufferings that afflict the whole man, and that is indeed Jesus' own intention. Hence he finds approval and yet at the same time is the "sign that is spoken against" (2:34 RSV), and the one who like the prophets is not accepted (cf. 4:24, 28 ff.).

It is likewise indicated that the Old Testament was already aware that here and now this comprehensive salvation is dawning, at first only in signs; there is not yet a universal end to suffering, and the sending of Jesus is aimed primarily at the Gentiles. For "in the days of Elijah in Israel, when the heavens were closed up for three years and six months, and a great famine came upon the whole land, there were many widows. And yet Elijah was not sent to any of them, but to a widow in Zarephath in (Gentile) Sidon. And in the days of the prophet Elisha there were many lepers in Israel, and none of them was cleansed, but Naaman the (Gentile) Syrian" (Luke 4:25-27; cf. 1 Kings 17:1 ff.; 2 Kings 5:8 ff.). This is not a refusal of earthly help (cf. vv. 31 ff.), but the deliberate intention specifically to give aid to foreigners. Because Jesus did not share the view that "charity begins at home," he earned a wrathful protest and had to deal with an attempt to lynch him.

The universal end of all suffering, when there will be no more hunger or thirst, when death, affliction, and sighing will flee away, and when God will wipe away all tears, is anticipated for the future by the New Testament along with Isa. 25:8, 35:10 (cf. 51:11), and 49:10 (Rev. 7:16; 21:4); and this is set in the comprehensive context of a new heaven and a new earth (cf. Isa. 65:17), where "all things will be new" (Rev. 21:5), and the creation itself will participate in the glorious freedom of the children of God (Rom. 8:19 ff.).

d) The Jewish modifications

The multilayered reception, but also the further development and modification, of the Old Testament utterances about suffering in Judaism will be indicated briefly at appropriate places in the following sections. There it will become evident that sufferings not only were seen as judgment and punishment, in keeping with the dogma of retribution, but in the Jewish theology of suffering they also serve for the expiation of sins, contribute to the increase of merit, or are understood as divine discipline prompted by love. Furthermore, and finally, in apocalypticism they are eschatological "woes" of the new aeon, a temporally and substantively limited, but necessary and promise-laden, transitional stage on the way to the coming glory. The New Testament is influenced by these trains of thought, particularly in the emphasis upon the eschatological hope and the attendant relativizing of suffering, but in part also in the understanding of suffering as judgment and beneficial discipline. But it neither affirms the assumption that sufferings affect man precisely in proportion to his guilt nor shares the opinion of Rabbi Akiba, that the question "What produces forgiveness for man?" is to be answered with the one word "sufferings." Nor does it simply agree with the view of 4 Esdras 14:16: "The weaker the world becomes because of age, the more man's sufferings increase."

2. The comprehensive dimension of suffering

a) Suffering as suffering of the whole person

The Old Testament tradition has already indicated that suffering indeed has many visages, but the experience of suffering and, accordingly, the conquest of suffering also affect man as a whole. What modern psychosomatic medicine has only slowly comprehended anew, and even in theology and church is still far from sufficiently considered or taken seriously, is for the New Testament clearly established. Suffering is suffering of the *totus homo*. "If one member suffers, all suffer together" (1 Cor. 12:26 RSV), related by Paul to the community and its members, applies also to the individual man. In suffering, man is always involved in sympathy as a whole person, not only in a physical sense, but also spiritually and psychically.

Corresponding to this holistic view of suffering, for example, is the fact that the individual anthropological terms and phenomena are used, particularly in Paul, as *pars pro toto* and that they mean man as a whole in a specific aspect. This is shown especially by the use of the word "body" *(soma)*, which Paul shows a preference for using in the context of pronouncements about suffering. If sufferings affect the body, they do not affect merely the outer shell or the outside of the unaffected inside or "real" person, but the "I" of the person. Equally as important as the often stressed fact that for Paul, "body" denotes the "I" and the person, is also, of course, the converse: that "I" and person include, *eo ipso,* corporeality; "body" thus is the concrete corporeal place where one experiences life and death, but likewise illness and suffering. When 2 Cor. 4:10 says that "in our body we carry about the dying of Jesus," this just says, as we shall further show, that the apostle so clearly bears the "stigmata" of Jesus' fate of death (cf. Gal. 6:17) that in his very corporeality he reflects that fate of suffering and death.

How strongly the whole man is held in view is confirmed also by other expressions that do not include the concept of "body." This is clear, for example, in 2 Cor. 7:5, where Paul describes his arrival in Macedonia with the words, "afflicted on every hand, battles without and fears within." The "outside" and the "inside" of a man form a unity and color each other. We must not let ourselves be deceived by the partially dualistic legacy found in Pauline anthropology (as e.g. in what he says in 2 Cor. 4:16 about the "inner" and the "outer" man). It is true that there are sufferings that are *primarily* physical or *primarily* psychical, as there are also *primarily* social and other kinds of suffering. However, they do not remain psychical or physical, but they are or become multidimensional and complex, and they manifest themselves not only in physical but also in psychical and spiritual terms, often from the very beginning. Hence Paul can say about the very same experience, "I found no rest in my *spirit*, because I did not find Titus" (2 Cor. 2:13), and "our *flesh* found no rest" (2 Cor. 7:5). If the "spirit" suffers, the "flesh" also suffers (on the suffering of the "flesh" cf. e.g., 2 Cor. 12:7; Col. 1:24; 1 Pet. 4:1); but conversely, a purely biological-somatic view of suffering likewise is inappropriate. "Spirit," "soul," "heart," and so on are also involved in the suffering. "Soul," for example, can denote man as a whole; it is not, however, conceived of abstractly, but corporeally. When the soul is injured (Mark 8:36), the man himself is injured and loses himself (thus the parallels in Luke 9:25). When Jesus' *soul* is "troubled, even to death" (Mark 14:34) or is anxious (John 12:27), it affects him as a whole person (cf. John 16:33: "in the world *you* have tribulation," and in 14:1, 27, in connection with "heart"). A "broken" (Acts 21:13) or anguished (Rom. 9:2) *"heart,"* a "pierced" (Luke 2:35) or faint (Heb. 12:3) *"soul,"* a sighing (Mark 8:12) or unsettled (cf. 2 Cor. 7:13) *"spirit,"* all these are only symptoms of the man who as a whole is troubled and filled with distress. So, just as man does not *have* a body or a soul, but rather *is* body and soul, so also in principle it is not that he has this or that suffering, but he himself suffers. But in any case, suffering does not affect him only peripherally, but at his very core.

This is also confirmed by the suffering itself. When a man would like to undo something that has happened (cf. the "bitter weeping" of Peter in Matt. 26:75), to escape from his self-contradiction, or when he is shattered in failure and guilt, then he suffers as a whole, even when he is not aware of this. Here we may only refer to Rom. 7:14 ff. where man is portrayed in his inner division and discord. "I do not understand my own actions. For I do not do what I want, but I do the very thing I hate" (v. 15 RSV). We may not understand this in terms of an anthropological division, as though here certain parts of man such as his will and his deed, or his body and his spirit, stood in contradiction with each other. The subject of the willing and the doing is always the selfsame "I". Man is in conflict with himself, in self-contradiction, and he suffers from this: "Wretched man that I am" (v. 24). Sin, which manifests itself in legalism as well as in antinomianism, in zeal for the law as well as in transgression of the law, has so taken hold in him and seized control that he himself is, as it were, expelled from himself and is no longer identical with himself; thus the "I" disintegrates. Of course this is said by Paul as he looks back from the perspective of faith, and it is neither simply the situation of the Christian nor identical with the empirical experience and self-analysis of the unredeemed man himself. But this does not rule out the fact that it provides some empirical points of contact for such a view of man and that the picture is colored from the perspective of the Christian's tribulations (cf. Gal. 5:17). In any case, the very act of turning away from God involves distress and calamity and brings the whole person into suffering (cf. e.g., Rom. 1:24 ff.; 3:10ff.), even though this cannot be calculated (cf. IV.2.a).

Thus there is repeated confirmation of the multilayered character, and yet at the same time the anthropological indivisibility, of suffering. Even though there is much that is not explicitly identified as suffering, it includes falling among robbers (Luke 10:25 ff.), as well as the sad lot of widows and orphans (James 1:27), the pain of parting (Acts 20:37-38), and tears (Hebr. 5:7, et passim); there is also the "anguish of the heart" (2 Cor. 2:4) and the divided state of the "I" (Rom. 7:14 ff.), as will become further evident in many other examples. This view of man as a totality has important consequences for the later question of the conquest of suffering. In the Stoic view, suffering is merely an external event, which does not at all affect man in his innermost center. Here the perspective is different, and hence a withdrawal inward, as though here one could find a refuge untouched by the storms of suffering, is no solution to the problem of suffering.

b) Common forms of suffering (catalogs of sufferings)

Any spiritualizing of suffering in particular misses the totality, reality, and harshness of the experiences. How far wide of the mark such an interpretation is, is confirmed by the Pauline catalogs of suffering. From among these, we shall quote here from 2 Cor. 11:23 ff., where Paul gives to the community his response to a challenge posed by the Corinthian heretics. It is true that there Paul at first, after he has sharply rejected the boasting of his Corinthian adversaries, appears to want to compete with them (vv. 1 ff.), yet he himself labels this foolish talk (v. 17). Then he immediately goes on to treat this with irony, and after two verses in which he compares himself with his opponents (vv. 22-23), he abandons this approach and only enumerates the abundance of his own sufferings, cares, and afflictions which he had to endure in his unprecedented devotion to the cause of the gospel. Paradoxically, his actual "more" is the affliction which turns the "catalog of boasts"into a catalog of sufferings.

> Are they servants of Christ? I am a better one—I am talking like a madman—with far greater labors, far more imprisonments, with countless beatings, and often near death. Five times I have received at the hands of the Jews the forty lashes less one. Three times I have been beaten with rods; once I was stoned. Three times I have been shipwrecked; a night and a day I have been adrift at sea; on frequent journeys, in danger from rivers, danger from robbers, danger from my own people, danger from Gentiles, danger in the city, danger in the wilderness, danger at sea, danger from false brethren; in toil and hardship, through many a sleepless night, in hunger and thirst, often without food, in cold and exposure. And, apart from other things, there is the daily pressure upon me of my anxiety for all the churches. (RSV)

The abundance of these enumerated sufferings, tribulations and difficulties, some of which, like the synagogue's punishment of thirty-nine lashes, were such torture that people frequently died while they were being inflicted, far exceeds the normal measure of what can be endured. But Paul is not exaggerating; this is shown in the parallels in various other catalogs (cf. 2 Cor. 4:8-9; 6:4-10; 1 Cor. 4:10-13) and in scattered individual utterances. This enumeration still is incomplete, as is made clear by the explicit remark in verse 28, but is also confirmed by the other catalogs of sufferings, in which, for example, homelessness is mentioned (1 Cor. 4:11), as well as evil reports and slander (1 Cor. 4:13; 2 Cor. 6:8), or hard physical labor (1 Cor. 4:12). Utterances about suffering outside these catalogs, which, for example, mention stoning (Acts 14:19) or fighting with wild beasts (1 Cor. 15:32), confirm or supplement the catalogs of sufferings. Of course, the forms of this suffering are dependent in part on quite specific situations or are even totally unique, like the extremely dangerous experience of Paul in Asia, which struck him so hard that it was beyond his power, and he expected to die soon (2 Cor. 1:8-9). It was much the same in the case of his encounter, mentioned in 2 Cor. 11:32, with the ethnarch of King Aretas in Damascus, who had the city gates guarded in order to capture Paul.

Other experiences, on the other hand, are typical and were also repeated elsewhere in primitive Christianity or are presupposed as realities of suffering that are common to humanity: imprisonment (in addition to 2 Cor. 11:23, cf. also Matt. 25:36; Rev. 2:10; 13:10; Acts 8:3; 16:23, et passim) and homelessness (in addition to 1 Cor. 4:11, cf. also Matt. 8:20; Heb. 11:38), to which may be added dispersion (Acts 8:1), exile (Rev. 1:9; cf. Acts 18:2), and being an alien (cf. Matt. 25:35; Heb. 13:2, et passim). Then further, vilification (in addition to 1 Cor. 4:12-13 and 2 Cor. 6:8, cf. also Mark 15:32; Matt. 5:11; 1 Pet. 3:9; 4:14; Heb. 10:33; 1 Tim. 4:10), with which are associated also reviling (1 Pet. 2:12; 3:16) and scorn (Mark 10:34; Matt. 20:19; Acts 17:18, et passim) and the suffering of blasphemy (a reading in 1 Cor. 4:13; Rev. 2:9; 1 Pet. 4:4); then beating with rods (2 Cor. 11:25; cf. Acts 16:22) or the synagogue's punishment by flogging (in addition to 2 Cor. 11:24, cf. also Matt. 10:17; 27:26; Acts 22:24, et passim), and finally hunger and thirst (in addition to 2 Cor. 11:27, 1 Cor. 4:11, and Rom. 8:35, cf. also Matt. 25:35; Acts 11:28; Rev. 6:8), loneliness (1 Thess. 3:1 ff.), and homesickness (Phil. 2:26), cold and exposure (in addition to 2 Cor. 11:27 and Rom. 8:35, cf. also Matt. 25:36; James 2:15), and the plight of the orphans and widows (James 1:27; Acts 6:1, et passim).

c) Political, social, and economic oppression

Although the above list covers the most common forms of suffering, apart from illness, that the men of New Testament times experienced and thought about, there are occasional references also to other things that caused distress or were experienced as affliction. First to be mentioned is the suffering that exists in political violence or oppression and that is presupposed, for example, in Matthew 20 as an altogether self-evident reality. "You know that the rulers of the Gentiles lord it over them, and their great men exercise authority over them" (v. 25 RSV), or "misuse the power of their office." As in Mark 10:42, this serves primarily as a contrast to the behavior within the community; yet we can also detect a certain undertone of opposition to the violence of earthly rulers that oppresses and causes grief to the peoples. The bloodbath among Galilean pilgrims in Jerusalem, initiated by Pilate, is recalled, though there to be sure without any such critical undertone (Luke 13:1 ff.). As a rule, it is assumed that the sword of the state only affects those who do wrong (cf. Rom. 13:4), yet the actual experiences of people in conflicts with the civil authorities also point in another direction (cf. Acts 12:1-2, and further III.3).

The exercise of power or even oppression acquires a more heavily social component where the Christians are reminded of their bad experiences with rich people who treat them cruelly (cf. James 2:6). In particular, the slaves of New Testament times must have had repeated personal acquaintance with beatings and mistreatment (cf. 1 Pet. 2:19-20), and even where there were only threats of such (cf. Eph. 6:9), it is obvious how vulnerable were the slaves to the arbitrariness and brutality of their masters. Oppression of others that is based upon social privileges and the misuse of economic power also becomes manifest where the accusation is made against the rich that they show off their power in court and publicly harass the Christian poor through court proceedings (James 2:6; cf. also Luke 18:1 ff.).

Distresses of an economic nature take many different forms. They can, for example, result from unjust socio-economic structures and consist of exploitation of workers in the harvest: "Behold, the wages of the laborers who mowed your fields, which you kept back by fraud, cry out; and the cries of the harvesters have reached the ears of the Lord of hosts" (James 5:4 RSV). Further, they can consist of the deprivation of a person of the essentials of life, and a person like "poor Lazarus" lies grievously ill before the door of a rich man who "feasts sumptuously every day," while the poor man must satisfy his hunger with the crumbs that fall from the rich man's table and must defend himself against stray dogs (Luke 16:19 ff.). They can arise, further, through the harsh and vexatious practice of collecting taxes, with which the feared tax collectors ("publicans") "unjustly extorted" their profits (Luke 19:8; cf. 3:14). They can also take the form of the confiscation of goods ("plundering of your property," Heb. 10:34 RSV); what is meant here probably is the loss of possessions decreed by civil authorities in a persecution. Finally, these distresses may take the form of an economic boycott, when, for example, the Roman imperial authority demands observance of the cult of the emperor and decrees for those who reject this state religion that no one "can buy or sell" (Rev. 13:17).

Here there is an alliance of religious and economic power (cf. also Rev. 17–18), particularly the extensive lamentation of the merchants and men of commerce who have become rich (18:11 ff.), after God's judgment upon "Babylon," from which the people of God are to withdraw, (18:4). But the religious activity itself can be misused and can become a pretext for the unscrupulous exploitation of others. Thus in Mark 12:40 the accusation is made against the scribes that they "eat up the houses of widows and make a show of their long prayers," thus either they make exorbitant charges for their long prayers of supplication or economic and religious interests form an alliance and in this way cause distress and injury to others.

d) Illness

The most common form of suffering, particularly in the gospels, is illness. Precisely here the unitary nature of suffering once again is made evident, and particularly its connection with psychical and religious circumstances (on Mark 2:1 ff., cf. V. 5), yet without the offering of a definition of the essence of illness, which indeed cannot be precisely defined in its essence down to the present time. In the accounts of healings in the Gospels, which are to be discussed later—and only in them is there any explicit discussion of illness—the description of the suffering is a typical feature. The duration of the illness in particular is frequently indicated: twelve years (Mark 5:25), eighteen years (Luke 13:11), thirty-eight years (John 5:5), from birth (John 9:1; Acts 3:2; 14:8). This does not mean that only long-lasting, chronic illnesses were regarded as suffering, but these indications evidently were intended especially to emphasize the gravity of the suffering and the greatness of Jesus' acts of healing. Occasionally there is explicit mention also of the fruitless attempts at healing or the dangerous and grievous nature of the illness, which caused the ill persons to "suffer terribly" (Matt. 17:15) or to "suffer fearful torments" (Matt. 8:6). Thus it is said of the woman who had an issue of blood, she "had suffered much under many physicians, and had spent all that she had, and was no better but rather grew worse" (Mark 5:26 RSV). Of course, we also encounter in such portrayals of illness various quite strange features, related to a world-view that is outdated, as in the story of the Gerasene demoniac (Mark 5:1 ff.), who lived among the tombs, could not be chained or bound, cried out day and night, and cut himself with stones (cf. further V.5). Among the disabilities and illnesses that we encounter, only a part of which of course can still be identified and diagnosed from today's perspective, are: fever (Matt. 8:14-15), leprosy (Mark 1:40 ff. and par.; Luke 17:1 ff.), epilepsy (Mark 9:14 ff. and par.), hemorrhaging (Mark 5:21 ff. and par.), paralysis (Mark 2:1 ff. and par.), demon possession (Mark 5:1 ff. and par., et passim), and blindness (Mark 10:46 ff. and par., et passim). Nevertheless, the concern of the Evangelists is not a precise diagnosis, but the fact that people "brought to him (sc. Jesus) all the sufferers, those who were afflicted with all sorts of illnesses and pains, demon-possessed, epileptics, and paralytics" (Matt. 4:24).

Illness of course has not only a biological and somatic side, but social and religious consequences as well. In an age without social security, illness often signified great social hardship and beggary (cf. John 9:8; Acts 3:2-3, et passim). The religious implications arise from the fact that according to the views of that time, illness and cultic disqualification go together; thus illness meant cultic defilement, and the persons affected by it were avoided and even ostracized. This was not for hygienic, but rather for cultic, reasons (cf. Lev. 13–14). When, for example, the ten lepers "stand at a distance" (Luke 17:12), this is not because of the danger of infection, but because they would cultically defile others (cf. Lev. 13:45-46). Hence illness was connected with social disintegration and religious distress. In Galatians, even Paul proceeds from the assumption that his could lead the Galatians to scorn or despise him, that is, there was the danger that the Galatians would see in the afflicted Paul a person possessed by demons and turn away from him with the gesture of spitting to signify their rejection of him (4:13-14).

e) Suffering at the hands of "religion"

This in itself is an indication that suffering can also take the form of a perverted religiosity. This is confirmed by other texts. The "weary and heavy-laden" to whom Jesus promises "rest" (Matt. 11:28) apparently are not suffering under physical afflictions or under the burden of their own sins, but under religious regulations that the Pharisees' exposition of the law has imposed upon them. All those who do not know the law are regarded by the official authorities as accursed (John 7:49). Included in this same connection is the woe pronounced upon the teachers of the law who "load men with burdens hard to bear," and yet themselves "do not touch the burdens with one of your fingers" (Luke 11:46 RSV and par.). Here too the "burdens" are the religious traditions and demands of the law, which, for example, because of their casuistry were bound to place heavy pressure upon all the uninitiated, while the religious authorities either did not offer any help and guidance or found a way to excuse themselves from the fulfillment of these demands. The religious blindness of the *homines religiosi* and the cause of suffering potentially connected with it are given especially pointed expression in the Gospel of John; there the disciples are warned of the hour "when whoever kills you will think he is offering service to God" (John 16:2; cf. also the "approval" of Paul the persecutor of the sufferings of Christians who were imprisoned and slain, Acts 22:19-20; and Rev. 11:10). The Christian community can explain such sufferings that are brought upon men in the name of God by the fact that people do not know God or Jesus (John 16:3).

However, there are not only the sufferings of those who as the targets of such misguided religiosity themselves are painfully affected, but also the shared suffering of those who strive in vain to change all this. According to Luke, Jesus himself wept over Jerusalem because it did not discern what would contribute to its own peace (Luke 19:41-42; cf. also 23:28-29). And Paul has "great sorrow and unceasing anguish" in his heart, indeed, he could even wish himself to be "accursed and cut off from Christ for the sake of my brethren" (Rom. 9:2-3 RSV), so gravely does he suffer from Israel's unbelief in relation to Christ. Elsewhere, too, compassion (i.e., "suffering with") is in fact experienced as actual suffering (cf. below, V. 4), and this is simply confirmation that suffering cannot be comprehended solely on the plane of individual distress but always affects others as well.

f) Suffering and death

This suffering-with-others that man experiences includes above all else his being affected by the death of others. Such suffering is expressed in the sorrow of widows and orphans (James 1:27), in grief (1 Thess. 4:13), in weeping (Luke 7:13; John 11:31, 33; 20:11) or weeping and wailing (Mark 5:38 and par.; cf. Matt. 2:18), in the custom of lamentation for the dead (Acts 8:2), and in the appearance of the women who observed the practices of mourning (cf. Mark 5:38 and par.; Luke 23:27; Acts 9:39).

But in the New Testament, suffering and one's own death are very closely related; indeed, one can say that all the afflictions and pains of the world are concentrated in death. Of course, life as a whole is moving toward death, but the close proximity of suffering and death to each other is shown by the striking observation that the Greek word for suffering *(pathein)* can also include dying, particularly when it refers to the death of Jesus (cf. Luke 24:46; Acts 1:3; 3:18; 17:3; 1 Pet. 2:21; Heb. 13:12), and sometimes it is explicated by the concept of "the suffering of death" (Heb. 2:9). The "passion" narrative includes Jesus' suffering *and dying*. And when Paul says, "I die daily" (1 Cor. 15:31) or "We are being killed all the day long" (Rom. 8:36; cf. 2 Cor. 4:11), this has specific reference to his sufferings. Illnesses, in particular, quickly bring one close to death (cf. Phil. 2:27). To be sure, not every illness is a "sickness unto death" (John 11:4), but illness and death are closely associated (cf. 1 Cor. 11:30; Acts 9:37). One could almost say that the real suffering of man is death, because even in life it displays its power, and this life is lived in the "land and shadow of death" (Matt. 4:16; Luke 1:79). Even though during the plagues of the end time a person may even long for death in order to escape the distresses, may "seek after it but not find it" (Rev. 9:5-6), still it is more characteristic that human life is marked by a fear of death (Heb. 2:15). Hence death, distress, crying, and pain will also be destroyed together (Rev. 21:4).

g) *The universal extent of suffering*

The utterly universal extent of all suffering becomes still clearer by the inclusion of man in the story of the sufferings of the unredeemed world. This is made the theme particularly of Rom. 8:18 ff. Here Paul feels obliged, in view of what he has said about the present reality of salvation, to incorporate into his thinking the opposite reality of worldwide suffering. In this context, he sees the suffering of Christians and of other men as "sufferings of this aeon" (v. 18) embedded in the sufferings of the entire creation, which is unwillingly subjected to nothingness and vanity (v. 20); but this is a subjection in hope, "because the creation itself will be set free from its bondage to decay and obtain the glorious liberty of the children of God. We know that the whole creation has been groaning in travail together until now" (vv. 21-22). This indeed is not to be understood analytically or ontologically, as though Paul here had learned of the agonized sighing and eager waiting of creation from nature itself. The "knowledge" (v. 22) is the knowledge of faith and is not gained from observation of nature or something of the sort, even though, of course, certain empirical points of reference and elements of experience are also involved, just as everyone is familiar with "collective" guilt and involvement in calamity. In any case, what concerns Paul is not a rational or speculative cosmology or etiology of the world's suffering, but the cosmic dimensions of blessing and disaster, of suffering and glory. The entire creation is involved in the fall and the redemption of man; this interconnection of destiny is already indicated in the Old Testament and in Jewish apocalyptic (cf. Gen. 3:17; Isa. 13:9; 4 Esd. 6:2 ff.; et passim). Guilt-laden man is the reason for the universal fate, but also for the universal hope ("for the sake of him who subjected it [the creation]," Rom. 8:20). Even those who already belong to the *new* creation are involved in this context of guilt and suffering of the entire creation. Paul always sees man, the old man as well as the new, as a member of the whole creation. Just as the new man will live in a transformed creation, the sighing and groaning are characteristic not only of men and of Christians, but of all creation, which therefore is waiting to share in the salvation of the children of God.

II. Christ's suffering

1. The sufferings of Jesus Christ

If one inquires as to the specifically New Testament view of suffering, one can only begin with the passion of Jesus, because it is above all *his* suffering and dying that is the theme of the New Testament. The very one who is appointed by God to put an end to all suffering is involved in the deepest distress and becomes the sufferer in a unique sense. "The Son of Man must suffer many things" (Mark 8:31). He did not merely teach this, but he himself suffered in his own body. His history is a history of suffering and pain, of rejection and humiliation, of ridicule and shame.

> Behold, we are going up to Jerusalem; and the Son of man will be delivered to the chief priests and the scribes, and they will condemn him to death, and deliver him to the Gentiles; and they will mock him, and spit upon him, and scourge him, and kill him; and after three days he will arise.
> (Mark 10:33-34 RSV).

Since Easter, Jesus Christ as the Suffering One is the one in whom we may recognize the *ecce homo* and the *ecce deus* as well. That is, the suffering and dying Jesus is "the man" (cf. John 19:5; Rom. 5:12 ff.), in whose suffering figure man can be discerned as he is, suffering and dying, wretched and forsaken; and in whom, paradoxically, at the same time, though veiled, the Word that became flesh (John 1:14; cf. 1:18), and "very likeness of God" (2 Cor. 4:4) has become manifest. But if God can be found in suffering, in his son and likeness, and his righteousness and love can be discerned therein (Rom. 3:25-26; John 3:16; et passim), this means, for one thing, that Jesus' suffering is not a refutation of God's promises, but his fulfillment in the context of the yet unredeemed world. But further, it means also that by analogy, under the conditions of the "sufferings of this present time" (Rom. 8:18) man, even as one suffering and oppressed, troubled and dying, may at the same time know himself to be beloved, known, and accepted by God ("as dying, and behold! we live," 2 Cor. 6:9).

> The idea that God has anything to do with affliction, and indeed in his Son has himself submitted to it, is in conflict with both the Stoic and the Platonic concept of God, according to which God is free from feelings and incapable of suffering. It conflicts also with gnosticism, which in its Christian forms steadfastly denied, in Docetic fashion, the incarnation and passion of Jesus. For example, in the First Apocalypse of James, Jesus says: "I have never suffered any pain, nor have I ever been afflicted." Particularly clear is the

"Second Logos of the Great Seth": "Yet I was not subjected
to death at all. They punished me (with death), yet I really
did not die, but (only) appeared to do so, so that I might not
be thwarted by them. . . . But I suffered (only) in their
imagination and according to their opinion. . . . It was
another—their father—who drank the gall and vinegar; it
was not I who was beaten with rods; it was another, Simon,
who bore the cross on his shoulders. It was another on whose
head the crown of thorns was placed; but I was being amused
in the heights at all the (apparent) abundance of the archons
and the seed of their error and the show of their idle
splendor, and I laughed at their lack of understanding"
(following *Theologische Literaturzeitung* 1975, 102-3).

But according to the passion narrative of the Gospels, Jesus did
not remain a stranger to suffering, but actually was "put to
shame." He is God's bearer of suffering, who was not snatched
away at the last moment into otherworldly glory, but "was
obedient unto death, even death on the cross" (Phil. 2:8).

a) "A passion narrative with a detailed introduction"

In New Testament scholarship there is a certain amount of
agreement in seeing in the Gospels, particularly in the gospel of
Mark, passion narratives that have been extended backward;
this has prevailed ever since M. Kähler somewhat provoca-
tively called them "passion narratives with detailed introduc-
tions." This—to continue with Mark's Gospel— is meant not
only to say something about the scope of chapters 14 and 15, but
also to give expression to the significance of this section for
shaping the entire Gospel. Indeed, the passion narrative is not
simply appended to the composition of the preceding chapters,
but it clearly casts its shadow over the entire Gospel. Even the
characterizing of John the Baptist, who in fact serves as the
forerunner of Christ, as one who is "handed over" (Mark 1:14) is
suggestive of the betrayal of Jesus. At the end of the first
complex of disputations, in 3:6, the Evangelist mentions the
Jewish authorities' resolve to seek Jesus' death, and especially

striking are the three predictions of his passion in chapters 8, 9, and 10. Of course, these are also predictions of the resurrection, but what is characteristic is that Mark interprets the tradition that has come down to him in the sense of the *theologia crucis* (cf. 9:9 with 9:12). All this is intended to show that Jesus' entire life takes its orientation and its meaning from the cross, and already, throughout his entire earthly life, he is the Suffering One.

The real text for the understanding of Jesus' suffering and dying, however, is not found in these allusions, references, and predictions that are scattered throughout the Gospel, but rather chapters 14 and 15. They are the key to the understanding of the Gospel overall. To the community in which the passion narrative developed, obviously of more importance than Jesus' activity as rabbi, prophet, or divine miracle-worker was the fact that he is the one who suffered, died, and rose again. Further, this does not immediately indicate that people connected the ideas of expiation, sacrifice, and substitution with this suffering and dying, for down to Mark 14:24 such ideas are absent even in the passion narrative. To be sure, this is for reasons of narration, because of the history of the tradition, and probably for theological reasons as well; it is not, as one occasionally reads even today, because even in that time people felt the ideas of sacrifice and substitution to be problematical and because the responsibility and maturity of man are thereby minimized.

For the passion narrative of the Gospels, the suffering of Jesus is not simply a special case of suffering in general, but it is in various respects unique and incapable of being repeated. The Synoptic Gospels even use the word "suffer" *(pascho)* only for the sufferings of Jesus. Much that is said nowadays about the significance of the earthly Jesus, that he is not a myth, a symbol, or an ideogram, or something of the sort, holds true in particular with reference to the passion narrative. It is not the disciples that are here portrayed as sufferers, but Jesus. Indeed, the passion narrative evidently is intended here to provide a deliberate contrast, when, for example, the account of the trial and the story of Peter's denial in Mark 14:53 ff. are deliberately interwoven, or the watching Jesus and the sleeping disciples in Gethsemane are set in confrontation (Mark 14:32 ff.). Jesus must travel his road of suffering alone, while the disciples on the other hand are offended (14:27), sleep (14:37, 40-41), deny (14:66 ff.), and flee (14:50), and at the climax of the passion narrative in the entire chapter 15 nothing more at all is said about the disciples.

In all this there is the declaration that Jesus, with his sufferings, is always leading the way for all who suffer, and it is *his* suffering alone that provides a foundation for the certainty that God is to be found here also, and precisely here. In his suffering and dying Jesus stands over against his friends as well as his foes; not only the officers and executioners, not only the protectors of law and order or the Zealot revolutionaries, but also those who belonged to him. It is precisely the account of Jesus' passion that thereby lets us discern the force of the Christ-story, a story which precedes faith and understanding and, furthermore, as passion is so singular and exclusive that here, at first, there is no notion of an example that has been set, but the givenness of the salvation that is wrought by this suffering is emphatically demonstrated. It probably is precisely through this history of the suffering and dying Jesus that primitive Christianity was preserved from a speculative mythologizing and Docetizing of the Christ-figure, and was itself, free from illusions, held firm to the reality of this world.

Not that here the historical interest is predominant and we have sources of greater historical reliability than elsewhere. Even the texts about Jesus' suffering and dying are stamped everywhere by the interest of faith. Here too the historical interest remains subordinated to the kerygmatic interest, that is, to the presentation of Jesus' passion as saving event. The historical dimension indeed has a corrective function, but it is not the foundation and the sole criterion of the accounts of the passion. Many factors and tendencies were operative here: among them, cultic needs (cf. the account of the Supper in Mark 14:22-25), political apologetics (cf. the exonerating of the Romans at the expense of the Jews), paraenetic aims (cf. the saying, "Watch and pray, lest you enter into temptation," Mark

14:38), a novelistic pleasure in narration (cf. the expansion of the story of the blow with the sword in Luke and John, with Mark 14:47), theological interpretation (cf. the "proofs from Scripture"), and others; though of course one cannot explain the passion narrative as a whole with only one of these functions. It probably still is best to think of the reading that took place in the assembly for worship as the "Sitz-im-Leben" of the passion narrative as a whole, though of course the extent of the narrative increased with the passage of time.

In recent times it has once again become stoutly disputed whether there is an earlier continuous narrative that underlies the passion narrative as we have it or whether it was first composed by Mark out of separate individual pieces. We need not discuss that question here. It is certain that the passion narrative, too, contains a large number of bits of tradition that originally circulated independently (cf. Mark 14:22 ff. with 1 Cor. 11:23 ff.); it is also certain that the share of the Evangelists in the process is greater than was earlier often assumed. But in my opinion, it likewise is highly probable that the passion narrative was very early related in continuity, even though the question of the scope of the pre-Marcan passion narrative must remain open, and most of the individual pieces probably arose independently apart from any continuous passion narrative. At any rate, only a passion narrative in context could, for example, provide an answer to the question of how and why this Jesus had been placed on the cross.

Some accents of the individual Evangelists may be stressed here. Others, such as, for example, the meaning of the Scripture, have already been mentioned (cf. I.1.a), and still others will be discussed in the following sections (cf. especially II.2).

As has already been shown, *Mark* oriented all of Jesus' activity to the passion and saw in it the center and the climax of that activity. Against the background of the secrecy that according to Mark surrounds the divine sonship during Jesus' active ministry, it is not accidental that Jesus makes an open confession of this divine sonship precisely at the moment of his deepest humiliation, when everyone saw in him only one who was broken and condemned. "The high priest asked him, 'Are you the Messiah, the son of the Blessed?' And Jesus said, 'I am, and you will see the Son of man sitting at the right hand of power, and coming in the clouds of heaven' " (Mark 14:61-62). This heaping up of the various christological predicates and Jesus' confident confession right there in the trial are together in their almost insurpassable sharpening of the paradox, highly instructive for the Marcan *theologia crucis*. Precisely the one who is devoid of all exaltation and splendor, the weak and condemned one, discloses himself to be Christ and Son of God. Nevertheless the passion also points beyond itself. The matter does not end with this paradox that the Judge himself is judged, but his messiahship, now hidden in his suffering, will be made manifest to all the world, just as Jesus never foretold his sufferings alone, but his resurrection as well (cf. also 14:28). However, according to Mark, this foreknowledge on Jesus' part about the resurrection and the parousia did not cause Jesus' way of suffering to become a matter of course. The paradox remains. The world indeed wants to "see" now and only then believe (15:32), but this is the very thing that is denied it. The question as to the legitimation of a messianic claim on the lips of one who suffers and is crucified remains, in the world's mind, unanswered, and only faith recognizes in the weakness of the crucified one the "King of Israel."

    In *Matthew* it is emphasized still more strongly than in Mark that even in his passion Jesus is possessed of power and exaltation and that he voluntarily takes upon himself his sufferings. If he had wanted them, Jesus would have had more than twelve legions of angels at his disposal (Matt. 26:53), but he remains the obedient and powerless one, whose straight and unwavering course reaches its climax in the passion. Other features, such as the emphasizing of the guilt of the Jewish people and their leaders (27:25; 26:67-68) or the expansion of references to scriptural passages (26:15; 27:9-10 or 27:34; 27:43) or explicit statements about the fulfillment of Scripture (26:54), probably are aimed at an apologetic in relation to Judaism.

    Luke has a still stronger view of the passion of Jesus as only a phase of salvation history on the way to the heavenly glory (24:26). It is true that he does not omit speaking of the "agony" of Jesus (22:44), and he even mentions the cold sweat that falls to the ground like drops of blood, but on the whole everything is more tempered. Jesus does not fall to the ground, as in Mark, but kneels in a liturgical posture (22:41). Moreover, as is to be shown further, Luke has reshaped the passion of Jesus in dependence upon the literature of martyrdom, and he represents Jesus as suffering as an example (cf. 2.b).

In *John*, finally, the passion is no longer an enigma, but is the hour of Jesus' exaltation (3:14; 8:28; 13:32) and glorification (13:31-32; 17:1, 4-5), as is shown by the concluding triumphal saying in 19:30 ("It is finished"), but also by Jesus' lofty bearing during the trial (18:18 ff., 28 ff. and elsewhere). The paradox that the Suffering One is the Son of God is interpreted to mean that his humiliation is at once also exaltation, and his pathway of suffering is a way of victory. Since his goal is already integrated into his pathway and the cross already lets his glory shine forth, there emerges the impression that the suffering does not seriously affect him, but rather he is exalted above it, and the cross is only the place of his return to the Father. In the view of this Evangelist, Jesus even says "I thirst" only "in order that the Scripture might be wholly fulfilled" (19:28), particularly since in connection with 19:30 this can signify, in a double meaning, the thirst to do God's will to the very end (cf. 4:34; 18:11).

b) Scandal and enigma

Jesus' suffering and dying was not only a central content of the primitive Christian faith, but also simply a stumbling-block. "Jesus Christ as crucified:" In this was summed up not only the message of salvation, but also the foolishness and offense of this message. "The word of the cross" is to the Jews an offense and to the Gentiles folly (1 Cor. 1:18). A suffering and dying messiah was not prefigured in the Old Testament and Judaism in any way; instead, it was a radical contradiction of the current messianic expectation (cf. Ps. Sol. 17-18 and similar passages). A person who hung on the cross was all the more bound to evoke ridicule and scorn (cf. Mark 15:29 ff.), and indeed to be regarded as one accursed by God (cf. the quotation

from Deut. 21:23 in Gal. 3:13). Even for non-Jews the message
of a person who had been put to death on the gallows—as the
Roman punishment for criminals and slaves the cross was
already offensive enough—was rather absurd and ridiculous.
But it was not only the Jews and the pagans; the disciples and
Christians also found God's action in Jesus' pathway of suffering
scandalous and absurd. All seek God, not in suffering and
lowliness, but in power and glory, on the conqueror's road and
not on the pathway of suffering.

The disciples themselves also therefore, full of blindness
and lack of understanding, are again and again brought face to
face with Jesus' destiny of suffering, especially in Mark. To each
of the three predictions of the passion, Mark appends a piece of
tradition that declares the disciples' failure to understand and
their incomprehension in relation to Jesus' pathway of
suffering. In Mark 8:32, the first prediction of the passion is
followed by Peter's protest. "Peter took him aside and began to
reprove him." But Jesus' reaction to this was, "Depart from me,
Satan, because you do not understand things that pertain to
God, but what pertains to man" (v. 33). In any case, regardless
of whether this verse originally was Jesus' answer to the
messianic confession of verse 29, in Mark's use of it, it is meant
to represent the resistance to a suffering Christ. This
resistance, however, is rooted not only in a different image of
the Messiah and of God, but also in the distaste for suffering on
the part of those who do not want to be involved in the suffering
of their Lord, because according to Mark, Jesus appends the
sayings about discipleship here (vv. 34 ff.). The negative
attitude on the part of Peter is symptomatic of all and is not
grounded in the peculiar temperament of this man; how much
this is true is shown in the reactions of the group of disciples to
the other predictions of suffering. While Jesus again and again
sets forth his declaration concerning suffering as the crucial
theme, the disciples continue to be marked by a lack of
understanding (9:32) or by consternation and fear (10:32);
indeed, they are thinking of how they can assure their own
places of honor in the kingdom of God (10:35 ff.).

Within the passion narrative itself, the resistance of the

disciples to that event of suffering that so radically shatters all their religious expectations and categories becomes fully evident. Jesus himself announces that *all* will be offended and fall away because "the shepherd" will be smitten (Mark 14:27). All then do flee and leave him in the lurch (Mark 14:50), a point which Luke omits. Even in the episode of the blow with a sword Mark does not see a serious attempt to liberate Jesus or an impulsive and desperate act, but rather the disciples' lack of understanding regarding Jesus' way of suffering and the cross (Mark 14:47). Indeed, Jesus is handed over to the Jewish authorities by a man who belonged to the innermost circle of his friends and was bound to him in table fellowship (Mark 14:18: "the passion within the passion"), and at the last, he is denied and cursed (14:71 is not a self-cursing but an anathema upon Jesus) by a man who had said he would even die with Jesus (Mark 14:31).

But we must go still another step further. In spite of the predictions of his passion and the voluntariness that is especially emphasized by Matthew and John (cf. e.g., John 10:18), according to the opinion of the gospel writers, even for Jesus himself the affliction was not simply self-evident and devoid of any problems. This is shown particularly by the Jesus under temptation of the Gethsemane pericope (Mark 14:32-42 and par.), where Mark probably has reworked an originally briefer account. It is true that here too Jesus is left alone by his disciples, but here he himself is the one who is being tempted. He is beset by the fear of death. Anxiety and disappointment seize him. He begins to tremble and to quail, and his soul is troubled even unto death.

To be compared with this also is Heb. 5:7, according to which Jesus in the days of his earthly life "offered up prayers and supplications with loud cries and with tears unto God, who could save him from death." Perhaps one may here adduce also the disputed passage in Luke 12:49-50. "I came to cast fire upon the earth; and would that it were already kindled! I have a baptism to be baptized with; and how am I constrained until it is accomplished!" (RSV).

However fire is to be understood here (fire of judgment?

suffering? the Holy Spirit?), at any rate baptism here, as in Mark 10:38, is suffering and death, which Jesus cannot avoid. He faces it with fear and dread (though it is possible that the intention is not to express oppressive anxiety, but the constraint).

In any case, in Gethsemane it is clearly Jesus' fear that is meant. If the "cup" signifies not only the cup of suffering, but also the cup of judgment and wrath (cf. Isa. 51:17, 21; Jer. 25:15-16; Ps. 75:8), then of course what is meant is not only the creaturely fear of death, but also the fear of God's judgment and wrath. But above all, it is clear that even Jesus did not concede in advance and without tension his agreement with the will of God; he did not give assurance of it without conflict, nor did he have insight into it by virtue of dogmatic axioms or postulates. Instead, this will, which led him into suffering, remained enigmatic even for him. And for this reason he fell to the ground—it is first in Luke that this becomes a solemn ritual of prayer—in order to pray. This prayer, however, is not an unquestioning submission; it is rather a plea that, if possible, the hour might pass and the cup might be taken from him. The use of the word "Abba" (in Mark only here) to address God indeed, on the one hand, accentuates the incomprehensibility of the suffering, but, on the other hand, of course, it affirms that this cup does not issue from some impersonal fate, but from him whom one can address as Father, and to whom one can remain obedient even in affliction and suffering.

This dialectic also appears to be in the foreground in Jesus' last saying on the cross. "My God, my God, why hast thou forsaken me?" It should be noted that in Mark and Matthew this is the only saying of Jesus on the cross (Mark 15:34 and par. = Ps. 22:1). This likewise is hardly to be interpreted in the sense of an agreement with God, as is often done when it is assumed that under any circumstances a biblical saying expresses harmony with God. Why was not unmistakable expression given to such harmony, as is done in Luke? Indeed, Luke has replaced the cry of desolation that is found in Mark, not without reason, with another saying from the Psalms, "Father, into thy hands I commend my spirit" (Luke 23:46). Moreover, the further history of the tradition, in which the words are weakened (as is manifest, e.g., in the Gospel of Peter, where Jesus' saying is given as "My strength, my strength, why have you left me?"), confirm that Jesus' words were understood not in the sense of a harmony but of a dissonance. Even in later exposition, which sought to restrict Jesus' abandonment and suffering to his body or to the lowest powers of the soul, the offensive character of the saying on the cross can be discerned.

What we are dealing with, therefore, is not submission to God, but uttermost desolation and profoundest distress. Even the question "Why?" which often is reproached by Christians, is not suppressed here, but is cried aloud, though, to be sure, it is addressed to God himself. In and in spite of a fearful event, it is not blind fate that governs, but the living God, who also can be addressed in the deepest depths of distress as "my God"; hence, this saying certainly is not expressive simply of naked despair or of pure meaninglessness. Jesus does not cast himself into the arms of despair, but into the arms of God, but precisely in desperation. The riddle of God's hiddenness in suffering, however, is not thereby diminished. That the God whom Jesus had not abandoned, and without whom Jesus could not be and is not even conceivable, now has abandoned him; that not only have Jesus' powers forsaken him, not only have his disciples fled, but God himself has withdrawn and "hidden his face from him" (thus v.24 in the same Ps. 22)—all this remains incomprehensible. This must silence all triumphalism, all *theologia gloriae,* and all enthusiasm, but also all know-it-all theology and accomplishments of theodicy. If anywhere at all, then here, in this suffering, God eludes our understanding and his faithfulness is concealed behind the mask of its very opposite. If anywhere at all, there is need here, in this radical end, of intervention from without, to break up this incomprehensible paradox. It is not to be denied that in the last saying of Jesus other motifs could also be at work, as for example, the idea of substitution. It is likewise possible that Psalm 22 as a whole had acquired, from the perspective of Easter, a significance, transcending the single isolated verse 2, and could signify deliverance from death. But even though it is true that the one who was forsaken by God was restored by God at Easter, it is not very likely that the very parts of the psalm that are not quoted are supposed to be central. In any case, the verse from the psalm that is quoted in Jesus' saying on the cross is not the conquest of suffering but the very peak of the passion; it is, so to speak, the summary expression of it all.

A counterpoint to this, of course, is the Johannine presentation, for in the Gospel of John, as in Luke, the last word of Jesus from Psalm 22 is lacking. Instead, John has Jesus dying with the triumphant cry of victory, "It is finished" (19:30). This is in keeping with the fact, already touched upon, that in John the Christology of glory is so dominant that the passion is represented from the outset as exaltation and under the sign of victory.

c) Eschatological saving event

From the perspective of Easter, primitive Christianity not only unfolded the enigma of the passion of Jesus Christ, but also its abiding meaning, its necessity, and its conquest. Here two things must constantly be emphasized. On the one hand, the cross of Jesus is not a mere point of transition, and his suffering no mere transitional phase. The cross rather continues to be the sign and signature of the Resurrected One, because the Resurrected One is proclaimed as the Crucified One (1 Cor. 1:23; 2:2). The Exalted One remains the "Lamb that was slain," to whom alone belongs power and praise (Rev. 5:12, et passim). But on the other hand, the cross is never seen in isolation nor is it even made the central theme as symbol of human suffering, but it has always been interpreted, as the cross of Jesus Christ, from the perspective afforded by the resurrection. It is not only the sign of suffering, but also of God's victory over suffering. From that perspective, primitive Christianity saw in the cross a divinely willed necessity. "Was it not necessary that the Christ should suffer these things and enter into his glory?" The Resurrected One asks the disciples on the road to Emmaus (Luke 24:26 RSV). The passion of Jesus corresponds to the divine plan of salvation, as is shown also by the predictions of his suffering (Mark 8:31 et passim). On the basis of the resurrection of Jesus, faith discerns in the passion, in spite of all its offensiveness and enigmatic character, not tragedy or accident, but the fulfilling of God's decree in the history of salvation.

Above all, with the aid of reference to the Old Testament, Jesus' suffering is to be represented as in accordance with Scripture: "The Son of man goes as it is written of him" (Mark 14:21 RSV). "What God foretold by the mouth of all his prophets, that his Christ should suffer, he thus fulfilled" (Acts 3:18 RSV). This kind of "proof," which as a rule is not very convincing to us nowadays, often enough had the Old Testament speaking in a Christian sense without justification in the text itself or only by doing exegetical violence to it (cf. I.1.a). This of course should not blind us to the basic intention, namely that here, contrary to all the apparent action on the part of men, there is a belief in God himself as the one who actually is at work in an eschatological way (cf. also the *passivum divinum* in Mark 10:33, or the many expressions that speak of God's giving Christ up for us, in Rom. 8:32; 1 John 4:10, et passim).

The same thing is also expressed in another way. For example, it has been noted repeatedly that the account of the crucifixion, with its precise specification of the hours (Mark 15:25, 33-34) hardly corresponds with historical reality (cf. John 19:4). To be sure, the time schema is not to be traced back to liturgical needs. It is due rather to the apocalyptic belief that everything, even to the very day and hour, is predetermined by God's plan of salvation (cf. IV.2.c). This is also confirmed by the connection of this schema of the very hours with the apocalyptic-eschatological events, such as the darkening of the sun (cf. Amos 8:9) and the rending of the veil in the temple (Mark 15:33, 38), and in Matthew the earthquake, the splitting of the rocks, and the opening of the tombs (Matt. 27:51 ff.). Jesus' suffering and dying accordingly is the onset of the end events as judgment (the darkness!) and grace (cf. the extending of the time "until the ninth hour").

Of course, Jesus' suffering and dying was interpreted in primitive Christianity in various ways as an eschatological saving event; here we can only refer to these, but they will be

developed somewhat more in detail with respect to the
sufferings of the Christians. A major role is played particularly
by the idea of atonement and substitution, which had already
been connected in Judaism with suffering and death (though of
course not the suffering and death of the Messiah! Cf. e.g., 2
Macc. 7:18; 4 Macc. 6:28-29, et passim): "Christ suffered once
for sins, a just one for the unjust, that he might bring you to
God" (1 Pet. 3:18; cf. 2:21). Here, with the sufferings of the
Christian in view, the emphasized "once" makes it clear that
the sufficiency of the salvation that is wrought by Christ's
sufferings is in no need of being supplemented. Because the
suffering Jesus did not suffer for himself, but "for our service
and benefit" (Luther), because he allied himself with the
"many" and "leaped into the breach" for them with his suffering
and dying, the suffering of the "many" is thereby relieved of all
anxiety and fear about whether it might possibly be meritorious
or about any saving and atoning significance. If Jesus' cross is
the only way of God to man, then even our own suffering does
not open up for us another way that will bring us close, or closer,
to God. Furthermore, as people who have been accepted by
God, we no longer need to interpret suffering as a possibility of
finding ourselves, of self-perfection, and of "glorying before
God."

However, in that Jesus vicariously bore the judgment of
God and wrought reconciliation and peace with God (Rom. 5:1,
10, et passim), he has all the more put an end to all rebellion
against God. If Christ "died for all" (2 Cor. 5:14), he died for the
suffering ones also, and himself suffering and dying, he also
accepted those who suffer. Even the sufferer may no longer
remain a rebel against God; instead, through the world-recon-
ciling and all-transforming effect of the passion of Jesus, he can,
even in his suffering, become a reconciled person and a "new
creation" and thus also, even with his suffering, live in the
domain of Christ. For if Christ has died and risen, in order that
he might be the Lord of the dead and the living (Rom. 14:9) and
the living might no longer live unto themselves (2 Cor. 5:15), so
also they can no longer suffer outside his lordship and for

themselves, and there is no such thing as a purely private life or a private suffering and dying (Rom. 14:7).

Because precisely the crucified one is God's power and wisdom (1 Cor. 1:18), this reevaluation of all values implies also a reevaluation of suffering, which in the sign of the cross acquires a new visage. Just as God has transformed the sufferings of Christ into life by forcing open the world of suffering and of death from without, so also help comes to the sufferer from without, and that precisely through Jesus' suffering and dying. "Although he was God's Son, he learned obedience through suffering and (thus) after he was perfected became the source of eternal salvation for all who obey him" (Heb. 5:8-9). The one in whom God made our sufferings his own, the one who had to enter into sufferings himself and participated in the sufferings of the world, thus brings salvation in a comprehensive sense and takes away the sting of suffering. Christ through his death in powerlessness liberates those who through the fear of death have fallen into slavery, and as the one who in solidarity with his brethren atones for their sins (Heb. 2:14 ff.). Just so, because suffering in the sphere of flesh and blood did not remain alien to him, as the one who "suffers with us in our infirmities" (Heb. 4:15), help is possible for him herein as well. "For since he himself was tempted and suffered, he is able also to help those who are tempted" (Heb. 2:18). Indeed, his suffering and dying now also makes it possible for those who suffer "to bear fruit." For his death, which, like the grain of wheat that dies, has produced "much fruit" (John 12:24), now, as such, an event in which his love becomes manifest, itself produces love (John 13:1; 15:12-13).

2. Conformity to Christ's suffering

As emerged in the preceding section, the sufferings of Christ and those of his people were set in relation to each other, for example, by the statement that the sufferer is able to help sufferers (Heb. 2:18) or that through his sufferings he "heals" the sufferings of others (1 Pet. 2:24). We shall now examine in more detail this correlation between the suffering of Jesus and the suffering of the Christians, which becomes manifest in various forms and even leads to the involvement of the Christians in his sufferings.

a) "Suffering with Christ"

Paul, in particular, made a close connection between the sufferings of the Christians and the suffering and dying of Jesus Christ, and he provided a theological foundation for the analogy between Christ's fate and the fate of the Christians even in suffering. Even when the correspondence between Jesus' suffering and that of the Christians is not as thoroughly thought-through in other texts in the New Testament as in Paul, still the matter itself is also brought to expression even there as well.

For example, the Gospels also are aware that Jesus' suffering and dying are inseparable from the suffering and dying of his people. Perhaps Jesus himself anticipated that the same destiny of suffering awaited the disciples as he himself faced. "You will drink the cup that I drink, and you will be baptized with the baptism with which I am baptized" (Mark 10:38-39). Here "being baptized" and "drinking the cup" signify suffering, drawing on figurative language from the Old Testament (cf. on the one hand, Pss. 42:7; 69:1; Isa. 43:2; and on the other hand, Isa. 51:17, 22; Lam. 4:21; Ps. 75:8). It is also stated indirectly in other words that following Christ always implies also following in suffering and involvement in the "Master's" destiny of suffering. "It is enough for the disciple that he should be like his master and the servant like his lord" (Matt. 10:25a). If suffering befalls the master, then it likewise befalls his disciples, who have bound themselves to his person and his cause. "Whoever does not bear his cross and go with me cannot be my disciple" (Luke 14:27 and par.). His way, on which they have been set as his disciples, is not to be abandoned, even in suffering, specifically, for example, in being maligned (Matt. 10:25b).

In such discipleship in suffering we are to think not only of extreme situations, such as martyrdom, but also of the everyday cross and affliction, as is made clear particularly in Luke 9:23 by the addition of the word "daily". "If anyone will come after me, let him deny himself and take up his cross daily and follow me." But of course the out-of-the-ordinary also is included, as for example, in cases of conflict, the painful and distressing separation from house and home, father and mother, brothers and sisters, wife and children (Matt. 19;2 and par.). "Anyone who loves father or mother . . . or son or daughter more than me is not worthy of me" (Matt. 10:37 and par.).

Mark in particular shows, by his connecting the predictions of the passion and his sayings about discipleship (Mark 8:31 ff. et passim)—this connection is particularly striking in contrast to the sayings about discipleship in the Logia source—that a constitutive aspect of faith in the cross is the readiness to take up one's own cross in following after the Crucified One. The same parallelism of Jesus' fate to that of his followers is also clear in the Gospel of John. "If the world hates you, know that it has hated me before it hated you" (15:18 RSV). The hatred and enmity of the "world" is grounded in the fact that the disciples, like Jesus himself (cf. 8:23), are no longer "of the world" (v. 19), and thus the hostile reaction of the world that is at enmity against God becomes unavoidable toward the disciples as well. The "servants" do not go beyond what their Lord has suffered (John 15:20; cf. also Matt. 10:24). His life and his "fruit-bearing" surrender of his life constitute the law of discipleship for those who follow him (John 12:24-26).

We cannot discuss here the religio-historical presuppositions of Paul's thinking about the correlation of Christ and the Christians. Instead, it must suffice to set forth the theological contexts of the subject. Of course, it must be acknowledged that even as regards substance there is a difference, depending on whether one interprets the Pauline utterances about the Christians' community of suffering with Christ in terms of the "corporate personality" or in terms of gnosticizing Adam-Anthropos speculations, from mystical or eschatological perspective. In any case, Paul sees in Christ that one who, like Adam, in universal scope determines the destiny of humanity and through his eschatological suffering and dying also places his followers in the "fellowship of his sufferings." The "sufferings of Christ" of the Christians signify not only their belonging to Christ, but also the eschatological efficacy and impact of his death. Therefore, Paul can sum up and interpret the catalog of sufferings of 2 Cor. 4:8-9 thus: "we always carry about in our body the death of Jesus" (v. 10). "Sharing in his *sufferings*" is "being made conformable to Christ's *death*" (Phil. 3:10). In this connection Paul saw this fellowship in suffering grounded in baptism, in which the old man "dies" and "is crucified" with Christ (Rom. 6:3, 6, 8; Gal. 2:19). In spite of the occasional ideas of judgment in the context of suffering (cf. IV.2.a), it does not follow from this that the sufferings of the Christian had their basis in additional sins of the "new" man or that the "being dead for sin" (Rom. 6:11), which was wrought by baptism, needed to be supplemented. It is not fellowship with sin but rather fellowship with Christ that draws the Christians into his sufferings and causes them to "participate" in the sufferings of Christ (2 Cor. 1:5; Phil. 3:10).

Such a fellowship in suffering does not mean a mystical or contemplative re-living of Jesus' passion, but a real participation in it. Hence it is clear, on the one hand, that it is not the sufferings as such, but sufferings as "Christ's sufferings" that are the sign of one's belonging to Christ. Above all, however, it is clear that these sufferings of the Christians in a certain sense correspond to the dying of Jesus Christ and therefore can also be called a "daily *dying*" (1 Cor. 15:31). For Paul, Jesus' death is not a datum that has been superseded by the resurrection, but a present, powerful reality (2 Cor. 4:12). It does not belong simply to the past, but is present in the sufferings of the Christians and is experienced as an eschatological occurrence in the sufferings of concrete historical life. Consequently Jesus' suffering and dying are to be related not only to ideas of atonement and substitution, but also to the distress and misery of the community in this world, and in this respect they have, not an exclusive, but an inclusive, prototypical significance. It is the Crucified One himself who involves the Christians in following in the train of his sufferings and includes them, whose subject he has become, (according to Gal. 2:20) in his fate. Thus Jesus' suffering and dying is not only a saving event that occurred *extra nos,* but it is also realized through the Christians' own "sufferings of Christ," which thus become transparent to Jesus' suffering and dying. Therefore, even down to the present time, a constitutive reflection of the preaching of the cross is always the weakness and folly, the lowliness and affliction of the community (cf. 1 Cor. 1:26 ff.; 2 Cor. 1:6, et passim), not only of the apostles (cf. 2 Cor. 11:23 ff.; 1 Cor. 2:2, et passim).

But if Jesus, death and resurrection belong together, then the involvement in Christ's fate also signifies the participation in the *"life* of Jesus" (2 Cor. 4:10). Because in Christ, precisely as the one who died in weakness, God's power has broken through triumphantly, Paul can and must speak not only of the abundance of Christ's sufferings, but also of the abundance of his consolation (2 Cor. 1:5). This is also the reason he breaks up the catalog of sufferings in dialectical fashion and speaks in antitheses: ". . . afflicted in every way, but not crushed; perplexed, but not driven to despair; persecuted, but not forsaken; struck down, but not destroyed" (2 Cor. 4:9-10 RSV; cf. also 6:8-10). Thus, as the "death of Jesus" is exhibited in their sufferings, so the "life of Jesus" is exhibited in their not despairing and their not being forsaken (2 Cor. 4:10). As much as the *death* of Jesus defines and determines Christian existence, just so much is the same true of his *resurrection:* "As dying, and behold! we live" (2 Cor. 6:9). Precisely in situations of hopelessness God's power of life is experienced. It is precisely in weakness that grace attains its fulfillment (2 Cor. 12:9).

Not that the two coincide! It is true that already, here and now, the power of the future resurrection of the dead reaches into the depth of suffering as the "power of his (i.e., Christ's) resurrection" in the present (Phil. 3:10), but the "life of Jesus" also has a future dimension (cf. further IV.1.c). The First Epistle of Peter accordingly addresses the persecuted communities: "But rejoice in so far as you share Christ's sufferings, that you may also rejoice and be glad when his glory is revealed" (4:13 RSV). But in any case, the participation in Christ's sufferings is a fundamental sign of those who belong to Christ, regardless of how this may appear in detail. If the crucified Christ is the foundation of the church, "the stone that the builders rejected" (1 Pet. 2:4), then being rejected and suffering is also a *nota ecclesiae* for the church that is built thereupon, and the church is a church under the cross. This cross and this suffering of the Christians do not establish the church, but they characterize it; they are not an accidental but a constitutive mark of the church.

b) Orientation to the example of the suffering Christ

The sotĕriological sufficiency of Jesus' suffering and dying, which as such cannot be exemplary, but is singular and unique, does not, however, exclude another prototypical and exemplary aspect of Jesus' suffering and dying; instead, it includes that aspect and gives it meaning. The New Testament contains various testimonies to this aspect. Certainly not as a summons to imitation in the sense of the copying of a model, because the grounding of our salvation that is wrought in Jesus' suffering and dying is not to be imitated, but this does not settle the matter. The sayings about discipleship that were mentioned in the preceding section also imply the idea of an example. One may compare, for example, the Lukan addition "behind Jesus" (Luke 23:26) or the ideas of correspondence in John, where the love that is demanded of the disciples includes, in correspondence with Christ, even the surrender of life itself (15:12-13; 1 John 3:16). Likewise, according to Rev. 14:4, those who have been purchased by the "Lamb" and join in the new song are those who follow the slain Lamb on his way of suffering, "wherever he goes."

As for Paul, the idea of following and that of example indeed have often been disputed, but here too the ideas can readily enough be recognized. Paul does not affirm a correspondence to Christ's suffering merely as a act *a posteriori*, but he adduces such mimesis also as a criterion of Christian conduct. This fact is attested, for example, by Rom. 15:3. According to this passage, everyone should please his neighbor, "for even Christ did not live to please himself, but as it is written, 'The reproaches of those who reproached you have fallen upon me.' " The passion of Jesus—reference is made to it by means of the quotation from the passion psalm (69:10)—is the point of orientation for the Christians also. Just as Christ devoted himself to the weak and those in need of help, and in his doing so incurred insults and disgrace at the hands of the world, so also the Christians, in devoting themselves to the weak, likewise are to endure slander. According to 1 Thess. 1:6 the Thessalonians, precisely because of their suffering, have become "followers" (literally "imitators") of the apostle *and of the Lord,* an idea which in Rom. 8:17 and Phil. 3:10 also includes a paraenetic motif. In any case, for Paul too, participation in Jesus' suffering and dying is not simply mere fate, in which the Christian comes under the shadow of the cross in a purely passive way. Even when the aspect of misfortune stands in the foreground, suffering still is at the same time an active "battle" (Phil. 1:29-30; cf. "struggle with sufferings," Heb. 10:32), which is correlated with the Crucified One.

Of course in the First Epistle of Peter, even more strongly than in Paul, the suffering Christ is claimed as prototype and example for Christian life and is introduced in paraenetic contexts. Thus the slaves who are treated harshly and unfairly by their perverse masters and suffer innocently are reminded of Christ's destiny of suffering as an example and incentive.

> Because Christ also suffered for you, leaving you an example, that you should follow in his steps. He committed no sin; no guile was found in his lips. When he was reviled, he did not revile in return; when he suffered, he did not threaten. . .
> (2:21-23 RSV).

Here in the "for you" lies the justification for the admonition to follow the example of Jesus, and thus the difference from any reproduction of a model. The author is concerned not only with an example, but also with the reasons and motivation for

Christian discipleship in suffering. Yet what is at stake above all
else is that the Christians follow this Christ on his way of
suffering and continue in his footsteps (cf. also 4:1). This is
confirmed by the fact that the author, by means of what he says
in verse 21a, c, here interprets in this exemplary sense an
already shaped christological tradition, which is distinguished
by style and content and is found in verses 21b, 22, and 24.
Anyone who follows after Jesus certainly is constantly aware of
Jesus' always being out in front and of the distance that lies
between the follower and the one whom he is following. But
this does not mean a relativizing of the orientation to the
footprints of Jesus on the way of suffering. This is here given
further specificity in the use of Isaiah 53 to say that Jesus
suffered as an innocent person and that what he suffered was not
just recompense (2:23). But this very thing also is demanded of
the Christians (3:9; cf. also 2:22 with 3:11). The context and the
use of the tradition that is appropriated, moreover, will show
that here it is not so much a matter of deducing from Christ's
sufferings the necessity of suffering for the Christians, but
rather, and conversely, Jesus' suffering is actualized in a
situation of suffering for the community. It is related to a
concrete experience of reality, and in its own way is set forth as
exemplary.

Further documentation is found in Heb. 13:12-13, where
within a series of admonitions we encounter the statement that
Christ "suffered outside the gate," that is, outside the sacred
precincts, by which he is understood as the one who perfects
and surpasses the Old Testament sacrifice. Then there is added
as a consequence, "Therefore let us go out to him outside the
camp and bear his abuse." This is, indeed, figurative language,
and there is disagreement as to what the "going out" means
here (separation from the synagogue or from Judaism? an
exodus from the earthly sphere into the celestial city?). It is
clear, however, that the leaving of the camp signifies abuse in
an analogy to "his abuse," and readiness to suffer shameful
martyrdom belongs to the community. In Heb. 12:2, also, the
reader is called upon to look to Jesus, the "author and finisher"
of faith, who took upon himself the cross and despised the

shame. Such a perspective on the crucified Jesus at the same
time brings him into view as a prototype and example. As the
ground of faith and the "source of eternal salvation" (5:9), he is,
as the one afflicted and obedient, also the type of the struggle
for the faith that is ordained for the Christians.

Finally, we must refer to Luke, who gave to the narrative
of Jesus' passion some features that are strongly marked by the
theme of example and that are oriented to the literature of
martyrdom, and quite clearly stylized Jesus' suffering and
dying as an exemplary martyrdom. This holds true, for
example, for the pericope on the crucifixion (Luke 23:33 ff.). A
comparison with the martyrdom of Stephen (Acts 7) will show
how strongly Luke understands Jesus' suffering and dying in
this passage. Just as Jesus, moveover, in contrast to Jewish and
in some measure to early Christian martyrs as well, does not rail
against the executioners and judges, but prays for them
("Father, forgive them, for they know not what they do," Luke
23:34), so also Stephen prays, "Lord, lay not this sin to their
charge" (Acts 7:60; cf. also 1 Pet. 2:23). And just as Jesus,
according to Luke, dies with a word of trust in God ("Father,
into thy hands I commend my spirit," 23:46), so also in the case
of Stephen, "Lord Jesus, receive my spirit" (Acts 7:59). This is
not supposed to mean that Luke utterly levels down what is
distinctive about the passion of Jesus and simply makes it an
interchangeable example of Christian *ars moriendi*. Even here
the analogy is rather a limited one; for example, there is no
parallel to the promise made to the thief on the cross (Luke
23:43). However, it is equally clear that the account of Jesus'
passion is meant to invite the Christians to accept their own
suffering and dying as Jesus had done and to orient themselves
to his example, which cannot be replaced by any other
example. Peter's and Paul's fate of suffering is in part
assimilated to the story of Jesus' passion (cf. Acts 12:3-4;
28:17-18), and elsewhere as well, in the portrayals of
persecutions of Christians, there are frequent allusions to Jesus'
passion, even to the language employed in speaking of them (cf.
the word "deliver" in Luke 24:20 and Acts 8:3; 22:4, *inter alia*).
In the next section, moreover, it will be shown that even in the

reasons and causes given for the suffering, a distinct parallelism between Jesus and his followers can be discerned.

III. Actual reasons for suffering

A substantive correspondence between the sufferings of Jesus and those of his followers consists not only in the fact and the mode, but in part also in the actual reasons for the suffering. Suffering "on account of the Son of man" (Luke 6:22) or "for Jesus' sake" (2 Cor. 4:11), or "for the sake of Christ" (2 Cor. 12:10; Phil. 1:29), "for his sake" (Mark 13:9; Matt. 5:11) or "for his name's sake" (Mark 13:13 and par.; John 15:21; Acts 9:16; 21:13; Rev. 2:3) also implies a suffering for the sake of the cause that Jesus Christ represents, and thus for example, "for righteousness' sake" (Matt. 5:10), "for the sake of the gospel" (Mark 8:35) or "for the sake of the kingdom of God" (Luke 18:29; 2 Thess. 1:5). In Mark 8:35 and 10:29, "for my sake" and "for the sake of the gospel" are set in parallel (cf. also Matt. 5:10 with 5:11). Anyone who suffers "for his sake" thus also falls victim to affliction for reasons similar to those in his case. Even Jesus himself was not persecuted and brought to the cross as a result of pure arbitrariness, mere misunderstanding, or unfortunate accident; instead, his sufferings resulted almost logically and inevitably out of the very center of his message and his life. Even if the reason for his suffering and dying can be deduced only in part, still they are closely connected with the content and claim of his word and his work. Precisely because it was not an obscure fate or an unexpected chain of hostile circumstances, but rather his message and his work that led him into suffering, his suffering itself, likewise, is an inseparable part of his message and his work.

1. Mission and ministry

Speaking in somewhat formal terms, one could say at the outset that suffering grows out of mission and ministry for God and for others. "The Son of man has not come to be ministered unto, but to minister and to give his life a ransom for many" (Mark 10:45). Even if this saying comes from the primitive church, it still is a fitting interpretation of Jesus' way, his suffering, and the surrender of his life, with which he took up the cause of "the many." One may also compare the other interpretations of Jesus' suffering and dying (cf. II.1,6), which in fact can all be summed up by saying that because he chooses to save others, he does not save himself (Mark 15:31-32), but remains faithful to his mission to the very end; because he wants to rescue others from suffering, he takes conflicts and sufferings upon himself (cf. the conflict over the Sabbath, e.g., in Mark 3:1-6, and on this see v.2). It is true that he did not consciously provoke suffering for the sake of some dogmatic axioms or press for martyrdom in a heroic pose, but he did not avoid the lurking danger and foreseeable sufferings when thereby he would have betrayed his commission or would have been obliged to compromise by diluting the truth of his message.

Even though there is no saving significance in the sufferings of the Christians, somewhat the same holds true for them as well. "Sheep among wolves" describes the disciples precisely in their mission (Matt. 10:16 and par.), and it is particularly from the perspective of this mission that their destiny of suffering comes into view. Occasionally the apostolic sufferings are even spoken of as having an expiatory function (e.g., with reference to 1 Cor. 4:13), but in my opinion this is based upon a mistaken interpretation. In the expression, "We have become like scapegoats of the world, like the offscouring of all down to the present time," the genitives denote the subject that forms this judgment, not the object for which Paul is being sacrificed. Even Col. 1:24 is not to be understood to mean that here a soteriological deficit in the sufferings of Christ is to be made up through the sufferings of the apostle. When it says there, "Now I rejoice in my sufferings for you and make up in my flesh what is still lacking in the sufferings of Christ for his body, that is, the church," underlying this is the idea of a definite apocalyptic measure of sufferings of the messianic age (on this, in addition to Rev. 6:11, cf. IV.2.c). Certainly the vicarious service of the apostle and of his sufferings benefits the community ("for you"; cf. also Eph. 3:13), but it remains without any soteriological or meritorious weight. When the suffering of the apostles in particular is strongly emphasized, this is because, especially according to Paul, suffering arises primarily out of service and existence for others.

According to Luke, even in his initial call Paul learns from the exalted Christ "how much he must suffer for my name's sake" (Acts 9:15-16), and at the last it is said that Paul did not regard his life as precious if only he might finish his "course and ministry" (Acts 20:24). The catalog of sufferings in 2 Corinthians 6 stands under the heading of *diakonia* ("In every way we commend ourselves as servants of God," v. 4), and all the sufferings enumerated in 2 Cor. 6:4 ff. and 11:23 ff. result from actions that the mission of the gospel brings with it. Accordingly, the sufferings are not regarded in and of themselves or seen as an opportunity for the development of character, but rather are bracketed with the ideas of ministry and witness. Hence there is in Paul's thought no distinction between sufferings in office and sufferings in a private sphere. But we are to understand from this perspective that the apostolic sufferings emerge in a particular fashion, and the apostle is "flooded" with sufferings (2 Cor. 1:5). Especially to be compared here is 2 Cor. 11:23, where the "I more," "far more abundantly," and "in far greater measure" are indeed used in a caricaturing way, but they are objectively correct. The "birthpangs," which the apostle suffers for the sake of the community in the mission (Gal. 4:19), are not to be compared with the sufferings of other Christians. But further, the same is true also in part of the cares and sufferings endured in the performance of the apostolic ministry, which he enumerates in the various catalogs of sufferings. Special tasks also bring special sufferings.

This, of course, does not mean that such service with suffering is limited to the apostle. Even in the synoptic tradition there are no sharp distinctions drawn between the sufferings of those disciples who went about with Jesus on the roads of Palestine and those of the disciples in the wider sense (cf. Matt.

10:5 ff. with 10:34 ff. and similar passages). One should not unduly stress the apostolic character of sufferings even in Paul. The Christians of Corinth have "the same sufferings" (2 Cor. 1:6) and those of Philippi "the same struggle" (Phil. 1:29-30) to endure as the apostle has. Even in 2 Cor. 2:14–7:3, where the apostolic office is the theme in a special way, the things that are said about suffering are not related exclusively to the apostle (cf. e.g., 2 Cor. 4:17). The paradigmatic significance of the apostolic sufferings also emerges clearly enough from such passages as Rom. 8:17 and 2 Cor. 1:5 and 7:3, as well as from 1 Thess. 1:6. The "equality" of the sufferings in this context of course is not so much to be found in their nature and intensity as in their character as "Christ's sufferings." Moreover, there is a mimesis of the apostle—and mimesis of the apostle (1 Cor. 4:16 et passim) is also mimesis of his sufferings! (1 Thess. 1:6)—or, as it is said later, emulation of the apostle in his sufferings (2 Tim. 3:10-11). Thus, particularly among the pupils of the apostles, witness and service to the word are not to be separated from affliction and adversity (2 Tim. 1:8, 12; 4:5).

But beyond all this, *all* Christians are commissioned for service, witness, and confession, which also has suffering as a consequence for them. To suffer "for the sake of the name" (and according to Mark 13:13 and par. and John 15:21 et passim, this is not limited to the apostles) means to suffer for the sake of the confession of this name, to "hold fast" in loyalty to the name (Rev. 2:13) and "not to deny" it (Rev. 3:8). But to confess means readily and openly to confess "before men" (Matt. 10:32 and par.), not to be ashamed of Jesus and his words "in this unfaithful and sinful generation" (Mark 8:38). It may possibly mean also to come forward, identified by a "seal" (cf. Rev. 7:4 with 13:16), but in any case to come forth with such public confession and witness out of anonymity and pluralism, and thereby to accept suffering. Thus, just as Jesus is the "faithful and true witness" (Rev. 3:14) and through word, deed, and suffering "in his testimony before Pontius Pilate made the good confession" (1 Tim. 6:13 RSV), other primitive Christian witnesses also were killed "for the word of God and for the witness they had borne" (Rev. 6:9 RSV; 20:4; cf. further IV.1.f).

What is involved in this public witness and confession and thus prompts affliction and persecution is to be discussed presently. Of course, one cannot exclude the role of human factors, all-too-human factors, in giving impetus to sufferings: for example, Jewish jealousy at the success of the mission and the growing influence of Christians (cf. Acts 5:17; 13:45; 17:5). Yet these factors, which are more in the foreground, are not the decisive ones.

2. The question of God and freedom from the law

If one inquires more specifically into the concrete reasons for suffering, various perspectives can be put forward. To the question as to the deeper reason for *Jesus'* suffering and dying, the answer is hardly to be gained from the account of the trial in the Gospels, but only from Jesus' authority, his message, and his manner of life. The account of the trial (Mark 14:53 ff. and par.), which was shaped from the primitive Christian confession, hardly allows us any longer to recognize the actual reasons, quite apart from the legal question as to the competence of the Jewish Sanhedrin to impose the death penalty and the numerous conflicts with the regulations for Jewish legal proceedings. For example, the saying about the destruction of the temple (Mark 14:58; cf. also 15:29) indeed in Matthew—differently from Mark—is not traced back to false witnesses (cf. Matt. 26:60-61), and actually probably goes back to Jesus. But whatever its original meaning may have been—it probably is to be understood in the sense of similar Old Testament and apocalyptic predictions (cf. Mic. 3:12; Jer. 26:18; Ethiopic Enoch 90:28-29, et passim)—it can hardly have been a valid point of accusation and condemnation. For Mark, at any rate, it was only meant to demonstrate that no proper point of accusation could be found (cf. 14:56, 59), and perhaps also a way of explaining Jesus' "silence" (cf. Mark 15:5 and Isa. 53:7). Of course, it is equally true that Jesus was not condemned because of a confession that he was the Messiah and Son of God. His message and his conduct indeed may very well have given occasion for regarding him as a claimant to messiahship, yet a claim to being the Messiah is not blasphemy, and no claimant to messiahship was ever tried for this reason. The combination of the various christological titles and Old Testament passages itself also demonstrates the primitive Christian character of Mark 14:61-62. The charge of blasphemy is either a reflection of the later dispute between church and synagogue or perhaps a sharpening and extrapolation of the conflict with Judaism into which Jesus himself actually was led.

This conflict, however, was not rooted in a formal messianic self-witness, but primarily in a different view of God and his law. Jesus in fact announces with authority that the God of Abraham, Isaac, and Jacob, in his eschatological turning to men, is independent of human observance of the law and of obligations to sanctified traditions (cf. Luke 15:1 ff.; 18:9 ff., and similar passages). Hence he set himself, in unprecedented sovereignty, above the limitations of the law, which for him was not simply identical with the will of God (cf. Matt. 5:21 ff.; Mark 7:15, et passim); further, he declared God's liberating yes even to tax collectors and sinners (cf. Mark 2:5, 7) and lived with them (cf. Mark 2:15-16). Also to be mentioned precisely here are the conflicts over the Sabbath into which Jesus was led because even on the Sabbath he relieved suffering and distress (Mark 3:4 and par.; Matt. 12:11-12 and par.; Luke 13:10 ff.). It is certain that this freedom in relation to the law aroused opposition. Thus, the first judgment for the death sentence by the Sanhedrin in Mark's account also stands at the end of the complex of "controversies" (2:1–3:6), which shows Jesus in conflict with his opponents because of his forgiveness of sins and eating with tax collectors, his failure to fast and his violation of the Sabbath (3:6; cf. also 11:18 and 12:12). In John's account, the violation of the Sabbath is explicitly named, along with the accusation that Jesus made himself out to be God, as the reason for the passion: "Therefore the Jews sought all the more to kill him, because he not only violated the Sabbath, but also called God his father, and thus made himself equal with God" (John 5:18). This is, to be sure, formulated thus from the perspective of the Christian community, but still it reflects the central conflict with the law and Jesus' claim to be speaking and acting in God's name and on God's behalf. In any case, the deeper reason for Jesus' suffering and rejection is the fact that Jesus confronted people with a God who, in the boundlessness and radicality of his goodness, appeared unsettling and dangerous to all devout persons, and who seriously disturbed the normal orders and standards of this world. And Jesus was, conversely, brought into suffering and to the cross in the name of the God who was regarded as the guarantor of that religio-ethical structure of law and world-order that Jesus called into question. All the depth and painfulness of the conflict becomes visible in the fact that the devout Jews accepted affliction and martyrdom precisely because of their faithfulness to the law (cf. 4 Ezra 7:89; 2 Macc. 7:2, 9, et passim), but Jesus must suffer because he proclaims God as the one who not only cares about those who are faithful to the law, but also those who have gone astray and have been rejected, those who suffer discrimination and are scorned.

    God's unconditional yes to all men, and thus the question of the law, continued to be a stumbling stone and a reason for persecution and suffering. The so-called "Hellenists" around Stephen probably were the first who once again were persecuted because of their freedom from the law and were driven out of Jerusalem. Attacks on the law and Moses, which, contrary to the portrayal in Acts 6:11-12, apparently were correctly charged against them, not only set in motion the persecution of Acts 8, but perhaps also prompted an expulsion from Rome. That is to say, it is entirely possible that the non-law-observing proclamation of the missionaries who had been expelled from Jerusalem reached even to Rome and created such a furor there that the Emperor Claudius put an end to these disputes with an edict and all the Jews and Jewish Christians had to leave Rome (cf. the reference in Acts 18:2, where, to be sure, the reason for the expulsion from Rome is not cited).

    The reason for Paul's persecuting activity, which he practiced before his conversion, may very well have been also the threat to these main pillars of Judaism (cf. Gal. 1:13; Phil.

3:6), which he as a "zealot for God" wanted to parry (cf. also Acts 22:3-4). But in any case, the persecution that later struck the apostle himself was provoked by his non-law-observing proclamation of the gospel. Since for Paul the cross of Jesus implied the end of the law (Rom. 10:4), and hence of circumcision as well, Paul preached simply the crucified one (Gal. 3:1; 1 Cor. 1:18) and no longer preached circumcision, and so he was persecuted (Gal. 5:11). Conversely he accused the Judaizing false teachers in Galatia of letting themselves be circumcised in order to avoid persecution and thus of obscuring the offence of the cross of Christ, which brings salvation without the law (Gal. 6:12). Indeed, it is the same story in 1 Thess. 2:15-16, where Paul writes to them that they suffer the same thing at the hands of their own countrymen as did the communities in Judea from the Jews, who not only killed the Lord Jesus and the prophets, but also persecuted him, in order to combat his mission to the Gentiles; and here that means his non-law-observing mission. Hence this suffering did not occur, as one perhaps could at first imagine, because of a so-to-speak "confessionally" distinctive confession, but precisely because of the universality of the offer of salvation. For Paul this always involved the obligation to the unity of the church. Thus, when the unity of Jewish and Gentile Christians was at stake, he undertook the dangerous journey to Jerusalem, and there in fact was arrested. But in any case, we can recognize that the real cause of suffering for Paul was the God whom he proclaimed, who justifies the sinners and the ungodly (Rom. 4:5) and thus dispenses with the law as a way of salvation. The deepest, most basic reason for his suffering is not political, social, or personal, but theological and "religious," even though it always has consequences in other areas and brings other causes and reasons in its train.

3. Critical stance in relation to the state

Of course Jesus was not crucified by the Jews, but by the Romans, and it is not accidental that the Apostles' Creed says, "suffered under Pontius Pilate." The fact of his crucifixion, which in fact was a Roman punishment, suggests that he was handed over to the Romans by the Jewish authorities on grounds that are no longer altogether clear. Jesus certainly was no political revolutionary or insurgent Zealot. On all the points of contact with Zealotism (the social dimension, readiness for martyrdom, eschatological character, and so forth), his distance from this anti-Roman resistance movement was too great to allow such an identification (cf. only the commandment to love one's enemies, in Matt. 5:44, or the injunction to pay taxes, in Mark 12:13 ff.). But we cannot exclude the possibilities that he consciously and deliberately approached the Zealots' position, particularly since many indications within the passion narrative argue for this view. Thus, he probably was crucified together with Zealot rebels (Mark 15:27), and his trial was connected with Barabbas, who according to Mark 15:7 was "in prison among the rebels who had committed a murder during an insurrection." One must also observe that he did not simply advocate an uncritical and unreserved yes to the Roman state, and his message contained thoroughly political implications and controversial material (cf. I.2.a), and perhaps even set in motion a messianic movement (which does not in and of itself also presuppose a messianic confession of Jesus!). John the Baptist appears already to have been imprisoned and executed for similar reasons even though in Mark 6:17 ff. the only reason that is mentioned for his arrest and beheading is that he had protested against Herod Antipas' having dismissed his first wife and married his sister-in-law Herodias. Once again we should recall (cf. I.1.a) the murderous command and the enmity of Herod (Matt. 2:16-17), who sees his rule threatened by one who desires neither scepter nor crown. But precisely thus it becomes clear that Jesus obviously could be the advocate of the poor and disfranchised only in flight and in affliction, not as a friend of the royal house; in any case, there was no thought simply of a peaceful and harmonious relationship with the state. But we can hardly go beyond conjectures in identifying possible specific points of collision.

Just as Jesus was dragged before the tribunal of Jewish and

Gentile judges, those in the primitive church also soberly reckoned with the prospect that Christians would be brought to account before the synagogues and punished as well as being "brought before governors and kings" (Mark 13:9; Matt. 10:17-18) for Christ's sake; that is that they would have to undergo conflicts with the Roman authorities. Of course, once again, it is hardly possible for us to discern more exactly the specific grounds of these conflicts. Uncritical servility indeed is already ruled out by the critical utterances about the practices of government (cf. I.2.c), but we can hardly say why the Christians actually were brought before the authorities. Unfortunately only a very little specific information can be drawn from non-Christian accounts, so that one can only state in general terms that the measures taken by the state apparently were designed primarily to serve the maintenance of public order and the civil cult. At any rate, one cannot yet speak of a systematically organized enmity toward Christians, or one based on principle. The Christian communities were far too insignificant for that. Moreover, attitudes of the agencies of the state and of the populace varied from place to place, and this fact must be takenn into account.

According to 2 Cor. 11:25, Paul was subjected to beatings three times by the Romans, and according to 2 Cor. 11:32-33 it was only by daring flight that he escaped a threatened imprisonment by King Aretas. But we do not know precisely what evoked these measures. Nevertheless, the punishment of beating, which was imposed by Roman authorities, shows that in spite of any loyalty toward the state, conflicts always had to be taken into account, a fact that is simply connected with faith and ministry. Thus in Phil. 1:13 Paul says that his chains have become known in the Roman praetorium (= the governor's palace?) as what he has to suffer for Christ's sake. Many are of the opinion that this signals a change in the judicial proceedings against him, that is, that the accusations that had been initiated against him, of causing riots, breach of public order, and the like, had proved untenable, and Paul had been able to make it clear to the court or to the assembled populace that he was in fact under accusation for the sake of the gospel. But this explanation is based upon conjecture. What is certain is only that his arrest was occasioned by the gospel (cf. also Philem. 13).

If the explanation for the expulsion of Aquila and Priscilla from Rome (Acts 18:2) that was given above is correct, then the edict of Claudius shows, in any case, that from the perspective of the Roman state, a danger to the public order and security was seen in the stir that was aroused within the Jewish community by the Christian proclamation (cf. also the division in the city, in Acts 14:4-5, but also 16:20). When Paul in 1 Thess. 2:14 says concerning the Thessalonians that they had suffered the same thing from their own countrymen as had the communities in Judea from their countrymen, we are not to think of persecution by agencies of the state, but by the pagan populace. It is possible that the Jews were involved in such actions, as is reported in Acts 13:50 about Antioch and in Acts 17 about Thessalonica. For example, according to Acts 17:5 ff. the missionaries were charged by jealous Jews before the rulers of the city with bringing the whole world into an uproar and acting contrary to the emperor's orders. Of course, according to Luke, such an accusation is nothing but slander. Nevertheless, with his apologetically motivated emphasis on the Christians' harmlessness and loyalty toward Rome, Luke avoided citing an actual reason. He is concerned rather with playing down the conflicts in the case of Paul and showing that Christians do nothing deserving of death or imprisonment (Acts 23:29; 25:25; 26:31), and that the charge of endangering the state is traceable to Jewish slander (Acts 18:12 ff.; 23:29; 25:18 ff.; 26:31-32). The portrayal of the representatives and agencies of the empire in a nonpartisan and even sympathetic attitude toward Paul (cf. Acts 16:37 ff.; 22:25 ff.; 23:29; 24:22 ff.; 25:24, et passim) of course stands in a certain amount of tension with Luke 12:11, where it is said that Christians also will be dragged before "authorities and officials" of the Roman governmental structure (cf. also Acts 27:24).

Even the First Epistle of Peter, which was written in a situation of impending persecution, tells more about the differences with the environment than with the civil authorities. Certainly no one from the community should suffer as a murderer, a thief, or a lawbreaker, but as a Christian (1 Pet. 4:5-16); that is, Christians are not to bring their sufferings upon themselves by coming into conflict with the penal law, but the cause or occasion should only be the fact of their being Christian. But to what extent and in what way this Christian profession possibly also brought with it suffering on the part of the civil authorities must also be left open here. Anyone who characterizes the bearers of civil power as "creatures" and thereby calls their divine dignity into question (1 Pet. 2:13), and who identifies freedom without fear as the ground and mode of proper respect (2:16-17), and thereby rules out a blind submission, must nevertheless always bear in mind that certain states will regard this as an impertinence and will react with countermeasures.

But it is only from the book of Revelation that we are first able to learn something more precise; this book was composed during the reign of the Emperor Domitian (A.D. 81-96), when the Christian faith collided with the Roman imperium and its cult of the emperor. It is true that even here the author usually speaks in general terms of those who are persecuted and slain "for the word of God and their witness" (Rev. 6:9) or "for their testimony to Jesus and for the word" (Rev. 20:4; cf. also 1:9); however, chapter 13 in particular makes it clear that it was not actually the Christian faith, as such, that was regarded as punishable, but rather the rejection, prompted by the faith, of the state-cult and of the religious veneration of the emperor. The province of Asia in particular, in which the seven churches specifically named in chapters 2 and 3 were situated, was a center of the cult of the emperor, the institutions and forms of which can be documented by an abundance of temples, cultic images, altars, coins, and the like. Hence, it is not surprising that Christian opposition and bloody persecution arose in the time of Domitian; already in his lifetime he claimed divine veneration as "lord and god" *(dominus ac deus),* and under him the imperial cult, as the official state-cult, serving the state's self-representation and its ideological-religious unity, underwent a significant heightening and expansion. Hence, for the seer of the book of Revelation, the state is not only the embodiment of satanic power on earth, but also a devilish caricature of Christ (cf. the parallel between 13:1 and 19:12, of 5:6, 12, or 2:8; and of 20:4 and 13:3). He demands *proskynesis* (13:4, 14), which belongs only to God and his Christ. But this means that the state demands what belongs to God. It has become a total and a deified state. But such a diabolic state, which by means of its imposing propaganda and the fascination that it bears also has a concern for the necessary state-ideology and the state-cult (cf. 13:14-15), consistently conducts itself in an anti-Christian manner, "wages war against the saints" (Rev. 13:7), and by means of its brutal harshness brings them into affliction and persecution (cf. Rev. 13:10, 15, 17).

4. Damage to economic interests

Thus the rejection of the cult of the emperor was not a purely private decision, set solely within the context of the preference of the individual, but with the given amalgamation of religion and politics *eo ipso* amounted to a political action and involved economic sanctions as well (cf. Rev. 13:17). Just so, the Christian faith likewise was drawn into suffering by virtue of the fact that it collided with economic interests. Jesus' cleansing of the temple (Mark 11:15 ff.) also affected the businesses of the money-changers and the sellers of doves. Certainly this was primarily an eschatological sign and not a protest against banking business in the temple or traffic in sacrificial offerings, but the chief priests and scribes must have felt themselves challenged, and that not only in a religious respect, by such an attack upon the market in the temple (v. 18); indeed, in Jesus' criticism of the law and of cultic thought, the ruling circles of the Sadducees and chief priests must have seen a danger to their economic basis also.

The first persecution of Christians by the pagans was also grounded in an interference with their financial profits. According to Acts 16:16 ff., Paul and Silas encounter in Philippi a slave girl who is a ventriloquist, and as such has a "spirit of divination" and brings in great profits to her master by her soothsaying (v. 16). Because this ventriloquism apparently is regarded as a state of being possessed, it leads to an exorcism. But thereupon Paul and Silas are seized and dragged to the magistrate, for "the hopes of their profits had vanished" (v. 19). This is evidently the actual ground and occasion for the animosity, even though the apostles then are accused before the authorities as Jews who set the city in an uproar and proclaim customs that are not allowed to Romans. In any case, beating and imprisonment follow.

Acts 19:23 ff. also illustrates the fact that the Christian faith can bring with it damage to certain kinds of business and thus can set in motion painful reactions. In this passage, there is an account of the rage of Demetrius the silversmith, who produces miniature silver temples of the goddess Artemis. This ancient manufacture of devotional objects brought considerable profit and prosperity (vv. 24-25). Therefore, Demetrius raised the fear in the circle of his fellow craftsmen that the Christian proclamation that "there are no gods made with hands" could mean a twofold danger, namely, that their business would fall into disrepute and that the sanctuary of the great goddess Artemis would be neglected (vv. 26-27). The whole story then takes a turn that is not altogether clear, in which Paul's fellow travelers Gaius and Aristarchus are dragged into the theater, while Paul is warned and remains otherwise unmolested, although 20:17 perhaps presupposes that he can no longer venture into the city (cf. also 2 Cor. 1:8 ff.; 1 Cor. 15:32). Even when the craftsmen are counseled to pursue their complaints in the civil courts (v. 38), it is still clear what material for conflict is present here.

Perhaps one may also mention here the warnings of James 2:1 ff., about giving preferential treatment in the community to someone on account of his wealth, even if one expects subsidies and prestige from the rich person. Of course, it is not certain whether the community that is addressed in verse 6 was experiencing social pressure and judicial oppression from the rich because of their being Christian. What is meant probably is only the oppression of the poor and not a legal proceeding against the Christians who are presenting a threat to wealth, because it is not until verse 7 that animosity toward the

Christians becomes the subject. Nevertheless it is self-explan-
atory that economically grounded distress was suffered by
Christians even without any specific connection with the
Christian faith, so long as these people themselves were
numbered among the have-nots (cf. I.2.c). Equally clear are the
admonitions to overcome such affliction (cf. V. 6).

5. Being different

Still another cause that occasioned suffering is the
Christians' being different from "the world," but also from "the
normal" and from what "they" do and regard as proper. There is
a very notable example in the case of Jesus himself, according to
which he remained essentially alien and misunderstood even in
the circle of a family. According to John 7:5, he found no
credence among his own brothers, and according to Mark
3:20-21, the members of his family said concerning him that he
was beside himself, and they sought to take him by force. Jesus
evidently lived and taught in a way that others could easily
discredit as being insanity. He simply could not be measured
by the usual standards, and his preaching and activity had to
bring him into conflict with any average Jewish family. The
saying that "those of a man's own household will be his
enemies" (Matt. 10:36) holds true even for Jesus himself. Mark
13:12-13 bears witness that hatred against Christ also will
divide blood-kin and set them against each other.

This is expressed even more clearly and more radically in
the Gospel of John. The hostility toward Jesus of the world that
is alienated from God, and accordingly toward his disciples as
well, ultimately stems from this remoteness from God on the
part of the world, in which the disciples no longer find their
sustaining foundation (cf. John 15:18-20). Because the disciples
are no longer "of the world" and therefore reject any conformity
to the world, the hatred of this world is directed against them.
In spite of the prominence of the dualistic manner of speaking
here, still it is evident that the hatred of the world is not based
upon an accident or misunderstanding, but that it has deeper

reasons and arises out of a fundamental estrangement in relation to God and his revelation. "They will do all this to you because of my name, for they do not know the one who sent me" (John 15:21). A church that does not evoke any contradiction and does not suffer must constantly allow itself to be challenged from this fundamental perspective with the question whether it is holding with sufficient fidelity to the "name" or has rather conformed, either in massive or in subtle fashion, to "the world."

In 1 Pet. 4:4, the view of the foreignness and unpopularity of the Christians who trouble the world as "aliens and exiles" (1 Pet. 2:11). is more concrete and not so much a matter of principle. There it is said concerning the "Gentiles," "They are surprised that you do not now join them in the same wild profligacy" (RSV), or "that you do not (any longer) plunge into the same stream of debauchery, and they revile you." The Christians now are swimming against the current, and their separation from earlier patterns of life (cf. also v. 3) stirs up conflicts with the world around them. Indeed this hardly means only a break with vice, but also a detachment from everyday customs and the common cultic practices and religion, for even the cultural and public life was in large measure (e.g., in theatrical performances, civil ceremonies, military service, and the like) permeated with cultic elements. Hence, we may not think that here we have simply religious reasons on the part of the Christian opposing nonreligious practices of the pagans. Instead, here even in everyday life different forms of belief come into conflict. For example, Christians, who reject the civil cult, therefore are accused not only of an offense against majesty, but also of godlessness.

Yet in whatever forms the differences are manifested, peculiarities and detachment always create resentment and alienation. Anyone who disrupts the existing scheme of things is regarded as an outsider, spoilsport, troublemaker, and the consequence is distrust, disparagement, suspicion. All this of course is expressed in various ways, but most prominent are defamation of moral character (1 Pet. 2:12; 3:16) and political suspicion (Acts 17:7; 21:38; 24:5). In this connection the apologetic intention of the passages cited certainly must be taken into consideration. But if Christians suffer "for righteousness' sake" (Matt. 5:10; 1 Pet. 3:4), still one may not simply assume that the understanding of this righteousness that occasions suffering is simply identical with the customary moralistic understanding of righteousness; indeed, in the suffering that is in accordance with that of their Lord (1 Pet. 2:23), for example, Christians do not repay like for like, evil for evil (1 Pet. 3:9; Matt. 5:44; 1 Cor. 4:12, et passim), or they accept conflicts which could normally be regarded as unnecessary and foolish.

6. Solidarity with the unredeemed creation

Although the causes and kinds of suffering that have been named are in part specifically Christian, and thus do not affect non-Christians, primitive Christianity, of course, also is acquainted with causes of suffering that apply to all men alike, therefore including the Christians. Here we need only to recall the examples of the reality of social and economic suffering that were cited in chapter 2, where the factors that cause suffering are in part sharply distinguished, when for example, the Christians are addressed with respect to their experiences with the rich, who oppress them as poor people and drag them before the courts (James 2:6), or as subjugated people who are enslaved (Mark 10:42), etc. Hence it is not true, at least for the New Testament as a whole, that the social causes of suffering are more or less suppressed. Of course, it is true that the New Testament sees other reasons for the sufferings of Christians in the foreground and never cites the social factors as the sole causes of suffering. There are also many other causes besides repressive structures and social antagonisms that are responsible for the suffering of people as people (not only as Christians!). One need only think of earthquakes, shipwrecks, or sexual difficulties. And we may think further of the utterances that stem from the wisdom-traditions, according to which man himself causes much suffering (1 Tim. 6:10; James 3:8; cf. v. 2).

In any case, these utterances refuse to seek the causes of suffering only outside the individual person in impersonal systems. The undeniable interactions between the human heart and the social structure are not thereby denied. But it is all the more true that such utterances are not limited to Christians.

However, the inclusion of Christians in the story of the suffering of this unredeemed world is expressed in an utterly universal way in Rom. 8:18-19 (cf. I.2.g). Even though Christians already participate in the hoped-for future and already possess the "earnest" of the Spirit, they too are still people who suffer, groan, and wait (v. 23). They too know not only the sufferings that arise out of service and commitment to Christ, but in solidarity with the creation, all the pains and fears, all the waste and the perils of death, of this world. Therefore, they too wait the "redemption of the body," the liberation from curruptibility and affliction. They too lack the power to change a white hair once again to black (Matt. 5:36) or to add anything to the length of their lives (Matt. 6:27). They too must be admonished, in view of everyday vexations and fears, not to be anxious about food and clothing (Matt. 6:25 ff.). They too therefore are addressed as those who "are a mist, that appears for a short time and then vanishes" (James 4:14). But the pain and trouble, the perishability and futility of man, who withers like the grass, are countered, of course, by the imperishable reality of the Word and hence by hope (1 Pet. 1:24-25).

IV. The meaning and interpretation of suffering

There is no theorizing and speculating about suffering in the New Testament. All "explanations" and interpretations based upon merely rational arguments of the "objective" reason, which could be gained from overlapping systems of coordinates and metaphysical contexts of meaning, are lacking. The knowledge and discernment contained in faith, of course, are

not simply dismissed in the face of suffering. Trouble that is
experienced is rather assimilated to faith, and in spite of all the
enigmas that remain, an effort is made to understand it
primarily from the perspective afforded by Christ's sufferings.
Since the sufferings of Jesus, who himself appears not to have
been very much concerned with integrating those sufferings
into an intelligible whole, the meaning of which however
became manifest *a posteriori* through the resurrection, the
sufferings of Christians too are not without meaning. Because
since Easter his sufferings can be thought of in connection with
the sufferings of Christians, there is now a divine proposal of
meaning, which of course does not seek to be explicated simply
in theoretical outlines, but to be proved in suffering and
understanding. Perhaps it is not accidental that the person who
has thought the most and most profoundly about suffering is the
one who like no one else in primitive Christianity was exposed
in surpassing measure to the weight of suffering and who lived
under conditions of hunger and thirst, "ill-clad and buffeted
and homeless," working hard (1 Cor. 4:10-11 RSV, et passim);
all this in the service of him who by suffering and dying wrought
salvation and sent his apostles into the world in the sign of his
cross. The Pauline interpretations of suffering were not thought
out at the writing-desk, but arose and were tested in his life with
Christ. The same may also be said of other New Testament
authors. From the perspective of the cross of Jesus, an
understanding faith is possible that is not obliged to consign
even suffering to absurdity or pure incomprehensibility. Hence
the crucial question even today in view of the New Testament
interpretations may very well be whether they will sustain one
in living and suffering. Here the very multiplicity of the
following interpretations is a warning against absolutizing one
of them or trying to bring them all together into a harmonized
system. They are highly paradoxical (cf. the relationship of
divine and satanic activity in IV.2.c and d). Anyone who is in the
throes of suffering obviously is not in a position to construct a
system. There really is only one thing that more or less strongly
prevails, the vision of the suffering Christ. This is the real
meaning, but also the real comfort.

1. Central New Testament interpretations

a) Fellowship with Christ

Accordingly, here once again we must list in first place, and pre-eminently, the fellowship with Christ in which Christians are set precisely through their sufferings (cf. II.2). Sufferings are a sign of one's belonging to Christ. Nevertheless, over against modern reinterpretations, it must be affirmed that Christ is not *eo ipso* present and suffering with all wherever there is suffering in the world but only where Christ is the subject of life (Gal. 2:20) is he the subject of suffering also. But there he actually is this; therefore persecution of the Christian community is persecution of Jesus, and thus Paul the persecutor of the Christians hears the exalted Christ say concerning his persecution of the community, "Why are you persecuting *me?*" and "I am Jesus whom you are persecuting" (Acts 9:4-5; 22:7-8; 26:15-16). According to Matthew 25, God or Christ indeed can be found in all those who are hungry and thirsty, the exiles and those who are ill-clad, the sick and those in prison; yet this is not said as a comfort for all who suffer, but as an encouragement for those who are to come to their aid and there encounter their Lord. However, it is precisely this fellowship with Christ that not only makes Christians capable of enduring suffering, but also gives the real meaning to their readiness to suffer. Hence sufferings have no intrinsic value and no meaning in and of themselves, and therefore any striving after suffering on one's own part and any martyrdom ideology is mistaken. With all the emphasis upon the voluntary character of Jesus' sufferings, sufferings are never minimized or glorified. Even the Christians' being included in the "dying of Jesus" is not, as such, given a positive evaluation and an independent significance. According to 2 Cor. 4:10, Christians bear about in their bodies the "dying of Jesus, in order that the life of Jesus also may become manifest in our bodies" (similarly 4:11; 7:3; Phil. 3:10). This final "in order that" clearly marks the distinction from any glorification of pain and suffering, even under the guise of conformity to Christ. Sufferings are rightly to be understood only from the perspective of the cross *and resurrection* of Jesus, that God slays in order to make alive. Just as in the crucified one God's power and wisdom are made manifest (1 Cor. 1:18 ff.), so in the sufferings of the Christians, under the mask of the "dying of Jesus" the "life of Jesus" becomes manifest. Only for this reason are the foolish and weak now the chosen ones (1 Cor. 1:25 ff.), and the suffering ones also the ones who are favored (Phil. 1:29), blessed (Matt. 5:3 ff.), and filled with the Spirit (1 Pet. 4:14). Thus it is not suffering as suffering that has the promise.

The New Testament also knows well enough that that naive opinion according to which affliction and distress allegedly teach one how to pray is unrealistic. Suffering as such does not lead into fellowship with Christ, but rather fellowship with Christ also has its outworking in suffering. It obviously is not a rule that suffering prompts reflection and the confession of one's sins (cf. Ps. 32). The scene with the reviling thief on the cross in Luke 23:39, e.g., shows unmistakably that people do not believe that inescapable affliction or even imminent death *eo ipso* will produce repentance and faith. In this world, trouble and affliction, as such, heighten the sensitivity neither for the suffering and dying of Jesus nor for that of others. Certainly the other one of the two who were crucified with Jesus is all the more a valid symbol for all those who, precisely when they are in misery and have reached their end, do not sink into cynicism and resignation, but gain hope because they choose to be "with him" (Luke 23:42-43), the crucified Christ. This means that the affinity between the cross of Jesus and the cross of the unredeemed world, its guilt and its affliction, is not called into question by the rejection voiced by the reviling thief on the cross. But suffering not only can open the way to Christ; it can also block that way. There is also a "worldly grief" (2 Cor. 7:10) that leads not to salvation but to death.

Thus, as much as it is true on the one hand that sufferings have no value in and of themselves, but rather are incorporated into a final event, it is equally true on the other hand that they are not regarded as a mere exception or anomaly. Certainly even the Christians of the New Testament period were inclined toward such an assumption, but they are warned, for example, by the author of First Peter: "Do not let the fiery ordeal surprise you, as though something strange were happening to you, but since you are participating in the sufferings of Christ, rejoice" (1 Pet. 4:12 ff.). Thus, sufferings are nothing surprising and extraordinary. This is not meant to speak in favor of a romantic minimizing of these sufferings, but rather to make clear that the close association with the afflicted and suffering Christ in the midst of sufferings makes it possible for Christians to rejoice. It is not some eternal plan of history nor an apocalyptic timetable, but fellowship with Christ that makes sufferings both unavoidable and understandable. But it is precisely for this reason that they contain a promise and give assurance, in this life and in the life to come, of comfort, joy, and life. Because the "life of Jesus" becomes capable of being experienced precisely in the destiny of suffering, and weakness is the paradoxical mode of the power of Christ, Paul can say that he will rather glory in his weaknesses (2 Cor. 12:5, 9). Because the power of Christ and fellowship with Christ reach their fulfillment in suffering, he says, "So I will rather glory in my infirmities, so that the power of Christ may reside in me. Therefore for Christ's sake I am content with my infirmities, injuries, troubles, persecutions, and afflictions. For when I am weak, then I am strong" (2 Cor. 12:9-10).

But all this holds true precisely because the dialectic of affliction and comfort, of weakness and strength, of sorrow and joy, corresponds to the dialectic of the death and the resurrection of Jesus, into which the Christians are incorporated.

Hence, even according to John, the two belong to Christian existence after Easter. The situation that has arisen because of Jesus' departure from the world is indeed in a special sense a time of sorrow and distress (John 16:16 ff.). "You will weep and lament, but the world will rejoice." But it is likewise true that "I will see you again, and then your hearts will rejoice, and no one will be able to take this joy from you" (John 16:20, 22). This means not only that the grief over the passion of Jesus will be transformed into the joy of Easter, but also (cf. the

intervening illustration of the woman giving birth, John 16:21)
that the joy "after a little while" arises specifically out of the
distress. The reason for this joy in the midst of lamentation,
distress, and desolation and the presumed triumph of the
world, however, is that Jesus will "see them again" (v. 22); that
is, the encounter with the Resurrected One, who addresses his
people in their weeping and their fear with his word (20:15, 19),
is possible since Easter for all Christians. Even though the
disciples still have fears, yet they may participate in their Lord's
victory over the world and in the midst of fear and affliction find
peace and assurance "in him" (16:33).

b) Vis aliena *("strange power")*

This conjunction of affliction and comfort in fellowship
with Christ means a constant dependence upon God and
looking away from one's self. Hence Paul can define the aim of
suffering and tribulations thus (2 Cor. 1:9), "So that we may not
place our confidence in ourselves, but in God, who raises the
dead." Similarly, in 2 Cor. 12:7 it is said that Paul was given a
"thorn in the flesh" (probably some kind of illness is meant) so
that he might "not be exalted overmuch," and in 2 Cor. 4:7, that
the treasure is hidden in earthen vessels "so that the excellency
of the power might belong to God and not come from us." Thus
all power and all confidence should be wholly and entirely
God's, and should in no wise be a human achievement or a
human possession. It is precisely in suffering that man learns
that he is not what he makes himself out to be.

Thus according to Paul, sufferings aim in the same direction
as the message of justification and the "word of the cross,"
namely, at striking out of man's hands all supports for
self-assertion and self-confidence, even though in the case of
justification, what is in view is the "alien righteousness" that is
promised to us by God, while in the case of suffering, on the
other hand, it is the "alien power." But in both cases, what is
involved is not something that is man's own, but the alien,
something that comes from without, given by God, a reality
extra se. This parallelism between the message of justification

and suffering is given expression particularly in Philippians 3, where Paul says to his opponents that he has given up everything of which by nature he could be proud (his belonging to Judaism, his irreproachable conduct, etc.) in order to gain Christ, "so that I might be found in him as one not having a righteousness of my own that is based on the law, but that which is based on faith in Christ, the righteousness that comes from God because of faith, that I might know him, and the power of his resurrection, and the fellowship of his sufferings; thus I become like him in his death, in order at last to attain to the resurrection from the dead" (Phil. 3:9-11). Thus there is a correspondence between one's being on the way, in cross and suffering, toward the resurrection, and the ungodly person's dependence upon justification. The dependence upon the power of the resurrection is equally manifested in the empty hands of those who have nothing to offer to God and in the suffering bodies of those for whom nothing remains but radical trust in God. In the afflictions of his sufferings the Christian is thrown back upon his own weakness, in order to remain dependent upon the self-disclosure of the One who calls into being out of nothing (Rom. 4:17; cf. 1 Cor. 1:28). Thus sufferings are not meant to produce evidence on our own behalf and prominence for ourselves, self-boasting and self-glorification, but the increase of grace, thanksgiving, the glorification of God (2 Cor. 1:11; 4:15). With respect even to the Christians, the declaration of empty-handedness always holds true, as is indicated in the catalog of sufferings found in 2 Cor. 6:10 ("as those who have nothing"), and this in a radical sense, that is, they have nothing even of an inward or religious nature. The "we live" in the midst of suffering and dying (2 Cor. 6:9), on the other hand, is not an expression of their own strength of life and in suffering, but is a gift of God.

Herein lies a significant difference from the Stoic understanding of suffering. For example, Seneca can write, in *Epistle* 71.26:

What then is really evil about torments and everything else that we call adverse? I believe that it is this: that the spirit

suffers under it, and lets itself be bowed and overpowered.
But this cannot happen to a wise person. He stands upright
under the burden . . . he knows his powers and knows that
he is born to bear burdens.

This distinctive clause, "he knows his powers" (*vires suas
novit*), stands in direct contradiction to what suffering is
supposed to achieve according to Paul, not to trust one's own
powers, but rather the *dynamis* of God. Paul does not extol the
superiority of reason and virtue over pain and suffering, as is
done even in Hellenistic Judaism (4 Macc. 8–12), but only
God's marvelous power. When Paul says, "We are more than
conquerors," he immediately adds, "through him that loved
us" (Rom. 8:37). He can do all things, even endure deprivation
and humiliation, only "through him who strengthens me" (Phil.
4:13). There is "triumph" always only in analogy to the triumph
of Christ (Rev. 3:21).

Accordingly, the endurance of suffering can be understood
only as a miracle of God, who guards one against the worst. This
is demonstrated by the following consideration. In the catalog
of sufferings in 2 Cor. 4:8 it is said that "we are afflicted but not
driven into a corner." However, in other catalogs of sufferings
(2 Cor. 6:4 and Rom. 8:35) these two terms do not stand over
against each other, but in parallel, as experiences that have
actually been endured. But this then shows how razor-thin
must be the distinction between the first and second elements
in 2 Cor. 4:8a, and thus between the experience of suffering, on
the one hand, and the preservation from the ultimate "being
driven into a corner and crushed," on the other hand. What is
maintained there as a minimum cannot be made the basis for
any sort of self-assurance and awareness of strength. The same
appears from a comparison of 2 Cor. 4:8b ("We are perplexed
but not despairing") and 2 Cor. 1:8 ("We were so overwhelm-
ingly burdened that we despaired of life itself"). In this radical
predicament no resistance on our own part will be of any help.
What sustains Paul is not his own ultimate will to resist; instead,
the one who preserves him from falling into the ultimate depths
is God alone. In this experience, it is by no means true that only

in the happy outcome is the divine saving intention served by suffering, but God works precisely *in* the depths and gives comfort *in* the affliction (2 Cor. 1:4).

Hence sufferings have a disillusioning and a critical function. In opposition to all self-assurance, they point the sufferer away from himself and toward God, who calls that which does not exist into being and raises the dead (2 Cor. 1:9). Resurrection of the dead is the sign and characteristic mark of God's activity even in the midst of the sufferings of the present time, and thus one can speak of it in the past tense as well as in the future ("who has delivered us from such a deadly peril and will deliver us"). God breaks through the power of death that surrounds and threatens man in suffering; he does this already now, in the midst of the circumstances of suffering in this world, and thus he gives us a basis for hope.

c) *Disillusionment and "eschatological reserve"*

But the disillusioning function of sufferings is exhibited also in another connection. Sufferings will not only point the sufferer away from himself and toward God, but also toward the future, and thus stamp "not yet" upon the consummation of salvation. To this extent they have an antifanatical function and are meant to hold Christians firm in hope in the face of all outward appearance. For Paul in particular, sufferings are not only a sign of one's belonging to Christ, but also a sign of this present age (Rom. 8:18). Thereby also, any minimizing or glorification of suffering is prohibited. In the earliest passage in which Paul offers a catalog of sufferings, this is clearly intended, over against the enthusiastic "already" of the Corinthian fanatics, to insist on the "eschatological reserve." In opposition to the "having-already-become-satisfied" and "having-already-become-rich" of the Corinthian achievement-enthusiasm (1 Cor. 4:8), Paul emphasizes that God has exhibited the apostles as "men who have been given over to death," and he makes this specific in a list of sufferings in verses 11 and 12. "Down to the present hour" (v. 11) he is suffering hunger and thirst, exposure, buffeting, and so on. Thus affliction still holds sway, oppression still prevails, there is still persecution, and there is still suffering (cf. also v. 13 and Rom. 8:22).

This means, however, that for Paul, sufferings are not only the paradoxical locus and mode of the new life and of the power of Christ, but also a characteristic mark of the *old* aeon. Suffering is not only "suffering with Christ," but also suffering for the yet-unredeemed world and the yet-unfulfilled "re-demption of the body" (Rom. 8:23); until this is accomplished, we "sigh and suffer anxiety" in this "earthly tent" (2 Cor. 5:4). Just as the "mortal body" (Rom. 8:11) and the "mortal flesh" in which, according to 2 Cor. 4:11, we bear about the "dying of Jesus" are assigned to this aeon, so also our sufferings not only signify our belonging to *Christus crucifixus*, but also to the "now" and to the "in part" as over against the "then" and the "perfect" (1 Cor. 13:10, 12).

Moreover, the blows and forces of fate that are enumerated in Rom. 8:38-39 confirm the transient and menacing character of sufferings. It is true that neither things present nor things to come, neither height nor depth, can separate us from God's love, but they obviously attempt to do so. In any case, sufferings are not simply a sign of the love of God and of the *theologia crucis*, but also of all that stands in opposition to this love, is in conflict with it, and therefore is an expression of the *theologia viatorum*. To this extent they are ambivalent. Hence, sufferings can also be understood as issuing from Satan (cf. IV. 2.d). Not until the future consummation will this contradiction disappear. Only the "new Jerusalem" is the place where "God will wipe away all tears from their eyes, and death shall be no more, neither will there be any suffering or crying or pain" (Rev. 21:4). Hence a present time that is free from affliction is an illusion so long as death, as the "last enemy" (1 Cor. 15:26), with his power still has not finally lost the battle and Satan still "buffets" (2 Cor. 12:7) and causes suffering (Rev. 2:10, et passim). Certainly the healings of the sick and the exorcisms signify for Jesus the in-breaking of the eschatological rule of God into this world of suffering and death (cf. Luke 11:20 and V. 5). The defeat of the satanic power of destruction, which has dawned with Jesus, indeed has set in motion the overcoming of the "strong man" and has shaken his dominion by breaking into his "house," but he is not yet fully deprived of his power (cf. Mark 3:26-27); therefore the devout still pray for the definitive coming of the rule of God (Matt. 6:10).

d) Testing

According to the New Testament view, of course, sufferings are not only to rid man of illusions, remind him of the transiency and fragility of all foundations and supports in this world, and point him to the only comfort in life and in death. They are also to test and exercise his faith, and to mobilize his powers of resistance and steadfastness. The insistent emphasis upon patient endurance, particularly in Hebrews and Revelation (cf. Heb. 10:32, 36; 12:1-2; Rev. 2:2-3, 19; 14:12, et passim), but also elsewhere (cf. Mark 13:13; Rom. 12:12; James 5:11; 2 Tim. 2:12), shows that in suffering, the Christian himself is at stake, in the midst of a not-yet-completed process, the meaning and outcome of which will remain undecided so long as this world-epoch lasts. The emphasis upon steadfastness is not to be taken as contradicting the preceding section. Even though Paul's view is by no means focused on any power of his own to bear up under suffering, still according to him the hour of suffering is also the hour of testing (2 Cor. 8:2) and of resistance (1 Cor. 4:12). God's helping presence does not dispense one from his own responsibility to bear and to stand fast, which therefore is connected with faith (2 Thess. 1:4; Rev. 13:10, et passim). His intervention does not occur alongside this bearing and standing fast, but *in* it, and renders it possible. Those who are afflicted, therefore, may know that in the affliction, which will not "go beyond their power," the "way of escape" is the "ability to endure it" that is given by God, and the power of conquest that is given to them has its turn in their bearing up (1 Cor. 10:13). Here it obviously is possible to speak only in paradoxical fashion in light of the subject.

Accordingly, other circumstances also can be seen. Thus joy in suffering, on the one hand, can be traced to the Holy Spirit (1 Thess. 1:6), but, on the other hand, the Christians also can be exhorted to rejoice. "Rejoice always" (1 Thess. 5:16, et passim). Moreover, the patience that is understood as unyielding "standing fast," on the one hand, comes from the "God of patience" (Rom. 15:5), who in accordance with his power "gives strength for all patience and endurance" (Col. 1:11; cf. also 1 Peter 5:10), but, on the other hand, there are repeated admonitions to be patient in suffering (Rom. 12:12, et passim), to refrain from dissatisfied grumbling that assails the sovereignty of God (1 Cor. 10:10), not to shrink back (Heb. 10:38-39), not to grow weary and slack, and not to lose heart (2 Cor. 4:16; Heb. 12:3, 5). Such patience that does not shirk the burden does not mean a merely passive and quietistic endurance, but it always involves an active impetus (cf. 2 Cor. 1:6; 1 Pet. 2:20). Hence, suffering is "struggling" (Phil. 1:29-30; Heb. 10:32); indeed, one may be called upon to participate in the struggle of suffering. "Be my companion in suffering as a brave soldier of Christ Jesus" (2 Tim. 2:3; cf. 1:8). But suffering therefore is also temptation (1 Thess. 3:3 ff.; 1 Pet. 1:6; 4:12; Heb. 2:18; Rev. 2:10). And for this reason, just before a catalog of sufferings that is interwoven with a catalog of charismata or "virtues" (2 Cor. 6:4 ff.), there can stand as a kind of superscription the words "in much patience."

This interweaving of sufferings and charismata certainly is not accidental. It is significant, as is the juxtaposition in the Beatitudes of the Sermon on the Mount (Matt. 5:3 ff.) of the poor, the burdened, and the sorrowing alongside the merciful and the peacemakers. Anyone who is "patient" in suffering obviously remains present, open, and active in relation to his own suffering, but also present, open, and active for others as well. The ability not to shake off one's own burden and the ability to help to bear the burdens of others (cf. Gal. 6:2) cannot be separated from each other; but one's own capacity to suffer always also bestows the strength to share in the sufferings of others (cf. further V. 3). Even in the catalogs of sufferings themselves, there frequently can be some obscurity as to whether the passive or the active motif is more prominent; for example, there is the question whether in 2 Cor. 6:5 the apostle is referring to deprivation of sleep and food, or more to the voluntary refraining from eating and sleeping. But in any case, the one who is suffering is not concerned solely with himself, but the testing of his faith in patience always includes also the testing of the love that "suffers all things" (1 Cor. 13:7). Hence in 1 Thess. 1:3 the writer can attach to the triad of faith, love, and hope, using the genitive forms, the other triad of work, labor, and patience: work, in which faith is worked out; labor, that is rooted in love; and patience, that is generated by hope; all these belong together. Patience is the sign of hope, which, however, does not remain idle or inactive, but opens itself to the affliction of others and forms a unity with the work of faith and love.

According to other statements found in the New Testament, sufferings and afflictions have the aim that "the genuineness of your faith, which is far more precious than perishable gold that is tested by fire, may be demonstrated" (1 Pet. 1:7). Thus faith demonstrates its genuineness in suffering as gold does in the fire. This is a familiar image. "As the crucible tests silver and the furnace tests gold, so the Lord tests hearts" (Prov. 17:3; 27:21; cf. also Wisd. 3:6). The salient point of this figure is the testing and proving, not refining and purifying (as it is, of course, in Pss. 12:6; 66:10; Rev. 3:18). Thus the author of 1 Peter does not intend to affirm a transforming power of suffering and to say that a pure and refined faith is little by little developed "in the fire" (cf. 4:12), that suffering liberates from all the dross of the world and sin and turns one's gaze from peripheral matters to the center; instead, he means to say that "in the fire" of suffering it is revealed what is faith and what is not. Sufferings ultimately only bring out what a person already is, a patient or an impatient person. Suffering is an exercise of faith, a putting-to-the-test, and the crucial instrument of testing (cf. James 1:3, 12). This testing, however, does not simply throw one back upon himself, but patience accomplishes "a perfect work" (1:4), leads to solid, effective work, and causes one to persist, even when "the love of many grows cold" (Matt. 24:12-13) or when one "does right and suffers for it" (1 Pet. 2:20); it causes one to "bring forth fruit in patience" (Luke 8:15)

and to combine patience with "works, love, faith, and service"
(Rev. 2:19; cf. 2:2).

Hope is a constitutive part of "patience" and "steadfastness" (cf. Rom. 8:25); without hope, suffering cannot be
endured. In Rom. 5:3-4 it is said, in a chainlike line of
argument, that Christians, on the basis of their justification (v.
1) and fundamental reorientation, not only rejoice in hope of
the glory of God, but "in tribulations also, knowing that
tribulation works patience, and patience produces character,
and character produces hope, and hope does not put us to
shame." Therewith, suffering is not merely removed from the
context of something that is meritorious and thus also of both
self-confidence and despair; the bold idea is suggested that it
ultimately gives strength to hope. The ascending scale of
tribulation, patience, character, and hope, which has the
appearance of a general truth, of course is anything but a
commonplace fact of experience (*per aspera ad astra*) or even a
didactic maxim ("Be grateful for anything that toughens you").
It rather gives expression to *faith's* knowledge about the
meaning of tribulations. Tribulations are intended to produce
patience, character, and hope. Of course, one may not place too
much emphasis upon the sequence of the individual links in this
chain, since here Paul evidently is referring back to a tradition
that could just as easily change the order, tracing patience back
to character (thus James 1:3). In either case, what is decisive in
such chainlike series, where apparently one feature is
developed out of another, is the beginning and the end, and
thus here, tribulation and hope. The pressure of suffering,
then, does not demolish hope, but strengthens and radicalizes
it, precisely because a hope that is, so to speak, given a hard slap
in the face by painful earthly reality bonds one all the more
firmly to God and grows more sure.

e) Hope

Nevertheless, not only do sufferings evoke hope, and to
this extent are to be affirmatively evaluated; they also cause us
to keep a watch for the end of sufferings, and to this extent they

are relativized by the hope of what is to come. This hope is grounded in and guaranteed by the Christ-event as well as by participation in the "sufferings of Christ" (cf. 2 Cor. 4:14; 13:4; Phil. 3:10; 1 Pet. 1:21; 5:1, et passim). Anyone who "suffers with him" will also be "glorified with him" (Rom. 8:17). Anyone who participates in the sufferings of Christ may also "rejoice and be glad when his glory is revealed" (1 Pet. 4:13 RSV). As far as form is concerned, this corresponds throughout to the Old Testament–Jewish heritage; and thus its form has no connection with the rationale for hope that is now given, in Jesus' death and resurrection.

Apocalyptic in particular has repeatedly emphasized that indeed the present time is filled with trouble, pain, and evils of all kinds, "full of grief and adversity" (4 Esd. 4:27), a "world of unrighteousness" (Ethiopic Enoch 48:7) and "tribulation" (Syriac Baruch 51:14), "trouble and labor with much exertion" (Syr. Bar. 15:8), and so on. It also emphasizes, however, that "what is present is worth nothing, but that which is future is of great value" (Syr. Bar. 44:8), and the present constriction can be endured only in light of the future liberation. After the author of 4 Esdras, for example, has stated that "the paths in this aeon are narrow and grievous and toilsome, wretched and bad, full of dangers and close to great hardships," he points his readers toward the future: "Why do you not take the future to heart, but only the present?" (7:12, 16). "For truly you who within this brief span of time in this perishable world . . . have endured much trouble will receive much light in that world without end" (Syr. Bar. 48:50; cf. also Wisd. 3:5).

In the Gospels, too, present affliction and future salvation are, in keeping with this tradition, repeatedly set over against each other. It is true that the good news of the coming rule of God is announced even now to the poor and miserable, so that it is already near to those who sit on the shadowy side of life, and they can live in its light; indeed, God is already coming to them now in Jesus, but the future, which promises to those who are suffering the coming blessedness and the heavenly reward, is dominant. Those who are reviled and persecuted should rejoice, because great reward awaits them in heaven (Matt.

5:12). "Whoever loses his life for my sake will find it" (Mark
10:39). "Whoever endures to the end shall be saved" (Mark
13:13). All those who now suffer, lament, and grieve will be
comforted (Matt. 5:4). The poor, hungry, weeping, and
persecuted will participate in the rule of God (Luke 6:20-21).
These are no mere delaying tactics, but this future even now
stands, with its promise, above the present that is filled with
suffering, and it is able to give strength and comfort.

Paul says, in corresponding terms, "that the sufferings of
this present time are nothing in comparison with the glory that
is to be revealed to us" (Rom. 8:18). That does not mean that
sufferings have become unimportant, insignificant, trifles. Paul
by no means treats sufferings as trivial—they remain oppressive and burdensome (2 Cor. 1:8; 4:17; 5:4)—but in the
light of what is to come, they acquire a different look and
significance. There is no comparison between them and the
coming glory in value and importance. In the light of the
coming *doxa* everything, even affliction, acquires its proper
perspective and dimensions.

> The slight momentary burden of suffering is producing in us
> in superabundant measure an eternal fullness of glory, when
> we look not at what is visible but at what is invisible. For
> what is visible is transient, but what is invisible is eternal.
> (2 Cor. 4:17-18)

Here too everything is to be understood only from the
perspective of the coming abundance of glory, from which
perspective the dimensions of suffering are diminished and
acquire different proportions of weight and time. What is
decisive is only what is to come and what will abide, the hope of
what now is still invisible (cf. Rom. 8:24-25). The person who
hopes is, by definition, one who hopes against all appearance,
one who maintains his hope even "against" all hope, even when
there is nothing to hope and to see (Rom. 4:17). What is
involved here is not the contrast of visibility and invisibility or
external and internal, but the contrast of present and future.

In this connection, 2 Cor. 4:16 also shows the difference
from the apocalyptic utterances that were cited, in that the

"renewal" does not begin only in the future, not only after and beyond the "wasting away" of the "outer" (= old) man in suffering, but in the very midst of it. Just as Paul in verse 17 grounds his certainty about this present renewal in the prospect of the coming abundance of glory, so in Rom. 8:31-32, conversely, God's saving action in the cross is the guarantee *apocalyptic* that God will "give us all things." Each calls for the other, and they provide reciprocal grounding, the one for the other. The paradox that the "life of Jesus" is manifest even now in the "death of Jesus" and that suffering and weakness provide the locus for the power of Christ is no more to be softened and played down than is the expression of hope that only the future will bring the "swallowing up of mortality by life" (2 Cor. 5:4). The interweaving and alternation of suffering and *doxa* is not an either-or, and therefore is not to be resolved one-sidedly in the sense of apocalyptic. In any case, Paul cannot speak of the present salvation and life without thinking at the same time of the still opposing reality of suffering or without reassuring himself of the future resurrection life along with the "power of his resurrection" that even in suffering is here and now effectual (Phil. 3:10); all that is mortal and painful will be swallowed up in that future resurrection life (2 Cor. 5:4).

In this context it is precisely sufferings that keep open the question of the "redemption of the body" (Rom. 8:23) and give urgency to the resolution of the tension between the "life" that is presently experienced in the depths of suffering (2 Cor. 4:10) and the "transformation of our lowly body into the body of glory" (Phil. 3:21). And it is precisely sufferings that allow us to see through the fragmentary and provisional nature of all that is temporal and direct our gaze to the expectation that we shall live with Christ (2 Cor. 13:4, et passim). It is this future life that gives breath and power even to the life that is concealed under sufferings. In the last analysis, it is only the hope of the resurrection of the dead that gives meaning to the fact that Paul hour after hour places himself in danger, "dies" day after day, and, for example, has to fight with wild beasts in the arena in Ephesus (1 Cor. 15:30-32); it is only this hope that makes it possible for those who mourn even now to mourn "as though they were not mourning (any longer)" (1 Cor. 7:30). God's power of life, in which Paul already trusts even now and which he is already experiencing even in the midst of sufferings, always brings into view the promise of the resurrection from death. Then and then only will God's power definitely and unequivocally be manifested as such and put an end to all sighing. The definitive solution of the question of suffering is only brought by God's universal rule, when he "shall be all in all," all his enemies have been disarmed, and even death, as "the last enemy," is annihilated (1 Cor. 15:26, 28).

Like Paul, the author of 1 Peter also, in the church's situation of distress, set hope before the eyes of the sufferers as a comfort. Already, in the eulogy at the beginning of the Epistle (1:3-12), we read that for the believers there is already prepared the eternal inheritance and salvation that will be revealed in the last time. "In it you will rejoice, you who now for a little time have to suffer various afflictions" (v. 6). It is true that the First Epistle of Peter, like James 1:2, knows also of a present joy in suffering. But this joy is explicitly distinguished from the coming jubilation at the appearing of Jesus Christ. The Christians are to rejoice even in the midst of the "fiery ordeal," because participation in the sufferings of Christ also guarantees a share in his glory, so that they "can rejoice, full of jubilation, at the revelation of his glory" (4:13). Thus Christian joy in the midst of affliction is not mere anticipatory joy, nor is it to be confused in fanatical fashion with eschatological jubilation. It is rather a prelude and a fore-glimmering of the "unutterable and exalted joy" (1:8 RSV) toward which the Christians are moving. Only then will the manifold trials and afflictions, in the presence of which true hope need not close its eyes, come to an end. Likewise for Paul there is joy even in affliction (2 Cor. 8:2), in sorrow (2 Cor. 6:10), and indeed always (1 Thess. 5:16), but the ground and object of this joy are not the sufferings themselves, but the nearness of the Lord (Phil. 4:4-5).

Finally, hope plays a major role—not by accident—in the book of Revelation, to be able to endure the time of suffering in persecution. Here again it is not a hope of an end to the affliction within time, but a hope of the ultimate freedom from affliction, pain, and crying (21:4), when those "who came out of the great tribulation" (7:14) "shall neither hunger nor thirst any more," when they shall be guided by the Lamb to the fountains of living water, and God shall wipe away all their tears (7:16-17). In 21:4 this wiping away of all tears is a consequence of God's bestowing upon the redeemed his biding nearness and presence. The end of affliction and distress, therefore, is found only in the presence of God, but the converse of this also is true: God's nearness and presence signifies the end of distress and death, as well as salvation in the universal horizon of a new heaven and a new earth (21:1). In one of the visions of the Seer that describe the future events and the tribulations of the end time, he hears the cries of the slain martyrs, whose souls are already at the foot of the heavenly altar, "How long . . .?" (6:9-10). Then they were given white garments and told that they "should be patient a little while longer, until the number of their fellow-servants and brothers, who yet must be killed as they had been, should be complete." This comfort is meant for the church under persecution. As in Col. 1:24, here the conception of a measure yet to be fulfilled is adopted; this is meant to say, above all, that the time of suffering of God's oppressed people is limited (cf. also the apocalyptic indications of time in 2:10; 11:2; 13:5) and is to last only "a little while longer" (cf. 12:12).

The theme of the imminent expectation of the end, which is sounded here and elsewhere and which has broken out again and again in the times of the church's suffering and persecution, cannot be set forth and discussed here with all its range of problems. It is, however, in my opinion, only an especially intense form of the expectation of the future. But in any case, one can no more dismiss the dimension of hope by pointing to the unfulfilled imminent expectation than by the modern denunciation of hope as a mere promise of better things in the hereafter or as a diversionary maneuver, aimed at stabilizing the status quo and drawing attention away from the true causes of suffering. Hope led, in primitive Christianity, not to paralysis, but on the one side, to the assimilation of suffering and the exercising of faith, and on the other hand, to the mobilizing of powers of resistance and to actions against suffering (cf. V). Because God's future definitively and universally puts an end to suffering, it is appropriate and requisite not only to endure sufferings in the resources provided by the divine offer of meaning, but also, here and now, to take action against suffering, however partial and fragmentary these actions may be.

f) Witness

As much as sufferings throw the Christian back upon faith and hope, or upon Christ, they always possess also in a peculiar sense the character of a testimony to others, even to non-Christians. The fact that no one suffers alone, but always in fellowship with Christ and with others, also has its effects on those without. When it is announced to the disciples that they will be brought before the local Jewish courts and will be beaten in the synagogues, as well as being brought before governors and kings, it is added, "to bear witness before them" (Mark 13:9 and par.). But what is meant here probably is not an influence on the authorities who are mentioned, by means of a suffering that bears a testimony, but rather a testimony of accusation; that is, the treatment of the Christians makes those responsible guilty and will bear "witness" against them on the day of judgment. In the parallel passage in Luke 21:13, on the other hand, those who are persecuted also become effective witnesses for the gospel, the power of which is demonstrated precisely in the aforesaid situation of suffering (cf. vv. 14 ff.; cf. also Mark 13:11). Of course we do not yet have here the later ecclesiastical usage, according to which a martyrdom itself is a *martyria* (= testimony). Still, Luke also indicates in the book of Acts that sufferings and persecutions do not hinder the spread of the gospel, but rather favor it (cf. the mission in Samaria, in 8:4, and elsewhere, 11:19, that begins in connection with the martyrdom of Stephen, 7:54 ff., and the persecution in Jerusalem, 8:1). It is not unintentional that in 16:25 it is said that the other prisoners were listening when Paul and Silas in prison at midnight were praying and singing hymns. But above all, it is no accident that the confession of the heathen centurion at the cross (Mark 15:39) occurs when he sees the crucified and dying Jesus. This does not mean that Jesus' heroic conduct had been so impressive that the nature of his martyrdom had moved the centurion to make his confession. What is meant is rather that the one who was dying here manifested thereby his divine Sonship, and consequently it can be recognized that contrary to all appearance, Jesus' death is not to be seen as a failure, but as a demonstration and testimony of his divine Sonship.

On the other hand, the words *martys* and *martyria* (= witness and testimony) themselves usually are restricted to reference to the testimony concerning the saving events that have come about through Jesus (Luke 24:48; 1 John 4:14, et passim) or will come about (Rev. 1:2). But because the witness also personally speaks out with this testimony with his whole existence and in so doing possibly risks his very life (Rev. 12:11-12), it is also necessary sometimes to speak of the "blood" of the witnesses, for example, of the blood of the "witness" Stephen (Acts 22:20) or of the "witnesses of Jesus" (Rev. 17:6). Even though the book of Revelation in particular approaches the martyrological concept of the "blood-witness" (= martyr), still the suffering of the witness is not itself actually the testimony. According to the New Testament sense, one suffers because one bears testimony as a witness; it is not that one is a witness because one suffers. Persecution occurs rather "for the sake of the word of God and of the testimony" (Rev. 6:9; 20:4; cf. further III. 1). Thus, the testimony is the ground, not the aim, of the persecution. When the "faithful witness" Antipas is killed (Rev. 2:13), when the two eschatological witnesses are "conquered and killed" (Rev. 11:7), if Rome is full of the blood of the "witnesses of Jesus" (Rev. 17:6), and the raging dragon is waging war against those who hold fast to "the commandments of God and the testimony to Jesus" (Rev. 12:17), what is testified to in each case still is not the suffering, but Jesus.

The author of 1 Peter likewise is a "witness of the sufferings of Christ" in the sense that he participates in them, and thus attests and confesses their reality by his own fate of suffering; however, it is not his own suffering that is the *martyria*, but the suffering of Jesus (5:1). Of course, one addresses others with this testimony, and hence is not concentrating upon his own suffering and his own piety but on the mission to the world; but at the same time he will point away from himself and his own suffering to the one for whose sake he is suffering.

In Paul's thought, suffering also acquires a witnessing function in relation to other Christians as well. Thus, his own daily submission to death in suffering leads to life for others (2 Cor. 4:12; cf. also 6:10). The significance of apostolic suffering for the "advancement of the gospel" (Phil. 1:12) also becomes especially clear where Paul relates that by seeing his imprisonment for Christ's sake others are encouraged to proclaim the Word fearlessly.

> It has become known throughout the whole praetorian guard and to all the rest that my imprisonment is for Christ; and most of the brethren have been made confident in the Lord because of my imprisonment, and are much more bold to speak the word of God without fear.
>
> (Phil. 1:13-14 RSV)

Thus standing the test in suffering is not of individual significance exclusively, but it is contagious. Suffering that has received consolation gives one the capacity to comfort others who suffer. Therefore God is praised as "the one who comforts us in all our trouble, so that we can comfort those who are in any kind of trouble, with the same comfort with which we ourselves are comforted by God" (2 Cor. 1:4). When Paul is comforted in suffering, this is done "for your comfort, which you experience when you patiently endure the same sufferings that we suffer" (2 Cor. 1:6 RSV). God's comfort is meant to flow through the ones who are comforted to the disconsolate, and not to serve only for one's own overcoming of suffering. Thus in suffering, too, God never acts only for the isolated individual, but always for the community (cf. 1 Cor. 12:26, and further V. 3).

Hence, on the one hand, sufferings are the real "commendation" of the one who proclaims the gospel, precisely because they direct attention away from the proclaimer to the power of God, as 2 Corinthians repeatedly makes clear; but just so, on the other hand, they can also confirm and strengthen the trustworthiness of the message of the cross. This holds true particularly for Paul's biography of suffering. Just as his entire existence is an authentic testimony and exposition of the gospel, so are his sufferings in particular, which he carries about as "wound-marks of Jesus on his body" (Gal. 6:17), a visible sign of his apostolic authority under the sign of the Crucified One. And when someone can write to oppressed communities as "your brother, who shares with you in Jesus the tribulation," as does the author of Revelation (1:9), or as one who is acquainted with suffering, not merely from hearsay, but himself bears witness, suffering the "sufferings of Christ," as does the author of 1 Peter (5:1), or when someone can identify himself even in the salutation of an epistle as a "prisoner of Jesus Christ," as Paul does (Philem. 1), this gives additional weight to the writings. However, not only apostles, but other Christians as well can, through their behavior in suffering as suffering witnesses of Jesus, become an "example" (1 Thess. 1:6-7; 2 Thess. 1:4) or, in their suffering, "imitators" of other communities (1 Thess. 2:14-15).

2. Secondary interpretations

In a few instances there appear, alongside the interpretations of suffering that have already been mentioned, other motifs as well, which are to be understood primarily out of the Old Testament–Jewish tradition, but which have only secondary and derivative significance. Some of them have, in fact, acquired a far greater import in the course of church history, and therefore are still today generally recognized and influential. However, according to the New Testament perspective, they should never be given independent status and should always be understood only within the framework provided by the foregoing patterns of thought.

a) Judgment and punishment

In the Old Testament as well as in Judaism the idea that sufferings result from man's sin and guilt and accordingly are to

be viewed as punishment and God's judgment is widespread
(on similar pagan views cf. Acts 28:3 ff.). The real problem, of
course, is not this connection of guilt and suffering, but the
principle, which in Judaism was often derived from it, that sin
and punishment exactly correspond. It is true that the author of
the Syriac Baruch, for example, could say, "What you are
suffering is less than what you have done" (48:5), and people
were aware of suffering as wholesome divine discipline (cf.
IV.2.b), but as a rule, people thought in terms of "measure for
measure." Therefore, when suffering strikes, one should first
examine his own deeds, and only if he found no sins or
omissions would he then think of the discipline of love. But in
the foreground there stood the doctrine of retribution.
Accordingly, the most severe sufferings and catastrophes
presuppose the gravest sins; indeed, one could draw inferences
from a man's sufferings as to the nature and gravity of his faults.

Even Jesus does not deny a connection between sin and
suffering, but he rejects any conclusion as to the particular fault
of the person smitten by suffering. According to Luke 13:1 ff.,
for example, this kind of conclusion is touched upon with
reference to two unfortunate events. Pilate had had some
Galileans killed and their blood mingled with that of the
sacrifices that they had offered. But according to Jesus, that did
not mean that the people who were murdered by Pilate were
more guilty than other people. "Do you think that these
Galileans were worse sinners than all the other Galileans,
because they suffered thus? I tell you, No, but unless you
repent you will all likewise perish" (vv. 2-3). What specific
event lies behind this is not certain, yet in my opinion it is not
necessary to assume a political background, as though the
Galileans had been Zealots and then Jesus would share some of
the blame because he had Galileans and Zealots in the circle of
his disciples. Jesus' answer then is not an implicit criticism of
political-zealot messianic dreams, but of the systematized
explanation of retribution and similar theories about suffering
that discuss the question of other people's guilt. The second
misfortune too, the collapse of a tower in the vicinity of the

fountain of Siloam (v. 4), is for Jesus only a call to repentance, not an occasion for bits of theological reckoning of accounts, processes of drawing conclusions, and attempts at explanation of human suffering. Any calculability and rationalizing of the causal nexus of guilt and punishment is rejected.

Of course Jesus does not actually wage a polemic against an all-too-mechanical application of that causal connection, but he turns the questioners' gaze back upon themselves. Those instances of misfortune are not special punishment for those affected, but they issue a summons to repentance for all. For the most part, of course, in vain! How little "success" sufferings and catastrophes usually have as examples that warn and call to repentance is shown in an especially graphic way by the book of Revelation. Even after the frightful punishment in which a third of mankind was killed, "the rest of mankind, who were not killed by these plagues, did not repent" (9:20 RSV), and even after still other frightful plagues, it is said, "they cursed the name of God who had power over these plagues, and they did not repent and give him glory" (16:9 RSV). While the "people of God" are summoned to an exodus, "lest you take part in her sins, lest you share in her plagues" (Rev. 18:4 RSV), even here strange sufferings and historical judgments prove to be inadequate to bring about repentance. Only when even in God's no the gracious yes can still be heard and it is clear that it is "the goodness of God that leads to repentance" (Rom. 2:4) does true repentance come about.

The story of the healing of the man born blind, in John 9, also points in a similar direction as does Luke 13:1 ff. Here the blind man first becomes the occasion of a conversation about the connection of guilt and suffering. The disciples ask Jesus, "Who sinned, this man himself or his parents, that he was born blind?" (v. 2). The principle that man is punished in the sphere in which he has sinned played a role also in connection with blindness; yet here it is complicated by the fact that the one affected had been born blind. Here too, of course, there were various explanations, two of which the disciples themselves cite. One of them corresponds to the general Old Testament–Jewish view that the guilt of parents is visited upon their children (Exod. 20:5; 34:7; Deut. 5:9, et passim). The other, that the child itself could already have sinned, perhaps is to be understood in terms of isolated rabbinical statements according to which a child can sin even in the womb. A further possible Jewish answer to the question of how one can reconcile with God's justice the fact that men are born blind and similarly handicapped consisted in the suggestion that God's wise foreknowledge seeks to prevent the full unfolding of evil tendencies.

Now it can be considered whether the disciples' question in verse 2 is meant to pose an impossible alternative and thus to demonstrate the absurdity of the dogma of retribution. But at any rate, Jesus' answer turns aside the question that presupposes the idea of retribution and replaces it with the declaration that neither the man born blind nor his parents had sinned, but he was born blind "in order that the works of God might be made manifest in him" (v. 3). Again, the intention is not to deny any connection at all between guilt and suffering (cf. also the warning given in John 5:14 to the paralytic who had been healed, "Sin no more, that nothing worse befall you"), but only the calculability and demonstrability of this connection. The tormented way of thinking that is oriented to the reconstruction of the past, that strives in vain to see through the network of cause and effect with the aid of a belief in retribution, and in so doing makes God a prisoner of a system of retribution, is to be dismissed and replaced by a perspective that looks forward.

This of course does not mean that here the general question of the why? is solved by a similarly general and timeless question of to what end? Jesus' answer, which otherwise corresponds to that in 11:4 ("*in order that* the son of man might be glorified"), instead is closely connected with the person and work of Jesus. Without this christological connection it has as little meaning as does the why question. The real light that Jesus bestows on the man born blind is himself (v. 5). It is not the Evangelist's intention thereby to deny the reality of the physical miracle of the healing of the blind man, but at the same time it becomes transparent to the miracle that Jesus as the light of the world and of life (8:12) opens the eyes of men in darkness. But in any case, the question about suffering is not answered with a reference to an ever-valid cosmic moral law, but rather by God's work in Jesus Christ. The idea of judgment, which is not excluded in Luke 13 and John 9, is also attested by Luke 1:20 and, in a very massive way, by Acts 12:33 and 13:10-11; moreover, it is also applied in 1 Cor. 11:30 to the sufferings of Christians. Here Paul traces instances of illness and death in the Corinthian community back to unworthy, unbrotherly conduct in the observance of the Lord's Supper and explicitly labels this "judgment" (v. 29). This judgment, however, is not regarded as a judgment of condemnation, but is distinguished from that and rather regarded as wholesome discipline. "But when we are judged by the Lord, we are chastened so that we may not be condemned along with the world" (v. 32 RSV). Thus the idea of judgment is not given an independent status, but judgment itself stands in the service of grace. According to 1 Pet. 4:17-19, too, sufferings belong to the judgment that begins "with the household of God." If one takes into consideration also verses 12-14, there is shown here within a little space the dual aspect of suffering, grace, and judgment together (cf. also 2:19 and 4:6). Nevertheless, one will have to say that seen as a whole, according to the New Testament, affliction is not regarded primarily as a sign of sin and judgment, but as a sign of provisionality and of salvation (cf. IV.1).

b) Divine "education"

We have already noted, in the passage cited from 1 Cor. 11:32, the idea of "being disciplined" in the sense of divine "pedagogy" that is meant to serve the improvement of man. As is already suggested by the closeness between discipline and judgment, one may not here cite, by way of explanation, the Greek educational and instructional ideal of the development of character or of intellect. Certainly Seneca can also say that God does not "pamper a good man, but tests him, toughens him, and fashions him for himself" (De providentia 17); but this has to do with the training of one's own powers of resistance to fate and the toughening, indeed the glorification, of the "brave man" *(vir fortis)*. When sufferings are viewed in the New Testament as an instrument of divine discipline, this is undoubtedly to be understood against the background of the Old Testament and Judaism (cf. Deut. 8:5; 11:2; 2 Sam. 7:14-15; Job 5:17-18; Ps. 94:12). A cardinal passage for these ideas, also appropriated in the New Testament, is Prov. 3:11-12:

> My son, do not despise the Lord's discipline
>   or be weary of his reproof,
> for the Lord reproves him whom he loves,
>   as a father the son in whom he delights. (RSV)

From the abundant Jewish documentation for the understanding of suffering as an instrument of divine education only a few items can be cited here. "He (i.e., God) warns the righteous man as a beloved son and disciplines him like a firstborn" (Psalms of Solomon 13:9). This discipline is aimed at improvement (Ps. Sol. 16:11) or expiation (Syr. Bar. 13:10), or at man's becoming "great at last" (Ecclus. 2:3) and experiencing great blessings (Wisd. Sol. 3:5); but even now it becomes "joy and delight" (1 QH 9:24). In contrast to the sufferings of the godless, these, as sufferings that are intended as discipline, are signs of divine approbation, because they anticipate the eschatological punishment and contribute not to destruction but to education (2 Macc. 6:12, et passim) and salvation (Syr. Bar. 48:6). "Blessed are all who are afflicted by your blows, for they will rejoice over you when they all behold your glory and will be able to be joyful for all eternity" (Tob. 13:14). The rabbis in particular were familiar with the understanding of sufferings as reproofs that are prompted by love, that stir us to improvement and purification, that contribute to the expiation of sins and the increase of reward, and that are meant to save us from condemnation hereafter.

The distinction between sufferings understood as discipline, on the one hand, and death and corruption, on the other hand, is also set forth by Paul with reference to Ps. 118:18. As in that passage ("The Lord has chastened me sorely, but he has not

given me over to death," RSV), so here also it is said within a
catalog of sufferings, "as chastened and yet not slain" (2 Cor.
6:9). Of course, nothing is said to suggest a meritorious or
expiatory significance of this discipline. Paul could never have
said, like the Talmud, that through discipline we gain the future
world. There is also lacking the idea that at the end the
unrighteous will suffer a terrible judgment. However, for Paul
too, the gracious God is also the disciplining God, whose
discipline is experienced in sufferings. The book of Revelation
too, appropriating Prov. 3:12, attests the same ideas. "I punish
and discipline all whom I love" (3:19). On the other hand, the
Deutero-Pauline passage in 2 Thess. 1:4 ff. is to be understood
more decidedly in the Jewish sense; here the persecutions and
sufferings of the Christians are understood as signs of the
righteous judgment of God, who by means of this present
affliction renders them worthy of the kingdom of God, while the
oppressors will receive their punishment only when the
circumstances of suffering are reversed (cf. also Luke 16:25).

The real representative in the New Testament of a divine
paideia, however, is the book of Hebrews; there we read:

> You have forgotten the admonition that addresses you as
> sons: "My son, do not despise the Lord's discipline, and do
> not become discouraged when you are chastised by him. For
> whom the Lord loves he disciplines, and he chastens every
> son whom he receives." It is for discipline that you endure
> suffering. God is treating you as sons. For what son is there
> whom the father does not discipline? But if you are without
> discipline, in which all have shared, then you are illegitimate
> children and not sons. Again: we have had our earthly fathers
> as teachers, and we had respect for them. Should we not then
> much more be obedient to the Father of spirits and (in this
> way) live? For they exercised their disciplines as they
> pleased for a little while, but he disciplines us for our good,
> that we might gain a share in his holiness. Any discipline
> seems at the moment, to be sure, not a pleasant but a painful
> thing, but later it brings to those who are trained by it the
> peaceful fruit of righteousness. (12:5-11)

The idea of *paideia*, which Paul touches upon only briefly, is here developed broadly. It is the central category of the passage, in which it appears no fewer than eight times. What is involved here is not the understanding of any and all suffering. Suffering under the sign of gracious divine discipline here is rather the consequence of the struggle that is ordained for Christians and of their "running the race with patience" (v. 1), and it grows out of their holding fast to their confession and the perils that threatened them as a result (cf. 4:14-15, et passim). Hence it is not necessary to think primarily about already experienced persecutions or painful blows of fate, as in 10:32-34—this period evidently lies in the past—but at least as much of weariness, disappointment, and resignation in ordinary, everyday practice of piety (cf. the preceding and following vv. 3 and 12-13). The "race" that is set for the Christians (v. 1) is a long-distance race, in which only those who are "trained" (cf. v. 11) will persevere.

According to the passage quoted, however, suffering is primarily the suffering of sons, whose sonship is grounded and mediated by the Son (2:5 ff.). But the Son himself had to "learn" obedience through suffering (5:8), being led step by step to "perfection." This certainly is to be understood primarily in soteriological terms (cf. 5:9 and 2:9-10), but it also makes it clear to the son in an example that sonship does not exempt one from the "learning" that comes by suffering. Here this is not merely a formal and secular idea, as it is repeatedly attested elsewhere in antiquity (cf. Herodotus I.207: "My sufferings have become instruction to me;" cf. also Aeschylus, *Agamemnon* 146-47, among others); instead, it is given content by the christological definition of the learning process. Because the Christians are sons for the sake of the Son, they too, like the Son, are subject to the *paideia* of God. In contrast to Proverbs 3, the address ("my son") in 12:5, therefore, is not simply the stylistic form of the wisdom-teaching; instead, those who are addressed are addressed *as sons* with respect to their sonship. But one aspect of their sonship is their being brought under discipline through suffering. Just as earthly fathers discipline their children in the process of training them, so God too enrolls those who belong to him in a hard school. We should not let ourselves be too greatly irritated by this parallel in our age of a repression-free, anti-authoritarian pedagogy. Here no pedagogical recommendation for the practice of corporal punishment is offered, but it is noted that reference is made even to fathers whose way of rearing their children was marked by limited insight and arbitrariness; the educational practice of these fathers is in no way praised, by no means in all particulars. Their harshness is neither subjected to criticism nor romantically glorified. It remains a painful occurrence, which to be sure—and here this parallel certainly will lack convincing proof for many—in the end proves to be beneficial (v. 11). But so much the more, in the author's opinion, in the relationship of the suffering Christians to God it is not rebellion but obedient submission that is the sign of those whom this God encounters as Father, even in their painful and distressing experiences. If sufferings are the mark and guarantee of sonship, then those who suffer are already, as those subjected to discipline, "accepted" and "beloved" (v. 6). This is the crucial point, even though there still is enough that is enigmatic, and the author offers no patented key to a rationally demonstrable teleology of all individual experiences of suffering.

c) God's will

Even apart from the biblical testimony it is known that affliction is not necessarily simply a case of meaningless arbitrariness on the part of the gods or of blind accidental fate, but can be "God's own arrangement" (Sophocles, *Oedipus Coloneus* 1694). But Jewish apocalyptic, in particular, is marked by a thoroughgoing determination of the course of time and sees everything that happens in heaven and on earth as predetermined in detail from all eternity, "He has overlooked nothing, even down to the smallest detail, but has . . .foreseen and foreordained everything" (Assumption of Moses 12:4-5; cf. also 4 Esd. 4:37). It is true that the divine "must" is related primarily to the events of the end (cf. Dan. 2:28-29), but included in this divinely predetermined category of all divine events are sufferings also, which in fact will increase at the end.

"In the last days the inhabitants of this world will *have* to be brought low by much affliction" (4 Esd. 8:50). "They *must* see many oppressions and afflictions" (4 Esd. 13:19; cf. also 1 QS 3:23, et passim). This foreordination evidently was perceived as a comfort: "Your spirit should not be troubled because of the evil times, for the Great and Holy One has determined days for all things" (Eth. Enoch 92:2).

The New Testament too, in spite of the fact that it likewise is acquainted with human action as causing suffering, can just as definitely identify God himself or his will as the cause of suffering. This finds expression particularly in the "must" that is adopted from apocalyptic. Such "must" certainly also accentuates other motifs as well, such as the moral commandment (1 Thess. 4:1; Acts 5:29), the fulfilling of Scripture (Matt. 26:54; Luke 24:44), the necessity of salvation (John 3:7, Acts 4:12), or the course of salvation-history (Mark 9:11; 13:10) and events of the end time (1 Cor. 15:25; Mark 13:7). But it is of interest here above all as an expression of the belief that even sufferings come from God's hand and are in keeping with his will; in this connection, however, various ones of the other motifs mentioned can also play a role here and there. Just as the Son of man "*must* suffer many things" (Mark 8:31 and par.), it is said also of Christians that they *must* suffer and through many tribulations enter into the kingdom of God (Acts 14:22; 9:16; Rev. 13:10, et passim). What is involved here is not simply a constitutive part of an apocalyptic timetable or a blind, impersonal necessity of fate, but rather God's plan. According to the New Testament, however, there comes into play also the dimension of divine freedom and of the distance from any compulsory, inescapable determination. In 1 Pet. 1:6 it is said—and this is not accidental—that those who are addressed "now for a little while may *have to* suffer various trials" (RSV; cf. a similar idea in 3:17: "if that should be God's will"). Thus, there is no dominant idea here of a mechanically operating cosmic law or a rationally calculable sequence of events, but God alone knows whether and when Christians *must* suffer. Possibly the "must," after all, is only an interpretation *a posteriori* and is utilized primarily when sufferings have already appeared and there is no escape, but a person still maintains God's purpose and saving intention, in spite of all the enigmas. In Rev. 13:10, for example, it evidently is presupposed that flight is ruled out and resistance to the imperial power is senseless (cf. v. 7). However, even there one should not adopt an attitude of resignation, but should cooperate, in assurance and with a free will, with what comes to him in accordance with God's plan. "If any one is to be taken captive, to captivity he goes; if any one slays with the sword, with the sword he must be slain. Here is a call for the endurance and faith of the saints" (Rev. 13:10 RSV).

It is noteworthy that the specific identification of the *will of God* in the context of the subject of suffering plays a rather minor role and except in Jesus' prayer in Gethsemane and in 1 Peter appears only in a very few places. We have already noted (in II. 1. b) in connection with Mark 14:32 ff. that Jesus' suffering is not *eo ipso* accepted, and a distinction is maintained between what Jesus wills and what God wills; thus, there is no utterance in advance, as wholly self-evident and a matter of principle, of the attitude of "May whatever my God wills be done always." The "if possible" (v. 35) shows that it is possible for the "cup" to "pass," and thus God is not impersonal fate, with whom any prayer would be meaningless, but the Father, with whom all things are possible. The submission to his will stands not at the beginning but only at the end. Moreover, it is not reached through any new insights—there is not a word to suggest that the enigma of his sufferings has been solved for Jesus or that he now has found another meaning for his situation—but through prayer and obedience. This is obedience, however, not in the sense of acquiescence in a will of God that has been fixed in advance and now has become manifest, nor in the sense of a resigned fatalistic yes to an inescapable fate, but the obedient yes to the One who as Father is near at hand and whose fatherly yes is the content of his will. Matthew has assimilated Jesus' prayer (Matt. 26:39) more decidedly to the petition in the Model Prayer (Matt. 6:10). There too, the prayer is not for the power to fulfill God's will or for acquiescence in it—this in itself shows the parallelism to the two preceding petitions, where what is involved in both cases is an eschatological event that will issue from God (cf. v. 6)—but rather that God himself may cause his will to prevail throughout the world.

To be sure, this will, as the will of the absolutely preeminent God, is not subject to man's critical prying—"O man, who then are you, that you should argue with God?" (Rom. 9:20)—but the crucial thing is not God's *potestas absoluta*, for which he owes no man an accounting, but his free mercy. It is repeatedly emphasized in the New Testament that God's will is not irrational and arbitrary, but a salvific purpose. "It is the will of your Father that not one of these little ones should perish" (Matt. 18:14; cf. John 6:40; Gal. 1:4, et passim). "God wills for all men to be saved and to come to the knowledge of the truth" (1 Tim. 2:4). There are equally clear and forthright statements about the will of God as the real criterion of the new life, about the way to test and to discern it (cf. Rom. 12:2), and above all about the doing and fulfilling of it (Mark 3:35; Matt. 7:21; 1 Pet. 4:2, et passim). This will that has salvation as its aim remains unwavering and steadfast.

On the other hand, where the New Testament speaks of God's will in the sense of the guiding and directing of human destiny, the way of speaking is much more reserved and marked by qualifications. "I shall come to you if it is the Lord's will" (1 Cor. 4:19; cf. Rom. 1:10; Acts 18:21, et passim); or, "If the Lord wills, and we live, we shall do this and that" (James 4:15). First Pet. 3:17 shows that, accordingly, even in connection with suffering, the will of God was spoken of more reservedly, that is, as a hypothetical case (in the Greek, the *optativus potentialis*) and an uncertain possibility. "If it should be God's will" (cf. 3:14, "Even if you should suffer"). This certainly does not rule out the possibility that those who suffer "suffer in accordance with God's will" and precisely for that reason can "entrust their lives to the faithful Creator" (1 Pet. 4:19), but it makes it difficult to trace any suffering directly to the will of God.

In addition to the passages from 1 Pet., Acts 21:14 also can be adduced here. When Paul, in spite of prophetic warnings and in spite of the urging of his companions that he should not go to Jerusalem (Acts 20:23; 21:4, 11-12), declares his readiness to suffer and die, these companions say, "The will of the Lord be done." This indeed demonstrates the apostle's great readiness to suffer, but it likewise bears witness to an almost fatalistic conception of the will of God that is typical of Luke: in Luke's writings there is also a strong emphasis upon God's "foresee-ing," "predestination," and "foreordination" (Acts 2:23; 4:28; et passim), against which all resistance is of no avail (cf. Acts 26:14; 5:38-39).

John 21:18 in particular shows that the will of God, which is superior to man, is not meant to condemn man to pure passivity or quietistic resignation. There, in a figure of speech, Peter's martyrdom is announced to him. "Another will gird you and lead you where you do not want to go;" verse 19 then interprets this to refer to the violent death toward which Peter was moving. But this does not correspond to his own will, but to that of someone else, to which he must conform. Thus although the ways of the Lord are not his ways, yet there follows the injunction, "Follow me" (v. 19). This clearly shows the relatedness of activity and passivity. If it is precisely suffering that demonstrates that someone else has become Lord over Peter, still this is to be consciously accepted and freely affirmed.

In view of the current Christian usage of language, which often makes a direct connection between suffering and the will of God, this reserve that the New Testament manifests needs to be noted. In it there is expressed, not only the awareness of God's sovereignty and superiority (cf. Rom. 9:18, 22), and all the more, not only the hope of being preserved from suffering in the individual case, but also the awareness that according to God's will, affliction actually should *not* be and not every affliction is in keeping with his will.

d) The work of Satan

In my judgment, the same is also indicated by the fact that God's adversary or the demonic forces are made responsible for suffering, as is the case particularly in the book of Revelation. In the letter to the church of Smyrna, for example, the Seer writes,

"Do not fear what you will suffer. Behold, the devil will put some of you in prison, so that you may be tested, and you will have tribulation for ten days" (Rev. 2:10; cf. further 12:12-13, but also 1 Pet. 5:8-9, where the devil is to be seen in the roving roaring lion that is concealed behind the sufferings). From the limitation of the imprisonment, of course, it is made clear that the sovereignty of the devil is limited and that in spite of the devil's machinations, God himself holds history in his hand, and indeed is following his own plan (cf. the *passivum divinum*, which points to the divine purpose and the divine concession). Similarly, in Rev. 13:7 the passive voice is used in speaking of the beast's attack upon the saints, "It was given to him to conquer them" (cf. also 11:7). Thus, in spite of all the satanic victories, the saints remain in the hands of God.

Along with the book of Revelation, we should here cite 2 Cor. 12:7, where Paul traces his sufferings to a buffeting by a messenger of Satan. "So that I might not be too exalted, a thorn in the flesh was given to me, a messenger of Satan, to buffet me to keep me from being too exalted." Here too the passive voice, "was given," is noteworthy; this once again shows that it is ultimately God who gives even Satan his power. At the same time, the doubled purposive clause at the beginning and the end gives assurance that the messenger of Satan ultimately must carry out God's commission and is in God's service. He is to guard Paul against undue exaltation.

Just as Paul in 2 Cor. 12:7 traces his illness to Satan, in the Gospels part of the responsibility for illnesses is placed upon the demons, which harass men with their destructive powers. The end of the demons' dominion, conversely, signals the dawning of the rule of God (cf. V. 5). This does not mean that every illness is regarded as caused by demons or as demon possession (cf. the differentiation in Mark 1:34); however, even persons who suffer physical affliction, such as the blind and deaf-mutes, can be regarded as demoniac (Matt. 12:22), or in the case of a woman who was bent and could not stand erect one could speak of an "(evil) spirit of infirmity" and of being bound by Satan (Luke 13:11, 16). Even if one demythologizes this ancient demonology, still it remains that illnesses stand in opposition to the dawning rule of God, and therefore, conversely, the "healing of those whom the devil has in his power" is a sign that God is with Jesus (Acts 10:38).

Now the problem lies in the fact that sometimes affliction is understood as the will of God and sometimes as the work of Satan, and thus the same phenomenon now can be traced to God and again to Satan. The same thing holds true not only for illness but also for temptation (cf. Matt. 6:13 or 1 Thess. 3:5), obstinacy, and blindness (cf. Rom. 9:18 or 2 Cor. 4:4), and even for such concrete experiences as the hindering of plans for a visit (cf. Rom. 1:13 or 1 Thess. 2:18). An explanation that strictly follows the history-of-traditions pattern, deriving one of these lines from the Old Testament (cf. e.g., Amos 3:6) and the other from the more strongly dualistic apocalyptic, cannot suffice, particularly since both traditions appear in one and the same author. But we are also forbidden to proceed from cleanly divided spheres of competence and realities of experience, because they are in fact the same phenomena for which now God and again the devil is supposed to be responsible. Moreover, it would be utterly out of harmony with the New Testament to concede to the devil and the powers of evil certain autonomous spheres, not subject to God, where they can reign and hold sway as sovereign. Finally, it is impossible simply to shift the distinction to the subjective point of view of the person affected, as though one saw it in this way today and in a different way tomorrow. It is indeed, for example, one and the same man, in one and the same situation, who in 2 Cor. 4:4 sees the devil at work and in 2 Cor. 3:14 sees God at work (cf. the passive formulation).

One can, in fact, see the distinction only in the different motivation, tendency, and intention of divine and devilish actions. Satan aims at the corruption of man (cf. 2 Cor. 4:4, "to keep them from seeing the light of the gospel," RSV), while God is aiming in all things at man's salvation. According to Rom. 11:32, God has subjected all to disobedience, "in order to have mercy on all"; here "everything" is working together "for good," that is, for salvation (Rom. 8:28). The affliction that is in accordance with God's will "produces repentance that leads to

salvation" (2 Cor. 7:10 RSV). God's *opus proprium,* the work
that is really his, is that of showing mercy, even in his *opus
alienum,* his strange work. This can lead to the inversion of what
is expected, as in Mark 8:33, where the hindering of Jesus'
suffering is characterized as satanic. Nevertheless, suffering
still is not God's own proper work, as is confirmed not only by
the eschatological expectation (Rev. 21:4, et passim), but also
and especially by the following section of our study, where the
conquest of suffering as God's work and God's commission is
central.

V. The mastery and conquest of suffering

Because the New Testament has something to offer in and
against suffering, it is not silenced in the face of the manifold
sufferings of this world; but what it has to say is not merely a
message of comfort, but is just as actively engaged in
combatting suffering. Hence, on the whole, suffering, as such,
is never made the theme, but is discussed in the context of its
possible mastery and conquest. Of course, even the *interpretation* of suffering, with all its various suggestions of meaning, is
a form of handling and mastery of suffering. For if the sufferer
comes to grips with his affliction and is able to wring some
meaning from it, he takes away from it its sharpness, even if it is
only that he now suffers while hoping against hope (Rom. 5:2-3;
8:24, et passim). And when those who suffer know that they are
suffering in fellowship with Christ (2 Cor. 1:5; 1 Pet. 4:13), that
nothing is able to separate them from the love that has been
made manifest in Jesus Christ (Rom. 8:35 ff.), and that "the
very hairs of their heads are numbered" (Matt. 10:30), the
suffering has taken on a new visage. Therefore our chapter 4
actually would have to stand under the general heading of the
following pages.

But primitive Christianity not only attempted to comprehend suffering and to integrate it into its faith and hope, but it also took direct action against suffering and, like Jesus, strove to soften it or to put an end to it wherever that was possible. Even though there was no explicit reflection upon the distinction between sufferings that can be eliminated and those that persist, with all the overlapping, such a differentiation still was indirectly achieved. Of course ultimately, there is no affliction that is regarded as intrinsically unconquerable, and in no affliction—not even in the temporary or curable kind—is one dismissed from the fellowship with Christ or removed from God's hand. The same God who comforts those who are bowed down also gives comfort, for example, through the arrival of a man who has long been missed and yearned for (2 Cor. 7:6). But most of all, Jesus himself not only pointed those who suffered to God's future, but in a comprehensive way stood up to the affliction and misery of this world and in accordance with the holistic view of suffering (cf. I.2) also brought to man holistic help and salvation. Wherever men fall among robbers or hunger or thirst, are strangers or ill-clad, sick or in prison, there his people are called upon to provide effectual remedies to such sufferings (Luke 10:25 ff.; Matt. 25:31 ff.). Nowhere, then, is there found any legitimizing of factors and causes that produce suffering, and nowhere is there any attempt artificially to prolong suffering. Because all glorification of suffering is lacking, we find again and again words of praise and thanksgiving when a person has been rescued from the peril of death (2 Cor. 1:10), from sufferings and persecutions (2 Tim. 3:11), or "from the mouth of the lion" (2 Tim. 4:17).

1. No pseudo-solutions

With some exceptions, the New Testament confronts suffering in an extraordinarily sober way and without illusions. This accounts for the fact that pseudo-solutions to the mastery of suffering are lacking or are subjected to criticism. But one also seeks in vain for current motifs of comfort of the environment and tradition. That the sufferings of other men are

SUFFERING IN THE NEW TESTAMENT

even greater than one's own (cf. Syr. Bar. 80:7), that the days of suffering will be followed again by days of joy (cf. Eccl. 3:1 ff.), that the good fortune of the ungodly will not last long (cf. Ps. 37:10, 35-36)—these and similar trains of thought are not found here. Even less is there any suggestion that one drink in order to forget one's distresses (cf. Prov. 31:6-7). Even the most highly moral and rational arguments of the philosophical writings of consolation, such as are found, for example, in those of Seneca to Polybius (cf. also those to Marcia or to Helvetia), are almost all without New Testament parallels: that it is the greatest comfort to think that all that a man suffers has been suffered by all others before him and will be suffered hereafter by all others (1:4); that no household on earth is or has been without sorrow (14:2); that pain is of no use (2:1), and tears do not set anything right (4:1); that one should conceal and master his pain (5:5), and the fulfillment of one's obligations does not allow one to feel pain (7:1 ff.); that one should have regard to public opinion and one's own position (6:1 ff.); that in view of earlier good fortune and the abiding remembrances of it, affliction is no injustice (10:1 ff.); that the body is only the "prison and fetter of the soul" (*To Helvetia* 11:7); that time heals all wounds (*To Marcia* 8:1); and so on. None of this is found in the New Testament. Even more alien to the New Testament are all attempts to find oblivion in schemes or labor, in indulgence or intoxication.

But the New Testament also avoids the way of suggestion and auto-suggestion, of mysticism and ecstasy, of cult and religiosity. We shall see further that a massive belief in miracles and magic appears relatively seldom, even though, of course, there can be no doubt about the New Testament belief in miracles. To be sure, it has often been asserted that mystical efforts to migrate into timelessness, to gain identity with deity, or to be mystically absorbed into deity, are not alien, at least to Paul; but this is based upon a misunderstanding that disregards particularly the abiding difference between the Redeemer and the redeemed in Paul's thought. It is true that ecstatic phenomena cannot entirely be denied, yet it is characteristic of Paul to return to his continuing illness and weakness precisely in the context of a visionary "heavenly journey of the soul" (2 Cor. 12). We hear nothing of cultic and sacramental practices in connection with overcoming suffering (on James 5:14 cf. V. 5); but even those who think here and there they can detect tendencies in this or that direction cannot escape the fact that the crucial categories still are different. Because affliction causes pain and death remains the "last enemy" (1 Cor. 15:26), furthermore, there is no martyr ideology or fanatical pursuit of suffering in the New Testament. Paul, for example, yearns for the redemption of the body (not, let it be noted, *from* the body! Rom. 8:23) and not for suffering. Indeed, he would be glad to have "less trouble" and not "trouble upon trouble" (Phil. 2:27-28).

2. The avoidance of suffering

How little affliction is sought after or yearned for, minimized or glorified, is illumined by the striking fact that there are various attempts and counsels to avoid suffering. In this connection, the starting point is the observation that is obvious to everyone, that man himself causes for himself and for others a great deal of suffering through his life and conduct. It is perfectly obvious that anyone who squanders everything in riotous living will end up in hunger (cf. Luke 15:14), that the person who is greedy for money will "pierce himself with many pangs" (1 Tim. 6:10), that the tongue can be "a restless evil, full of deadly poison" (James 3:1 ff. RSV), capable of utterly universal destructive effects, and so forth. It is not accidental that there are numerous parallels for these and similar utterances in the rules for living found in the Old Testament–Jewish wisdom-teaching and in the Hellenistic popular philosophy. However, the New Testament authors see in such causes of suffering the symptoms of a more profound disruption and perversion of human life. That is, the sentences that were quoted above were written with the primary concern, not the avoidance of suffering, but rather the avoidance of sin. But sin is not an abstract and theoretical phenomenon, its power is exhibited also in its perceptible effects that ruin lives (cf. Rom.

1:24 ff.). When Paul describes the universal sinful plight of man, this sounds in some places, not accidentally, like a catalog of sufferings, even though in this case the victims of the sins are other people:

> Their throat is an open tomb; they lie with their tongues. The poison of asps is under their lips. Their mouth is full of cursing and bitterness. Their feet are swift to shed blood. Ruin and wretchedness are in their paths, and they have never known the path of peace.
>
> (Rom. 3:13-17)

Thus anyone who wishes to do away with suffering must take into account the fact that sin will cause renewed suffering. Accordingly, admonitions such as James 3:8 ff., and similar ones, aim at limiting the spread of suffering brought on by one's own deeds, in oneself or in others, by a kind of blockade of sin. But even where Christians in this world that is filled with sin and suffering are threatened by others, there is the possibility of avoiding unnecessary affliction. Moreover, one who knows that even in doing good Christians may expect to suffer (1 Pet. 2:20) still would like to spare his communities unnecessary suffering, as does the author of 1 Pet., for example; and he hopes that this will be accomplished primarily through a proper manner of life (2:12; 3:13, et passim; cf. also the quotation from Ps. 34:12-16 in 1 Pet. 3:10-12, and on this see I.1.c).

The exhortations to guard against self-induced affliction become, particularly in the late New Testament times, quite homey and prosaic, plain and in set phrases, but there is also an altogether too appropriate criticism of these paraenetic utterances about a "rational" manner of life. Hence, before any disparagement of the exhortations of this sort in the so-called Pastoral Epistles, it should be noted that the author is writing in a time when there is a danger that the church will slip into the speculative, ascetic, and apocryphal, and when, in the author's opinion, only a respect for the "natural" order and pattern of life is a safeguard against unnecessary suffering. As an example, we may cite the high regard for moderation. "But if we have food and clothing, with these we shall be content. But those who desire to be rich fall into temptation, into a snare, into many senseless and hurtful desires that plunge men into ruin and destruction" (1 Tim. 6:8-9 RSV). Typical also is the attitude toward the enjoyment of wine; one should not be addicted to an excessive use of wine (1 Tim. 3:3; Titus 1:7; 2:3), but then with reference to abstinence from wine it is said, "No longer drink only water, but use a little wine for the sake of your stomach and your frequent ailments" (1 Tim. 5:23 RSV). This "middle way" certainly is not simply the way of Jesus, yet it should not be overlooked that, on the one hand, Jesus was reviled as a "glutton and winebibber" (Matt. 11:19), and thus asceticism was not his program, but on the other hand, his conduct of life was characterized by a very modest and frugal style (cf. Matt. 8:20, et al.).

Sometimes the way of avoiding suffering is described as a balancing of two attitudes, both of which indeed bring with them trouble, but one of which is less painful than the other. According to Paul, for example, the affliction of married people can only be intensified in the approaching tribulation of the end-time, and for this reason too—though of course his main reason was another—he advised against marriage. "Those who marry will have troubles in the flesh [i.e., in the earthly and creaturely humanness, physical existence, and contingency]; but I would like to spare you that" (1 Cor. 7:28). But on the other hand, Paul takes into account the reality of sexuality and knows that a person can be consumed in the fire of sexual desire, and for this reason he advises those who are thus concerned to marry, for "it is better to marry than to burn (i.e., in the flames of sexual desire)" (1 Cor. 7:9; cf. also 7:36). Of course, the real criterion is usually not the measure of one's own suffering, but that of others. Therefore it is better to suffer than to cause someone else to suffer (cf. 1 Cor. 6:7). Those who utter curses and abuse, for example, are not to be repaid in kind, but restraint is commanded in order to halt the unwholesome chain-reaction of the *action* that causes suffering and then is followed by the *reaction* that causes still further suffering (Luke 6:28 and par.); this is not because the painful experience is to be handled internally by oneself, but because the vicious circle with its pain-producing automatic reaction is to be overcome by the good (cf. also Rom. 12:21, et passim). Nevertheless, one's own suffering is not made obligatory under all circumstances.

This is shown, even more clearly than in the avoidance of suffering, by the frequently discussed subject of *flight* from suffering, usually that of persecution. From the very earliest period, when people still lived in the expectation of the imminent end, the saying is handed down: "When they persecute you in this city, flee to another. Truly I say to you, you will not go through all the cities of Israel before the Son of man comes" (Matt. 10:23). This motif of flight is also encountered elsewhere (Mark 13:14; Matt. 24:16, 20; Rev. 12:6), and it certainly is fully understandable only in the context of the eschatological utterances. But it nevertheless makes it clear that there are legitimate possibilities of avoiding suffering. The driving motive here is not a lack of readiness to suffer, but rather the idea of mission and ministry, for example the missionary obligation to other cities as well; that is, the disciples; missionary commission takes precedence over the motif of suffering. It is not suffering but the mission that is of prime importance. A yearning for martyrdom that is more interested in one's own perfection than in service to others is foreign to the New Testament. In the commissioning of the Twelve (Matt. 10:16-17), Jesus explicitly commends to the disciples the proverbial cunning of the serpent and self-protection against men (Matt. 10:16-17), which certainly does not mean flight from the world or a renunciation of their commission (cf. 10:27), but it does show an awareness that there are also unnecesary confrontations and sufferings.

According to the Gospel of John, even Jesus himself, when people wanted to stone him as a blasphemer, "hid" himself in order to escape them (John 8:59; cf. also Matt. 12:15). This "hiding" may indeed be subject to a twofold interpretation (cf. 7:10; 12:36), because Jesus and his revelation have eluded the world's grasp; there may also be the idea of a miraculous disappearance, because Jesus' "hour had not yet come" (cf. 7:30; 8:20; 10:39). But whatever the motivation of the hiding was, Jesus escapes suffering and death, even though it is only a postponement. In Matt. 2:13 ff., Joseph's secret flight with Mary and Jesus to Egypt is even traced to an explicit message from an angel, which was designed to save the child's life from Herod's persecution. Of course, it is God's intention specifically with this flight to preserve him for his mission, which indeed is a mission to death, and to fulfill his promise. The flight, which makes Jesus even as a child a refugee and a hunted prey, thus is something temporary, which moreover is itself already an indication of Jesus' destiny of suffering; and thus to this extent it is at one and the same time preservation and suffering.

We hear a few times in primitive Christianity of a flight of the apostles (Acts 9:25; 14:5-6). Paul himself tells in 2 Cor. 11:32-33 about a flight over the city walls of Damascus in order to escape the persecution of the ethnarch of Aretas, who had the city gates under guard. Since Paul relates this in the immediate context of a catalog of sufferings, one can accordingly count the flight itself, even here, among the sufferings. To this extent, what is involved is not so much a flight from suffering as a flight which itself is undertaken in the service of the gospel and is intended above all to be a precaution against the ultimate penalty or even against imprisonment.

On the other hand, it is equally clear that there are boundaries to this possibility of fleeing which one may not cross, as becomes evident particularly in the case of Jesus himself. He could not very well have avoided the conflict with the Jewish authorities; indeed, without that confrontation with them he probably would have won far more followers. But in the crucial issue there was for him no "tactical move," no compromise, no watering-down of his message, and thus also no avoidance of suffering. Jesus was no "hireling" (John 10:12), who flees in the hour of peril, but "the good shepherd," whose main concern is not his own safety, but the welfare of the "sheep," and who in fact lays down his life for them (10:11). But he also demands the same of his followers (15:13-14). Above all, the *status confessionis* rules out any "denial" and timidity in the face of suffering.

The best known and most memorable example of such "denial" is that of Peter, who in the court of the high priest did not dare to confess his Lord. The same man who, according to Acts 4:20, says before the Sanhedrin, "It is impossible for us to keep silent about what we have seen and heard," is so disconcerted by the mere assertion of a girl that he too was a companion of Jesus, that he cursed his Lord (Mark 14:66 ff. and par.). It is worth pondering that a rather innocent, perhaps malicious, but by no means inquisitorial or aggressive, assertion brings about Peter's fall. Situations in which a confession is called for, not before emperor and king, an imposing tribunal or audience, but before an altogether unceremonial everyday forum, are evidently the ones that really are dangerous. It is not a readiness to die and a confession in the limelight of the public that is most of all demanded, but steadfastness and readiness to suffer in apparently unimportant moments. Here we are called upon to stand, perhaps to suffer, and with Heb. 10:39 to confess: "But we are not of those who shrink back" (cf. also Rev. 21:8).

Flight from painful situations is also forbidden where obedience to God's commandments or to love would thus require. Here again, it is not the avoidance of distress that is the supreme good. Thus it is better "to go into life maimed or lame than with hands or feet to be cast into eternal fire" (Matt. 18:8; cf. 18:9; Heb. 11:25, but also Jesus' first temptation in Matt. 4:3-4). "We must obey God rather than men" (Acts 5:29), even when this brings sufferings upon us. Impermissible "flight" occurs then primarily when, in a situation where the demonstration of love is called for in the presence of distress, one passes by the person who has fallen among thieves (Luke 10:31-32) or refuses to share the sufferings of others (cf. the examples in V.3).

Nevertheless, the examples of people taking flight show that one does not in these cases seek to suffer, but rather endures suffering and in so doing, from case to case, gives careful consideration to the question of when suffering is necessary and when it is not. Paul, for example, would rather depart and be with Christ (Phil. 1:23), because in this world-epoch he lives as one who is oppressed, groaning, yearning for the Lord (2 Cor. 5:1 ff.); but he knows that for the church it is more needful for him to remain alive, because even his suffering brings benefit to them all, "for advance and joy in the faith" (Phil. 1:24-25). Painful rifts and tensions in the family can be altogether necessary in conflicts for the sake of the kingdom of God (Luke 2:48-49; 12:52-53; 18:29), but not divorce (cf. Mark 10:2 ff.) or escape from a mixed marriage, even though this marriage certainly brings with it suffering (1 Cor. 7:12-13). It is equally wrong to attribute to God's will the distressing efforts at intimidation on the part of the privileged husbands (cf. 1 Pet. 3:7) or the disheartening exercise of the *patria potestas* (cf. Col. 3:21). And when a wayward member of the community had to be corrected and punished, this person was not to be "overwhelmed by excessive sorrow" (2 Cor. 2:6-7 RSV; cf. 7:8 ff.).

Finally, because suffering is of no value in and of itself and need not be accepted in every case, there are also primitive Christian protests and complaints against it (cf. Acts 16:37; 22:25; 25:10-11, et passim). In this connection, reference should be made not so much to the rehabilitation demanded by Paul when he was "publicly beaten without trial and put in prison," as to the fact that he appealed to his rights as a Roman citizen. The same is true where Paul protests against his being scourged (22:24 ff.), which was about to be done without an investigation. In 25:10-11, Paul even appeals to the emperor. Even though the legal and historical questions that are connected with the claim to the rights of Roman citizenship and the appeal to the emperor are not yet fully clarified, and Luke presents all this primarily in the perspective of political apologetics, in any case, Roman law here is claimed as a protection against affliction and persecution. To be compared also is Paul's reaction when the high priest struck him on the mouth (Acts 23:2-3). In this connection, of course, it is hardly possible to overlook the tension between this response and the admonition found in Matt. 5:39 and Luke 6:29. But according to John 18:23, Jesus himself responded, when he was struck in the face by one of Annas' servants: "If I have said something wrong, then show that it was wrong; but if it was correct, then why do you strike me?" In contrast to the Synoptics, where Jesus suffers ridicule and mistreatment in silence, here he reproves the injustice that is done to him. In the opinion of the Evangelist, this is done not so much in protest against what he suffers as in testimony to Jesus' being in the right and innocent.

Jesus' real protest against suffering, then, is made on behalf of others, and it is made primarily in the context of the dispute over the Sabbath, both in word and in deed. Jesus not only heals on the Sabbath, but he also accuses the Pharisees of having made the Sabbath, which should be a boon and an opportunity, into a yoke and a burden, when, for example, they forbid the plucking of ears of grain. But the Sabbath "was made for the sake of man, and not man for the sake of the Sabbath"(Mark 2:27). This leads consistently even to such cases of healing as in Judaism are forbidden on the Sabbath, because no immediate danger to life is involved, as for example, the healing of a withered hand. However, according to Jesus, who does not abide by this rule, and in freedom and out of love heals even such an illness as does not involve a danger to life, the commandment to do good and to relieve suffering applies in cases other than emergency. When he asks, "Is it permissible on the Sabbath to do good or to do evil, to save life or to kill?" (Mark 3:4), this implies only the alternative of doing good *or* evil, of serving life *or* death. In concrete terms, this means that the person who does not do good to those who are suffering is doing evil to them, and anyone who does not oppose suffering and diminish it is actually increasing it. But anyone who dares to take action against the suffering of others, and in so doing calls into question the structures and taboos that cause suffering, must himself reckon with the prospect of thereby bringing trouble upon himself (cf. Mark 3:6 and III.1,2).

3. Solidarity and sympathy

These last examples have already indicated that the real response of Jesus and of Christians to suffering is the attempt to overcome the sufferings of others or to share in them. Such solidarity in suffering is not a self-evident thing, not even among those who themselves are suffering. Affliction can also render one dull and callous; indeed, it can even break the closest of family ties and promote a boundless self-seeking attitude. But Jesus was not only bound to his disciples in a community of destiny that included all the relationships and circumstances of life, but he also had a great sensitivity for the sufferings of others who were not involved in his fellowship. The help he offered did not consist in the preaching of *a-pathy* but in the preaching and actualization of *sym-pathy* with the lowly and tormented, in the sharing of suffering and in active assistance. And hence, he likewise urged his followers to join with him in taking action against the destructive powers of evil and of suffering, of sickness and of death, in this unredeemed world.

For example, he encountered the outcasts and the disenfranchised by joining them in table fellowship. Thus we hear in Mark 2:15-16 that he "sits at table with taxgatherers and sinners." "Taxgatherers" in Judaism, however, were hated and isolated, because they ruthlessly collected the taxes and were in the service of the Roman occupying forces, so that they were placed on the same level with the godless heathen (Matt. 5:46-47; 18:17). The term "sinners" meant those who led an immoral life, did not respect the law, and thus were excluded from the fellowship. For a devout, law-observing Jew, table fellowship with such persons was impossible and contaminating. "Do not eat and drink with sinners" (Tobit 4:18; cf. Jubilees 22:16); "Let your companions at table be righteous men" (Ecclus. 9:16). People observed this rule (cf. also Acts 10:28; 11:3). Against this background, Jesus' conduct takes on a shocking and provocative, but also a liberating and integrating character. He breaks through the restrictions of the commandments of purity (cf. also Mark 7:15) and sets himself above convention and prejudice, in order to rescue men from their isolation and to draw those who are religiously and socially disqualified into his presence. This is further reflected in Luke 14:13, "When you give a feast, invite the poor, the cripples, the lame, and the blind." Of course, this table fellowship is not exhausted in solidarity among men, but it is also a symbol of one's acceptance by God, in whose name Jesus promises forgiveness (Mark 2:5). "This man receives sinners and eats with them" (Luke 15:2). Therefore, it is said concerning Jesus' going into the house of the taxgatherer Zacchaeus, "Today salvation has come to this house" (Luke 19:9). But this also implies the breaking-through of social or cultic fences. Thus, those sick persons who live as outcasts, exiles, regarded as under God's punishment, who like those suffering from leprosy are treated the same as dead, find compassion with Jesus (Mark 1:40 ff.; Luke 17:11 ff.). Further examples of such an attitude of solidarity in the face of hunger, illness, and other distresses and sufferings will be found particularly in the following section (4).

The motivation for, and the criterion of, such practice that seeks to overcome suffering is the commandment of love, which Jesus intensified in the form of the commandment to love one's enemies. As the highest commandment, taking its place before and above all others (Mark 12:28 ff.), the commandment of love is the decisive stimulus toward the relief of suffering. This is illustrated in an especially impressive way by the story and example of the good Samaritan (Luke 10:30 ff.), where Jesus uses an exemplary case to show what it means to love one's neighbor as oneself (10:25 ff.). It has frequently been pointed out in the exegesis of this passage that the inquirer in Luke 10:25 inquires about the extent and the boundaries of his obligation to love, while Jesus on the other hand tells the story from the perspective of the man who had fallen among thieves. One should transpose oneself into the situation of the sufferer who is dependent upon assistance. The fact that it was specifically a Samaritan who gave help to the man lying beside the road half-dead takes on special importance in view of the irreconcilable hostility between Jews and Samaritans. Precisely the one from whom, according to the usual norms, the victim could least have expected help, set himself above conventions and prejudices and discovered in the man who had fallen among thieves the person who was dependent upon his love and assistance. The affliction that disregards all religious, racial, and social boundaries also demands a love that transcends all boundaries. A solidarity with sufferers that would limit itself to the circle of the family or friends, of one's own confession or race, is not Jesus' intention. Just as God sets no boundaries to his love, but causes the sun to shine and the rain to fall even upon the ungodly and the unrighteous, so also one's enemy is to be included in one's love (Matt. 5:44).

Jesus obviously does not see in this any excessive demand, as he then lays undivided claim to man's readiness to sacrifice and to give aid, and he is not of the opinion that distresses and sufferings are merely to be allayed out of our surplus. This is shown in the little scene with the gift of the poor widow who places only two small coins in the offering, but is praised by Jesus in contrast to the larger gifts of the rich, "For they all have given out of their surplus, but she has given out of her poverty, all that she had, her very livelihood" (Mark 12:44 and par.).

In primitive Christianity the sharing of suffering was practiced above all within the community itself as brotherhood in practice. The community was conscious of being the body of Christ, which is marked by solidarity, not by a leveling uniformity (Rom. 12:4 ff.; 1 Cor. 12:12 ff.). This means, for example, that all differences that divide and, all the more, all racial, social, and sexual discrimination are outmoded (Gal. 3:28; Col. 3:11), and there is mutual respect among people. But above all it means that the individual members of this body are not isolated and do not withdraw from each other. Even though the idea of the organism is only of secondary importance, still it clearly shows the reciprocal fraternal obligation of the members among themselves. What affects one member of this body also affects all other members. "If one member suffers, then all members suffer together" (1 Cor. 12:26). Just as no one can live and suffer by himself, because he is always related to his Lord (Rom. 14:7-8), so also with his suffering he is integrated into the fellowship of the members of Christ's body. In this body indeed all are involved in some way in suffering, though not to the same depth, but in such a way that there are some at hand who can give the others a helping hand. Belonging to Christ and his body rescues one from isolation even in suffering. Here suffering is never solely an individual fate; instead, the suffering of an individual always signifies also the suffering of the community. Therefore the community is admonished by the apostle to practice solidarity and to stand together in joy and sorrow, in laughing and weeping. "Rejoice with those who rejoice, and weep with those who weep" (Rom. 12:15).

Now it is not certain whether we may make this apply only to the members of the community. But here Paul obviously is not at all reflecting on the limits of solidarity. Certainly verse 13 says that one should contribute to the necessities of the *saints*, but verse 20 at least goes beyond this, when Paul there admonishes, "If your enemy is hungry, give him something to eat; if he is thirsty, give him something to drink." The basic principle, however, is that one should bear the burdens of others (Gal. 6:2), and indeed should do good to all, but especially to one's comrades in the faith (Gal. 6:10). This is not a confessionalizing of love, but it is an indication that love does not begin first with those who are some little distance away, but with those nearest at hand.

Solidarity is exhibited first of all in one's allowing oneself to be drawn into the suffering and taking a share in it. "Where is one weak, and I am not weak? Where is one offended [or: caused to stumble] and I do not burn [with sympathy]?" (2 Cor. 11:29). Paul takes upon himself what other members of the community suffer (cf. also Gal. 4:19-20, et passim). Their affliction is to be his own. Similarly, it is also said of Christians that they share in his trouble (Phil. 4:14). This also includes one's not being "ashamed" of another in his suffering, as for example, when he is under suspicion (cf. Mark 8:38) or is in prison (2 Tim. 1:16), but rather stands by him and, for example, visits him (cf. Matt. 25:36). In that time, too, to sympathize with prisoners or to visit them must have been seen as a compromising rather than an innocent act, and indeed must have included the risk of being imprisoned oneself. Nevertheless, there were those who "suffered with the prisoners" (Heb. 10:34).

One's own experiences of suffering indeed can impel one to solidarity with other sufferers. Thus, those who are addressed in the book of Hebrews, who "have endured a hard struggle with sufferings, sometimes being publicly exposed to abuse and affliction, and sometimes being partners with those so treated" (10:32-33 RSV). But anyone who has to suffer affliction in his own body does not leave others in the lurch and understands the admonition, "Remember those who are in prison, as though in prison with them; and those who are ill-treated, since you also are in the body" (Heb. 13:3 RSV; cf. Col. 4:18). He knows at once that this cannot mean only a sympathy or a spiritual kinship, but a participation in the fate of the sufferers in word and deed.

But affliction that is shared not only binds together individuals within a community, but also various communities throughout the world. The knowledge that "the same experience of suffering is required of your brotherhood throughout the world" (1 Pet. 5:9 RSV) manifestly makes it easier to bear one's own fate of suffering (cf. also 1 Thess. 2:14). But where there are not such "like sufferings," there is the consciousness of being challenged beyond the boundaries of one's own community, to leap actively to the aid of one's suffering brethren in the *oikoumene*.

Thus, in a certain sense, solidarity tends directly toward equality. For in 2 Cor. 8, Paul offers as the aim of his collection, of which we shall have more to say, "that there may be equality," and that the person who has much should not have a surplus, while the one who has little should suffer no lack (v. 14-15). This obviously was not understood as an illusion or as utopia. Primitive Christianity was too sober for that. There is no dream here of a society that is free from affliction, but suffering that can be eliminated is to be eliminated as far as that is possible. Thus quite thoroughgoing distinctions are made with respect to sufferings and the provision of help that is prompted by them. For example, in the discourse on the last judgment, there is an enumeration only of realizable possibilities: the hungry are to be fed, the thirsty provided with drink, strangers given shelter, the naked clothed, the sick and imprisoned ones visited (Matt. 25:31 ff.). It could indeed be asked, for example, why there is not a call to *heal* the sick or to *liberate* the prisoners, but "only" to visit them. But healing the sick obviously was a charisma not at one's disposal, not granted to everyone. And liberating the captives was neither in the mind nor in the power of that little flock who were to come to the aid of "the least of these my brethren" in their affliction.

However, the examples cited are not aimed at a legalistic copying. Hence, it would be a narrow biblicism if one were to say that because the good Samaritan gave specific help to the man who had fallen among thieves and did not campaign for the building of a safer road between Jerusalem and Jericho, today also one should not attempt to wage a preventive struggle against suffering by changing structures, but only from time to time bind up wounds in specific situations of suffering and provide care for the days immediately following. In Luke 10:25 ff., indeed, no unattainable heroism is preached, such as would so easily give an excuse to the person who is called upon to give aid, on the grounds that, in view of the immeasurable amount of suffering, any help would be only a drop of water on a hot stone. Furthermore, this passage does not advance the punishment of robbers and the improvement of "internal security" as an excuse for refusal to act in solidarity, nor does it advocate work on the change of structures to the benefit of all those who suffer and are disadvantaged to the neglect of the specific neighbor in need. Instead, quite soberly, prosaically, and with courage to undertake the provisional and fragmentary, what is possible and necessary for a sufferer today is done. The person who is placed alongside the sufferer as his neighbor certainly is not to be discouraged by being confronted with excessive demands, and all the more, he is not to be satisfied with utopian programs for the future, but a preventive, institutionally governed assistance for suffering people is altogether in keeping with the New Testament, particularly when the church itself can become the active subject in such measures of assistance.

Hence it is not appropriate to pose the alternative of either a spontaneous or an institutional manifestation of solidarity; but it is proper to make a certain distinction between those sufferings that in light of the limited means available necessarily challenge the community to intervene, and those that perhaps can be managed by the persons affected or by their families themselves. In the regulations concerning the care of widows, for example (1 Tim. 5:3 ff.), there is first of all an appeal to the family. Support of the widows is in the first place a matter for the kinfolk, and anyone who does not concern himself for the widows in his family is denying the faith. Young widows—and there were many such in that time—are urged to remarry. Only the "genuine and solitary widows" are to receive support from the church; the others are to be supported by their kinfolk, and "the church not be burdened, so that it may assist those who are real widows" (v. 16). To be sure, the author connects the church's charitable activity not only to social but also to moral conditions and apparently even to a collaboration in the church, but there is a good bit that is not entirely clear here as to details. Nevertheless, it is clear that the church here is assuming a regulated obligation for assistance for one of the classes that in that time suffered social, economic, and legal disadvantages. If such institutionalized regulations are first encountered only in the late period of primitive Christianity, still the idea of fellowship and solidarity that underlies them is attested in all parts of the New Testament.

4. Material assistance

Thus it is already shown that fellowship in suffering does not mean merely a fellowship in feeling, spirit, and attitude that is exhausted in inward or verbal sympathy, but it is manifested also and primarily in material things such as money, food, and the like. A solidarity that does not open hands and purses for the support of those who suffer is subject to criticism. This is very emphatically evident in some passages in the New Testament. "But if any one has the world's goods and sees his brother in need, yet closes his heart against him, how does God's love abide in him?" (1 John 3:17 RSV). Here it is not the attitude that counts, but the deed. "Let us not love in word or speech but in deed and in truth" (v. 18 RSV). Thus even the Johannine writings, which frequently appear to understand everything worldly as only unreal, want to see love related in a very real, earthly, and physical way to the suffering brother in his everyday needs.

But the Epistle of James in particular emphasizes that human goodwill and an attitude of fellow-feeling will not suffice, but also that even pious words are not enough: "If a brother or sister is ill-clad and in lack of daily food, and one of you says to them, 'Go in peace, be warmed and filled,' without giving them the things needed for the body, what does it profit?" (James 2:15-16 RSV). Anyone who dismisses those who are lacking necessary food and clothing with good words and wishes is not relieving affliction but rather increasing it. What is involved here is not a protest against soothing phrases and pious ways of speaking (we have here, e.g., the Old Testament-Jewish farewell wishes). Even proper, well-meaning words do not suffice in the face of the suffering of persons in distress, because they simply do not feed those who are famishing or warm those who are freezing. The sufferer is in need not only of verbal, but also of physical, material support.

Jesus himself quite obviously takes as his starting point the position that one must come to the aid of suffering people with active assistance. One must not pass by someone who has fallen among thieves and is lying half-dead beside the road (Luke 10:25 ff.). It makes no difference for what reasons the priest and the Levite nevertheless did so—there are many speculations about this: fear of cultic uncleanness or of danger to themselves, and so on; some have even suggested a reluctance to intervene in an alleged divine judgment!—such behavior that turns one's back on a person who has fallen into distress and need cannot be justified in any way. The Samaritan, on the other hand, does what is needed to alleviate the distress; he binds up the man's wounds, brings him to the nearest inn, and arranges for his food and lodging, assuming the expenses for his further care. Thus, the exemplary conduct of that Samaritan does not consist of his selling all he had at once, but with his personal intervention and his financial means helping the robbed and injured man to his feet again and guaranteeing his sustenance for a certain time. What was really needed here was not a spectacular action, but the fulfillment of needs of the specific case. Even "a cup of cold water"—of course worth more at certain times in dry Palestine than among us—is a relief deemed worthy of mention in Matt. 10:42. To be compared also is the emphasis upon hospitality (Matt. 25:35; Rom. 12:13, et passim) that is to be practiced, for example, toward apostles and missionaries who were away from home on official business, so to speak (cf. 3 John 5-8), but also toward all others, which, particularly in times of persecution, was especially important for refugees and exiles (cf. 1 Pet. 4:9; Heb. 13:2).

The fact that what is called for here is not something exaggerated and excessively demanding upon people, but something that is simply obvious, does not mean that such concrete readiness to give help will not have to go to the very limit of one's own minimum for existence. Even the simple but crucial demands of John the Baptist radically call in question an affluent society that is oriented exclusively to its own interests, when those demands are seen in the context of the society of that time. "Anyone who has two coats should give one of them to him who has none, and whoever has food should likewise share" (Luke 3:11). The extraordinary and the obvious are not to be separated in Jesus' view, either; indeed, Jesus is still more radical (cf. Luke 6:29), though equally free of bombast and pathos. His warning against riches in any case is not based solely upon the fact that one cannot serve both God and Mammon (Matt. 6:24) and that the "deceitfulness of riches" can "choke" the word (Mark 4:19). It rather is aimed also at help for the poor. One's own imperiling by wealth is always also an imperiling of the destitute or socially weaker neighbor, whose distress the rich person ignores. The challenge to the rich young man to sell his possessions and "give to the poor" (Mark 10:21) to be sure may not be universalized, but it is quite certain that it was Jesus' intention that one's earthly possessions should be used in the service of love for people in distress (cf. also Luke 16:9; 19:8; but also Matt. 5:42; Luke 8:3, et passim). Even though according to

1 Cor. 13:3, one can give all one's possessions to feed the poor
and still not have love, still this reference to the ambivalence of
concretely practiced love should not ease anyone's conscience
about refraining from such expenditures to feed those in
distress or about spiritualizing love.

In the primitive church the fraternal bond appears from
time to time to have led even to the sale of land and houses in
order to be able to help the needy with the proceeds. Luke has
generalized such individual cases when he writes that "no one
said that any of the things which he possessed was his own, but
they had everything in common" (Acts 4:32 RSV). "There was
not a needy person among them, for as many as were possessors
of lands or houses sold them, and brought the proceeds of what
was sold and laid it at the apostles' feet; and distribution was
made to each as any had need" (4:34-35 RSV; cf. also 2:44-45).
But since in the following verses (4:36-37) Luke tells of an
individual case which, if it had been the general rule, did not
need to be mentioned (cf. also Acts 5:4; 12:12), and evidently in
4:32 ff. also it appears that such sales only occurred from time to
time, it has often been surmised that the expansion into a
general description must be credited to Luke, who here is
idealizing the picture of the primitive church (perhaps also with
extra-biblical examples in mind). But it is sufficiently clear that
common worship and common life can also include common
possession of goods and that in any case they inevitably lead to
the dissolving of isolation even in economic and material
matters, in order thereby to be able to meet the need and the
affliction of the world, including the economic realities found
there. Certainly there is a total absence of legalism (cf. the
reference in 5:4 to the voluntary character of these actions) and
of any programmatic scheme, and of course, all the more of any
intention of a revolutionary alteration of the society that
surrounds the little company; but it is so much the more
impressive that Christian community can also include community of goods.

Usually, of course, people have taken another way. Paul in
particular does not call for a renunciation of property in

principle, but for a voluntary community even in the realm of earthly goods, as for example, in the collection for Jerusalem, which Paul then brought to Jerusalem under personal danger—in fact, he was arrested while there (cf. also Acts 11:29, according to which the Christians of Antioch determine, in the case of a great famine, that each of them will contribute, according to his ability, to the support of Judea). One can gain a good insight into the collection particularly in 2 Cor. 8-9. It was for Paul certainly above all an act of faith, to document the unity of the church, but it was likewise an economic and financial help for the Jerusalem church. Precisely here is found the "proving of the genuineness of love" (2 Cor. 8:8; cf. also 8:24) that goes beyond the means of the givers (2 Cor. 8:3) in supplying needs (2 Cor. 9:12). The recipients are not only supplied with material gifts, but the contributors have simply given themselves (2 Cor. 8:5); but this was done precisely *in* the concrete deed of love. Correspondingly, the churches also undertook to gather financial support for the imprisoned apostle (Phil. 4:14). Fellowship and doing good belong together (Heb. 13:16).

Christians cannot stand by idly to look on either innocent or self-induced distress. Paul, for example, is willing to make good the damages owed by the refugee slave Onesimus to his master (Philem. 18-19). As a rule there is not even any reflection on whether the suffering is to be attributed to one's own fault or not. Whether the man who fell among thieves was foolish, whether the tax gatherers and prostitutes were driven by stark need or by greed to an unrestrained collection of taxes and to prostitution, whether those in prison had been justly or unjustly imprisoned, and so on—all this remains open, immaterial, unimportant. The only significant and urgent considerations are the giving of assistance, readiness to sacrifice, solidarity.

5. Healing of the sick

Jesus cannot be charged with the interiorizing and assignment of a transcendent character to salvation, as is often the one-sided representation in Christianity; on the contrary, he is strongly committed to the view that the liberating power of the rule of God concerns the body as well as the soul. Particularly impressive demonstration of this is provided by Jesus' healing activities, according to the healing narratives in the Gospels. As was shown in I.1.c, the messianic hopes of the Old Testament that are taken up in the Gospels show how salvation and healing are connected, as are word and deed with Jesus (cf. Matt. 11:5 and par.). Already in the Old Testament the "healing of broken hearts" is as much a part of the proclamation of the good news as is the abundance of earthly and material blessings and benefit (Luke 4:17–19). Accordingly, Jesus' "compassion" is just as much concerned with physical hunger (Mark 8:2), illness (Matt. 20:34), and death (Luke 7:13) as with the aimlessness of those who "have no shepherd" (Mark 6:34; in Matt. 9:36 this is further interspersed with the words "harrassed and helpless"), with sin as much as with illness. He makes the whole man well (cf. John 7:23).

In the story of the healing of the paralytic (Mark 2:1 ff. and par.), the word of forgiveness and the act of healing are placed side-by-side from the very outset. It is true that the debate over the right to forgive sins in verses 6-10 only arose as a secondary development, but the word of forgiveness and the word of healing belong together from the very first, and thus they illustrate the healing of the whole person. This is not intended to say that in his heart of hearts the sick man did not yearn for healing but for reconciliation with God, that healing necessarily presupposes forgiveness, or that one must first become healthy in soul before the body can recover. Jesus also healed without forgiving. Healing and the forgiveness of sins *can* coincide, but they do not necessarily do so. Not every sick person is *eo ipso* a sinner (cf. also James 5:15, "and if he has committed sins") But because illness and sin can be associated or interwoven, forgiveness also can be an element in recovery, so that one may not play off the word of healing and the word of forgiveness against each other. The fact that the proclamation of the gospel and the healing of the sick belong together is confirmed by summaries like Matt. 4:23 and 9:35 as well as by the proverb in Mark 2:17: "It is not the healthy ones who need a physician, but those who are sick. I did not come to call the righteous, but sinners" (cf. also Mark 5:34; 10:52).

Even when one allows for a critical stance and for methodological caution toward the miracle-tradition, which in its style appropriates typical characteristics of form from ancient miracle-stories, there can be no doubt that Jesus healed sick people and drove out demons. This is confirmed even by his adversaries, who, of course, are of the opinion that in this connection he is in league with the devil (Mark 3:22). From this it is evident that miracles, as such, are ambiguous (cf. also Mark 13:22, et passim); yet Jesus himself saw in his healings and exorcisms the defeat of Satan's rule and the bringing-in of the rule of God. "But if it is by the Spirit of God [Luke: the finger of God] that I cast out demons, then the kingdom of God has come upon you" (Matt. 12:28 and par.; cf. also Mark 3:27; Matt. 11:20 ff. and par.). Thus Jesus connects the casting out of demons with himself and his message of the in-breaking kingdom of God. But precisely at this point it becomes evident that what is involved in the dawning of this kingdom of God is not solely the so-called salvation of souls or the hereafter, but the salvation of the *totus homo*, the whole man, here and now. Of course, in the background there is also the ancient belief in demons, but what is crucial is not this outmoded demonology. The crucial thing is rather that men who were bruised and suffering at the hands of evil forces are snatched from the grasp of the antigodly powers. The signs of the dawning rule of God are not turned into vapor in an abstract or spiritualized form, but people are affected even in their physical condition and as whole persons they experience liberation from their various bondages and enslavements.

Of course, the precondition of such becoming well and free is "faith," by which is meant confidence in Jesus' marvelous power (cf. Mark 5:34, 36; Matt. 8:13; 9:28) and prayerful belief in God (Mark 11:22), but also an impetus of activity, for example, the overcoming of difficulties (Mark 2:4-5), un-

daunted crying for help (Mark 10:47-48, 50), and indeed a
desire (Mark 10:51; Matt. 15:28). Among the things identified
as wonder-working are Jesus' effectual word (Matt. 8:16; Mark
1:25, 27, 41; 5:41; 9:25), his touch, and the laying-on of his
hands (Mark 1:31, 41; 8:23 or 5:23; 7:32, et passim), but also
practices that are comparable with the methods of primitive
folk medicine (Mark 8:23; 7:33). In spite of the fact that the cases
of healing illustrate the authority and uniqueness of Jesus, still
it is assumed that the disciples also (see below), and indeed in a
certain sense *all*, are called to engage in healing activity (cf.
Luke 10:37), and thus any tendency to make a confessional
restriction of this activity is rejected (cf. Mark 9:38-39).

Jesus' proclamation and practice that eliminated or
alleviated suffering were taken up and carried on by his
followers. The disciples themselves obviously were taken by
Jesus into his mission and empowered to heal (cf. Mark 3:15;
6:7, 13 and par.; Matt. 10:8). The stories in the book of Acts
indeed are in part characterized by a massive belief in miracles
(cf. Acts 5:15; 19:12), but they indubitably show that the
primitive church too was conscious of an obligation to contend
against physical suffering. There are reports of healings
performed by Peter (Acts 3:1 ff.; 5:14 ff.; 9:32 ff.), Philip (Acts
8:7), and Paul (Acts 28:8-9). Paul himself knows of the charisma
of healing the sick, though of course he speaks of it only in the
enumeration of charismata (1 Cor. 12:9, 28, 30). And Paul
certainly shows, with all his awareness of the physical nature
and the wholeness of the human person, that healing is a marvel
that is not merely at one's disposal, and that the failure of
healing to occur need not be in contradiction to salvation and
grace (cf. 2 Cor. 12:7 ff.); however, he did not simply accept
illness in Stoic fashion, but pled that it might be removed (cf. v.
8), and he speaks of the "mercy of God" when he sees someone
restored to health who had been ill and in danger of death (Phil.
2:27). According to James 5:14, the sick person is to call to
himself the elders of the community, and they are to make him
well by means of prayer and anointing with oil. Here, instead of
a charismatic gift that refuses to be at everyone's disposal, what

is in view evidently is an institutional connection of such healing powers.

But everywhere it is presupposed that illness is an evil and distress that injures God's creation and therefore calls for "mercy" (cf. Matt. 20:34; Mark 9:22). Accordingly, there is not the recommendation, as there is in Seneca *(Epistle to Lucilius* 78), that the sick persons concentrate on intellectual activities and scorn the pain. We do not read here, "Is it nothing when you endure illness with self-mastery?" *(ibid.).* The struggle against affliction and illness is not won by means of a rational or moral appeal to the sick, and not only from within, but however much the sick person himself also is summoned to activity (cf. also the following section), from without, by means of the healing word and the healing deed, by liberating absolution and the helping hand. Hence salvation and healing, the transformation of *psyche* and *physis*, recovery in body and soul, are not seen as alternative choices by primitive Christianity.

6. Prayer and supplication

Even in the context of the narratives of healing petitions and prayers play a major role. Those who are sick "beseech" Jesus themselves (Mark 1:40 and par.) and "cry to him" (Mark 10:47; Matt. 9:27), or others plead for their kinfolk (Mark 5:22-23; 7:26; John 11:3) or for others (Matt. 8:5-6; Luke 7:3; Mark 6:56; 7:32). But even outside the healing narratives, we read of people crying out to Jesus in distress, as for example Peter's "Lord, save me!" (Matt. 14:30; cf. Matt. 8:25: "Lord, save us, we are perishing"). Prayer is mentioned particularly in connection with healings performed by Christians (Acts 9:40; 28:8; cf. Mark 9:29). According to James 5:14, prayer is offered "over" the sick person "in the name of the Lord," which means, under commission, at the call, and in the power of the Lord. According to verse 15, any "prayer of faith" can heal a sick person. In addition to the healing of the sick, in the primitive church prayer is offered for all sorts of desires: for the Holy Spirit (Acts 8:15; cf. Luke 11:13) and for the coming of Jesus

Christ (1 Cor. 16:22; Rev. 22:17, 20), for liberty in proclaiming
the word (Acts 4:29; cf. Eph. 6:19-20) and for the abounding of
love in knowledge (Phil. 1:9; cf. James 1:5), but also for healing
(2 Cor. 12:8) or for liberation from prison (Acts 12:5; cf. also Acts
26:29; Philem. 22), for deliverance from the danger of death (2
Cor. 1:10-11) or similarly grave perils (Rom. 15:30-31; cf. also
Rev. 6:10).

The person to whom it is given to bear trouble and
misfortune is to pray (James 5:13), and indeed obviously to pray
not only for an inner willingness to suffer or the strength to
endure, but also for the removal of the distress. It certainly is
not a small thing when prayer drives out anxiety (Phil. 4:6) and
even in suffering does not leave one discouraged (Eph. 3:13);
but in James 5, even a greater effect is attributed to prayer, as is
shown in the following examples from verses 14-19, where by
the power of prayer even the heavens themselves are unlocked
and opened up (cf. also v. 4, according to which the cries of the
exploited workers in the harvest have reached God). The
"prayer of faith" is able to accomplish "much," even though
obviously not everything (v. 16).

The fact that James speaks of the "prayer of the righteous" (v.
16) shows that the one who is praying is the poor man ("righteous"
and "poor" are frequently synonymous: Ps. Sol. 10:6; 15:1, 6-7),
but also that prayer and the doing of righteousness belong
together (cf. also 1 Pet. 3:7; James 4:3); so also prayer does not
exclude visiting the sick and the use of medical skills (if we may
understand the anointing with oil as medical treatment; cf. Mark
6:13; Luke 10:34), but includes them (v. 14). Moreover, James 5
places one's own prayers and the intercession of others together
(vv. 13-14). In any case, prayer is always also intercession—in
Rom. 15:30 it is even called "striving together" (cf. also Col.
4:12)—and does not serve the cause of religious individualism.
According to Paul, prayer in the worship service is not simply
"private," but it is to serve the edification of others, and therefore
prayer with the mind is greatly preferred to praying in glossolalia
(1 Cor. 14:13-15).

The primitive church was aware of having been empowered for its comprehensive praying by Jesus, who had taught his disciples to pray. According to Matt. 7:7 ff., man can and should turn to God in prayer with everything and should be certain of being heard, because God is Father, and praying to him is as natural and appropriate as a child's request of its earthly father (cf. also 6:8). The Lord's Prayer in particular lets us see the intention of Jesus. First are the three eschatological petitions, which ask for God's eschatological saving action, that he, who is addressed as Father and as the subject of what is requested, may universally and definitively establish his saving and beneficent rule and may prevail. Thus, just as the salvation of man is included in this eschatological manifestation of his rule, so all the more does the petition for daily bread express the conviction that ordinary, everyday things, but also suffering, distress, and the cares of this world are in God's hands. Correspondingly, in the petition for forgiveness, we are not to leave out the guilt for our own deeds that cause affliction, but accordingly also our own forgiveness is to be extended to those who have caused affliction for us (cf. Matt. 5:44; Luke 23:34; Acts 7:60). Similarly, the temptation into which one desires not to be led, and the evil from which one desires to be delivered, certainly would include suffering (on the tempting character of suffering, cf. Rev. 2:10, 13, and on the evil from which one desires to be "delivered," cf. 2 Cor. 1:10 and 2 Tim. 3:11; 4:7).

Of course, the petitions of the Lord's Prayer are not a canon of all the potential contents of prayer. Rather, "Whatever you pray for and request, (only) believe that you will receive it, and it will be given to you" (Mark 11:24 and par.). In Luke 11:5 ff. and Matt. 7:7 ff., also it is promised that the prayer of supplication, without any restriction, will be heard. In *all* matters man should turn to God. He is encouraged to do this, precisely in concrete situations of distress. Of course, it is presupposed that one will not seek to have his own way and to justify himself, but will submit and surrender himself to God (cf. Luke 18:14); however, this does not imply any reduction of petitions to the achievement of an inner peace and submission to God's will, but rather a childlike trust toward the God who wills to give to his children *nothing but* good and who can give help in difficulties and crises, losses and sufferings. The person who prays is suffering and is aware that he does not have what he needs.

Apathy and inability to pray, on the other hand, are closely related to each other, as Stoic thought teaches us. Wherever the only content of prayer is a fatalistic resignation to one's destiny, the pallor and chill of philosophical meditation are dominant, not a disregard for reserve and detachment, a disregard commended by Jesus in the parable of the importunate friend, not the "importunity" and "boldness" (Luke 11:8) with which we may come before God. Certainly this is itself a help, when affliction need not be silent or fall dumb, but can be articulated. However, in a hopeless situation one does not experience liberating and effectual help in the articulation as such, not in a monologue within oneself in the face of a blindly and coldly governing Providence or in an atmosphere of impersonal mysticism, but only in a lively, vital dialogue with the divine Thou, which is not achieved in an attitude of spectatorship and detached reflection. Certainly God is free in his hearing us, but he is free as the Father who is concerned about his children and who gives to them the assurance that he will turn all things to the best.

However, Jesus not only encouraged his followers to pray, but he himself also prayed, specifically in suffering. We hear of his intercession in John's Gospel (cf. the so-called "high priestly prayer" in John 17), but also in Luke 22:31-32. While Satan shakes the disciples like flour in a sieve, Jesus counters this satanic threat with intercession, that later on, after his "conversion," Peter may strengthen his brethren. But above all we should recall here the prayer of Jesus in Gethsemane (Mark 14:32 ff.). We have earlier shown that this prayer does not express a submission to unalterable processes of fate and an assent to God's inscrutable decrees because anything but submission to what is unchangeable would be without meaning (cf. II.1.b). Rather, Jesus' profound grief and his drawing back in the face of suffering and death is just as seriously meant as his prayer that the "cup" might pass from him. All things are possible, not to him, but to the Father. As much as this intensifies the inexplicable character of his destiny, still at the end there is the obedient yes to the "cup" that the Father proffers. But this is something different from the shattering of his own will and a resigned submission to the divine will. The "not as I will, but as thou wilt" is rather an affirmation and unconditional trust *in the midst of* fear and pain, affliction and powerlessness. Nevertheless, beyond all this the readers of the Gethsemane story are meant to be aware also that the depth of loneliness in which Jesus watched and prayed alone is overcome by his drinking the cup. Precisely because the one who stood before God with prayer and supplications, with loud cries and tears (Heb. 5:7), was heard and exalted on Easter, he now is able to help his "brethren" in their sufferings (Heb. 2:17-18; 4:15).

Prayer accordingly is not affirmation on principle, but a cry out of the depths. The context of prayer is the sighing and groaning of the unredeemed creation, out of which itself the "unutterable groanings," that the Spirit himself makes his own, cry out all the distress of the need of redemption and urgently call for the new world (Rom. 8:23, 26). It is prayer that puts us in the place where man in the last analysis, unable to discern God's governance, stands before him with empty hands and waits for God himself to intervene and to comfort the sufferers (Matt. 5:4). At the same time, in prayer it becomes manifest once again that the transforming power of love, which is expressed in intercession even for the persecutor who is causing the suffering (cf. Matt. 5:44), always remains oriented to the other person, to be able effectually to hasten to his aid in his suffering (cf. James 5:14). But above all, prayer, in its waiting and hoping aspects, points to the coming of the Lord who "makes all things new" (Rev. 21:4-5), the coming that will put an end definitively to suffering. In harmony with his ministry, there is here and now a twofold obligation: in the paradoxical correlation of "suffering" and "living" ("as dying, and behold! we live") that is sustained by the assurance that no power on earth, not even suffering, can separate us from God's love in Jesus Christ (Rom. 8:38-39); and at the same time in the affliction-conquering practice of those who because of the transforming encounter with the Crucified and Resurrected One strive to relieve the suffering of those who have fallen among thieves.